ALONE
IN AMERICA

ALONE
IN
AMERICA

The Search for Companionship

by LOUISE BERNIKOW

1817
HARPER & ROW, PUBLISHERS, New York
Cambridge, Philadelphia, San Francisco,
London, Mexico City, São Paulo, Singapore, Sydney

FIRST EDITION

Designer: Nancy Sugihara

Library of Congress Cataloging-in-Publication Data

Bernikow, Louise, date
  Alone in America.

  Includes index.
  1. Social isolation. 2. Single people—United States. I. Title.
HM291.B395   1986   302.5'45   85-45178
ISBN 0-06-015505-1

86 87 88 89 90 HC 10 9 8 7 6 5 4 3 2 1

For Bruce, for believing

Contents

Acknowledgments

Imagine sitting alone at a desk writing about loneliness. Strangely, the work of this book put me in profound touch with other people. I owe everyone who helped an enormous debt. Those willing to have their names used are mentioned in the text, but I want to record special thanks to the friends with double roles—they agreed to speak on the record and they prompted, suggested, discussed and encouraged, as friends do: Mary Bacon, Drs. Frances and Paul Lippmann, Toby Marotta, Dr. Elizabeth Milwid, Tom Peters and John Tirpak. To those who preferred anonymity in helping me unravel the problem of loneliness, an equal measure of absolute gratitude.

And gratitude, too, to Edward Klein, Martin Arnold, Jon Nordheimer and Clifford May at the *New York Times Magazine* for instigating the report on which this book is based; to Kathy Robbins, my dear and inspiring agent, and Hugh Van Dusen, my wise editor; to the friends whose care and counsel made the difference between the impulse to turn away and the impulse to persevere: Maggie Anderson, Arthur Blaustein, Larry Deitz, Anna French, Ruth Gruenthal, Walter Kiechel, Jane Little, Jim Landis, Honor Moore, Dr. Elizabeth Mayer, Dr. Owen Renik, Miriam Schneir and JoAnn Stone.

I know Sargent Shriver slightly. When he was campaigning for Vice-President, he asked me if I had any ideas. You remember that there was plenty of money around, but as far as ideas went, both parties were in a state of destitution. So I told him, and I'm afraid he didn't listen, that the number one American killer wasn't cardiovascular disease, but loneliness. I told him that he and McGovern could swamp the Republicans if they would promise to cure that disease. I even gave him a slogan to put on buttons and bumpers and flags and billboards: Lonesome No More!

The rest is history.

—Kurt Vonnegut, *Palm Sunday*

Alone in America is factually accurate, except that names, locales and individual traits have been altered in some instances.

CHAPTER 1

Introduction

"The impulse is to turn away"

It begins in the oddest way, three times removed from human life. A man is talking, but he is not present; I hear his voice on a tape recorder. He is not speaking to me, but to a group of psychiatric residents. He presents the case of a woman who grew up in a good family and a good home, went to excellent schools and, all her life, was unable to form close ties with anyone. In school, she had few friends; at the university, she was lonely and isolated. Her academic work substituted for people. By the time the doctor saw her, she was in her thirties, there had been "no direct sexual contact with anyone," and she had "little to do with anyone around her." The doctor's interest, he says, is in helping her, trying to establish contact, "hoping an attachment would develop." As a psychoanalyst, he is interested in loneliness, which he describes as "mysterious" and "baffling" and essentially uncommunicable. He comes back, again and again, to the words "secretiveness," "yearning" and "fear."

He is compassionate and puzzled by the mystery of extreme loneliness. He is also unusually honest about his own desire to turn away from it. At times, treating this patient, he felt "burdened by a fear of being in her loneliness. I was afraid of entering her world and never getting out of it. Sometimes I wanted to get out of the office and call somebody up and say, 'Hello, how is it out there?' "

He offers no easy answers. The only progress he can report in this case is the slow establishment of some contact, the forging of a tentative link for her through him, to the rest of humanity. He doesn't snap his fingers and insist that the patient mobilize herself and get out and meet people. Another psychiatrist I know had said such a thing to a patient and only understood how facile and unknowing he had been when his lover died. Years after his intense mourning had passed, this psychiatrist spoke of that specific loneliness and said he hadn't understood before. Not at all.

Not everyone who feels lonely becomes psychotic or profoundly withdrawn. The loneliness heard by mental health workers, family therapists, drugs counselors or just sympathetic friends is not always so extreme, not always related to a lover's death and not always seen as critical. Most people don't speak of loneliness. They dial the weather report just to hear a voice. They call suicide prevention hotlines feeling not suicidal, but lonely. They watch television night after night, saying good night to Dan Rather when he says good night to them, catching up with all their ersatz neighbors on evening soap operas, deluded into an intimacy with the characters and their problems and their pets and their furniture that disappears with a click the minute the television set goes off. The screen goes dark fast.

But the psychiatrist is alive, a place to begin. It was difficult to find a starting point, to articulate something as uncommunicable as loneliness. The reason for beginning and continuing and wishing, often, to turn away, was clear. Not only is loneliness a common experience at one time or another in most people's lives, but it seems hidden away, implied between the lines, insidiously woven into the fabric of most of our social problems. Loneliness propels inordinate numbers of people to abuse alcohol or drugs or other people. Loneliness fills the average workdays of many citizens, and perhaps more, certainly different, kinds of loneliness add to the burden of those who are out of work. It is like the Emperor's nakedness—obvious to everyone, unuttered.

The psychiatrist had study and experience of the ways the psyche works that he could bring to bear in his attempts to understand and to help. I had different tools. Accustomed to investigating and reporting what is going on, I was able to travel across the country, talk with people whose work illuminated some aspect of loneliness, follow a chain of leads from one person to another—"real people" as well as experts, Americans who were willing to tell their stories—and come back to tell the tale.

The tale is disturbing, but not entirely bleak. In what many described as a desert of loneliness, there were oases. Acknowledging the problem, we are searching for solutions. A teenager learns, in fits and starts, to substitute a person for the drugs that have been his best friend. Men and women try to adjust their expectations of each other on the tumultuous terrain of changing definitions of what a man is and what a woman is and what each might be for the other. People in all geographies and all situations learn to help each other, providing more hope for managing loneliness than the words of all the experts combined. There were things that held us together in communities and things that tore us apart. My job was to chronicle them.

The voice of the psychiatrist that had been so disembodied on a tape recorder comes alive on a steep slope looking down at water spotted with the red and purple of a California sunset, the Golden Gate Bridge in the clear distance. Dr. Otto Will is sweeping the walk. We descend the slope, terrace by terrace, toward the house. Each terrace contains a different kind of vegetation, all unknown to me. Dr. Will's wife was once married to a landscape architect. I have seen, before he turned to lead the way down, a rising belly over slim hips and legs, a tall man, in very good shape, aging. His reputation is extraordinary, but confined largely to the psychiatric world and, within that, to the hospitals at which he has taught and the people he has worked with. He publishes little. He is interested in healing, not fame. Descending, I feel like the characters in old lapis lazuli carvings, except we are not going up the mountain together, but down.

The room is paneled with warm wood and hung with Indian and Mexican rugs. There are tiny figures scattered about the bookshelves and the desk, animal figures, just as Freud had. Dr. Will has something of Freud's aura, that is, he is interested in culture and history—witness the many artifacts on the walls, the shelves and the desk—and he sees the forces shaping our psyches as being in the world as much they are in primal scenes and constructs like ego and superego. He is attentive to and genuinely interested in literature and artists' visions. He mentions F. Scott Fitzgerald as a chronicler of adolescent loneliness and then Ibsen's Peer Gynt as the lonely outcast. And he wonders about how loneliness varies from culture to culture. In Nigeria and Colombia, where he has done some work, the family comes to the hospital with a mentally ill patient, remaining there to provide comfort and companionship. Nothing is more alien to American psychiatric medicine. Does this mean the people of Nigeria and Colombia are less prone to loneliness, surrounded, as they are, by numbers of people? Perhaps not. The family at the bedside may, in fact, be the cause of the patient's illness. He doesn't know and neither do I.

I am wary of the definite. Although it makes sense to think of what appears to be an epidemic of loneliness in America in terms of concrete facts and figures—there are now more people living alone than before, more older people surviving and moving away from their families, later marriages, opportunities for women to live on their own and embrace a kind of independence hitherto denied them—although the statistics point to something important in the way we live, they tell only the rough outline of the story. We are now asked, from time to time, to fill out surveys saying whether we are very lonely, somewhat lonely or never lonely, rated on a scale of one to ten. I miss something reading the results of the surveys, some kind of understanding that lies in the shadows, in nuances surveys cannot quantify and shadings statistics cannot hint at.

What interests me is understanding the problem of loneliness and particularly the loneliness of this time and place. So I find myself at the other end of the spectrum from all the quick-fix therapies, books and articles now on the market. I am often reminded of snake oil peddlers, listening to talk shows tell people that if only they did this or that—join a video dating service, buy a pet or a plant, learn how to talk with people—that loneliness would disappear, be conquered or be cured. These things may help, the way aspirin helps headaches, but for many people they do not. If you think you can buy snake oil to cure your problem, then you don't need to think about yourself very much—just shell out the money— and you don't need to think about the structure of the world in which you live.

The problem with trying to "fix" loneliness is that the theory rests on suffering people knowing they are suffering and looking for relief. I hardly found this to be the case. Loneliness, for most people, is a great source of shame. It is denied. It is covered up. The impulse is to turn away from lonely people, who somehow threaten to draw us into deep quicksand, and to turn away from the idea of our own loneliness.

Dr. Will is a healer, but he has, like the rest of us, his limitations. "There are things I can listen to as an analyst," he says. "I can listen to anything about sex. I can listen to 'I hate

Mommy,' 'I hate Daddy,' 'I want to have sex with my mother,' but I find it hard to listen to loneliness."

The room is still. Sunset scatters russet shafts of light through two large windows, across his face and into my eyes. I shift. Just before the doctor was born, his father came down with tuberculosis. His mother took her ailing husband to New Mexico where, perhaps, the climate was considered a balm to his illness. When Otto Will was born, he was sent to live with his grandparents until he was three years old.

The impulse is to turn away. Dr. Will finds it hard to listen to lonely patients because of the remembered suffering of his first three years, the sense of what was lost. This is a small, wise observation to turn over and over like a paperweight full of swimming snowflakes: "You can't have loneliness without relatedness. It implies a memory of something lost."

I have been thinking about our history and our myths. In the nineteenth century, Alexis de Tocqueville saw us as a nation of citizens "locked in the solitude of their own hearts." American heroes are always loners—Johnny Appleseed, the lonesome cowboy riding the range, the solitary private eye, the self-made businessman who battles his way to the top without aid or comfort. As schoolchildren, we were taught to admire Thoreau for living without companionship or society at Walden Pond. These are male heroes. Few women in our history are admired for going it alone. I can hardly think of American heroines without seeing them in the context of other people—Betsy Ross in a community, other brave women with children clinging to their skirts. Even the famous outlaw, like Belle Starr or the heroine in *Bonnie and Clyde,* has a man by her side or in her gang. For women, being alone is punishment; the lonesome cowboy hero or soldier or explorer or politician is matched only by figures like Hester Prynne in Hawthorne's *The Scarlet Letter,* a woman outcast because she has stood against the values of the community.

Dr. Will remembers his family as I talk about heroes who are alone. There were two grandfathers, both Lone Ranger kinds of men. He moves easily from grandfathers to male friends. One, there was one, a friend he had known in the war, where so much male intimacy is forged, who did, one day, say "I love you." He said it, however, obliquely, to someone else. "I love this man," he said, referring to Dr. Will, but speaking to someone else.

One researcher found that when he asked men about their close friends, one named a war buddy who had been dead ten years. I remember a long walk with an intellectual and sensitive man in his early forties, the river on our right, the first buds of spring popping out on the trees, the man catching me up on the changes of the decade in which we had not seen each other much. What he remembered—what I remember from that conversation now years later—was a camping trip with a male friend, a mountain, a cold night and a sudden storm. One sleeping bag got soaked. The two friends huddled through the night in the other one. This, he said, was a cataclysmic turning point in his life. My friend had had four wives by then, an interesting slew of children ranging from an infant to a few beginning to make their marks on the world. His career had taken several startling turns. Yet "cataclysmic" applied to the night on the mountain, the conquest of his fear, the ability to be close to another man.

Another friend talked about a skiing trip on yet another mountain. Men's stories of companionship most often take place outdoors—mountains, forests, battlefields, playing fields—while women's are almost always set indoors and, more likely than not, in kitchens. My friend had spent the day with three other men, none of whom he had much in common with, aside from skiing. One was a carpenter, another a plumber, the third a lawyer. It was a day of good, hard skiing, a beer at the end and a return to separate homes, separate lives. My friend was happy. He had experienced companionship and friendship. And a good day's skiing. There had been no personal conversation. He knew nothing of the other men's private lives—how they lived, what they were going through. He had no hint of who they loved or hated, what they dreamed about, what kept them going or set them back, all the things most women would, after a day spent together, have begun to elicit. It didn't matter. A woman finds this hard to understand. Her definition of "intimacy" is different, her expectations of friendship, companionship and, often, love take different forms. So do her satisfactions. Lacking a connection that feels to her like a connection, a woman will say she is lonely. Men seem to be speaking a different language.

The forms of friendship men build in adolescence don't seem to change in mature life. Men in the park on Sunday afternoons horsing around with footballs often look as though they are clinging to what was, shouting and back-slapping just as their sons, on adjacent fields, pass, run and tackle with their friends. It is not the waning athleticism that seems sad, but the sense that these men can enjoy and care for each other only in the ways they did as boys. Grown men at business conferences together often behave like adolescents. At an elegant hotel in Palm Beach, eight executives who started out at the same firm and had gone separate ways—many now owned their own companies—met for a yearly reunion. They ogled women, whom they called "girls." They poked each other in the ribs. Their talk, to my shamelessly eavesdropping ear, was competitive: "Well, our earnings last year were . . ." "Well, we brought in this new consultant who said we had the best . . ."

A man says he doesn't know what happened, but that he "used to have a concrete, sharp feeling for a man friend and that seems to disappear as a man becomes more of a man." He disdains my disdain about male forms of intimacy. "There are things that are understood between men," he says. "They don't need to be talked about. They might be expressed with a touch on the shoulder or a joke."

For women, the opposite of loneliness is almost always having someone to talk to. The stereotype of the adolescent girl tying up the family telephone for hours chatting with girlfriends is not mythological, nor is it confined to adolescence. Married men are generally confounded about what their wives find to talk with their women friends about so endlessly. This female emphasis on talk as connection may originate in childhood. Some studies show that mothers not only hold girl children closer to their bodies than they do boy children, but that they talk more to girls. Anyone who has watched children playing together knows that girls' play is, on the whole, more sedentary. Boys horse around and run around. Girls pour tea or talk to dolls.

The female idea of connection is generally based on identification and sharing. Women tolerate differences less well than men do, having been socialized to be "nice" and to "get along" with people. "I feel the same way," "I have the same dress," "I know just what you mean" are common phrases among women talking together. Men learn more thoroughly to set themselves apart from other people and to feel more comfortable in a mode of competition rather than identification.

Some of the loneliness around the country came down to this gender difference. Women and men lamented not being "in love," not being able to "find someone." People in marriages were often lonely, the women particularly, saying, "We never talk." Men didn't understand what they meant by "talk" because they thought they did it. In a recent episode of the television serial *Dallas,* three relationships were depicted this way: there was trouble; the woman said to the man, "We have to talk"; and the man either turned his back, took a drink or walked out of the room.

Ah, but I was talking easily with a man in Northern California, in a large-windowed study, about these very things. Women, Dr. Will said, were surely more capable of intimacy. This capacity came because, as mothers, they were "so close to the beating heart of a child." Pregnancy, in his view, qualified a person for intimacy. The room tipped. One of his patients had lived in such icy silence that even the sound of the curtain at the window moving in the wind had disturbed her. Now the curtain moved disturbingly for me. I have, by choice, carried no child. Was I therefore, by his definition, incapable of intimacy? And other women who had not had children? He rose in my mind like the ghost of Freud, making biology destiny. As with many women, identification is comfortable for me, and moments when the "fit" is not what I wish, the harmony broken, are difficult. I felt suddenly very lonely in that room. This might seem a luxury to people who spend days with no living soul within reach, men working at jobs where they stare at dials all day, young mothers pushing prams over empty streets, but I felt unbearably lonely. It was the feeling many people in this book tried to articulate—the loneliness of not being known, of not fitting, of not being right.

And then I recovered. The room righted itself. If I thought of nonloneliness as being in absolute accord with this man, I was doomed. We were different—in gender, generation, temperament and history. Given his childhood experience of being sent away by his mother, I understood why the baby's heart beating in the mother's body was, perhaps sentimentally and romantically, his idea of the key to intimacy. To be different was not to be disconnected. I had begun to learn something about loneliness. I climbed the hill up to the road, wiser and grateful.

I thought, at first, that I knew what loneliness was and that it belonged to the world of losers, like the scrawny old woman in a rundown hotel in south Miami, her door barred, a meager store of groceries still in their paper sack. Or the man shuffling up a Manhattan street, stubble on his face and darkness under his eyes, going to the candy store, buying a newspaper, trying to say hello to children on the street who turned away, then going home alone. But I came to find loneliness more and more among people we like to think of as winners, like the sharp commodities broker on the way up, bicycling to work in a herd of cars knowing he would have no real conversation with anyone at work that day, or the woman who left the security of a Los Angeles company to start one of her own in a town on the Russian River in Northern California, was close to her husband, saw the work thrive, and yet suffered because she had no women friends.

I had no working definition. The dictionary says that loneliness is a longing for companionship or society, but declines to say how much companionship, how much society, satisfies the longing. I knew that "alone" and "lonely" did not mean the same thing, that some people were perfectly happy to spend time alone or to live alone. Instead of loneliness, this happy condition was called solitude. Being physically alone had little to do with feeling lonely. People told me they were lonely in offices full of people, in marriages, hanging around on street corners with gangs of alleged friends. Loneliness takes different shapes, is expressed in different languages and coped with or not by very different behavior, depending on who the people are, where and how they live, what they imagine life ought to be, what resources, real and imagined, are available for pulling themselves out of loneliness, for engaging the problem.

People mean very different things by loneliness. Some are lonely eating alone, reminded of something that isn't there, a family, an idea of family. Some are perfectly happy eating alone, but can't go to movies by themselves. Big cities make some people lonely; others feel empty and alone in nature, missing the human presence of city life. Lonely means "nobody cares about me" often enough, a lack of relatedness to other people, feeling shut out. It sometimes means wanting a mate or it means being married and having no friends. Many people use the word to describe a feeling of being adrift in the universe, atomized, living in a world that comprises only the self.

Usually, loneliness was described as a condition of space—

empty space, the feeling that no one is home, the physical panic of reaching out and finding no one there. Listening, I had the sensation of large land masses coming apart and people actually falling into the cracks. The land masses were the bonds dissolving in the lives of lonely people—families disintegrating, grandparents moving to Phoenix or Miami, parents divorcing. Friendships broke because someone was transferred to Houston or got a better job in Atlanta. Neighborhoods dissolved because they were "upscaled"—the shoemaker left, the lady who had always sat on her stoop purveying neighborhood gossip couldn't afford to live there anymore. People lost their jobs: were fired, forced into early retirement, let go when the factory closed, sent away when the farm went into receivership.

But I came to see that, for many people, loneliness was an experience of time. "Not knowing what to do with yourself" was the way it was usually put. Children rattled around in empty houses. Teenagers rattled around in the streets. People sat at telephones, waiting for someone to call. Life became a month of Blue Sundays, days that made people vulnerable to the fantasy that everyone else was with someone and not lonely, that lovers were having brunch and families were having picnics and the world was elsewhere knit together.

It was always a personal, private experience, particular to each one of us. It was spoken of in all the psychological terms that have become an easy part of our vocabulary—"lack of intimacy," "learning to relate," "escaping narcissism" and "learning to communicate." Few Americans saw loneliness as having a social dimension, being related to the way we live, to the changing conditions of our world, to the economy or the state of technology. Solutions, then, were private.

In loneliness, people turned to telephones. A Puerto Rican woman in Miami spends hundreds of dollars asking her sister in New York what she puts in the rice. A market researcher moved to Houston has astronomical bills for calling home to Buffalo at Thanksgiving and Christmas, spending almost entire days on the telephone. The telephone company is not unaware of this and has, in all its recent advertising campaigns, exploited it. First there was "reach out and touch someone"—for a price. The current campaign is "I can't live without you."

Throughout the advertising world, selling products and services other than telephones, the pitch is so often about moving people closer to each other or giving them the illusion that they are not so very much alone. In Houston, a real estate developer advertised his condominiums as places for making friends. Almost all alcoholic beverage commercials promise companionship. A Silver Spring, Maryland, adult community tries to lure senior citizens away from Florida and closer to families left behind by running an ad that shows a child's handwritten note: "Dear Grandma and Grandad. I liked it when you lived here and we played on Sunday. Please come home."

The illusion of companionship sits waiting in the television set. We keep our televisions on more than we watch them—an average of more than seven hours a day. For background. For company. In Cleveland, one station's pre-emption of a daytime soap for an address by the President was met by a howl from viewers.

Cleveland was where I started thinking about the loneliness of certain places. I tried to be mindful that this subject was not open to tourism, that I couldn't see, by walking around, the high school kid feeling he didn't belong anywhere or the couple married twenty years lying in the same bed night after night without touching. Still, some places seemed lonelier than others. Seattle, for example, has an unusually large number of citizens trained in cardiopulmonary resuscitation. In Seattle, it is considered a civic virtue to know what to do about cardiac arrest, and nearly 40 percent of the population does know. Although there are surely people in Seattle suffering their own private agonies of loneliness, it does seem to me that the context of civic life is the antithesis of loneliness.

People think it important to care for one another. They are prepared to save each other's lives. Seattle has the highest rate in the country for recovery from cardiac arrest. Since so much talk about loneliness is couched in metaphors of the heart—metaphors considered literal by some medical experts who relate heart disease to loneliness quite precisely—I think Seattle's program addresses the question of loneliness better than the pages and pages of singles advertising in most other cities' newspapers do.

In Cleveland, the cab driver shuttling between the airport and downtown hotels had lost two sons to that city's failing economy. He sounded like parents who have lost their children to war. Cleveland's version of war is a decline of almost 25 percent in the population in the last decade. The cab driver has five other children still living with him, but he is a man forlorn.

The sons have gone to Houston. At the time he told me this, Houston's unemployment rate was under 4 percent and the city was a lure for workers who had lost their jobs in industrial northern states. But the jobs in Houston were for skilled labor. "If you have skills," Houstonians said, before their city, too, saw unemployment rise, "we can absorb you." The cab driver's sons had no skills. They had not found work. What they had brought with them—clothing, guitars, belt buckles, flasks—would, I expected, end up out near the petroleum refineries in Pasadena, Texas, down near Gilley's bar, where rows and rows of pawnshops testify to massive dashed expectations. In Cleveland that wintry day, the circus announced it would skip the Midwest because people couldn't afford to come. Imagine the loneliness of a town without a circus.

Houston was lonely in a different way, a place where people had come seeking to connect themselves to pots of gold and The American Dream and where lonely meant deeply disappointed. Mary Bacon, a judge in Houston's criminal court, said that many defendants who take the stand in her courtroom "can barely speak, so unaccustomed are they to having anyone ask them anything about themselves and wait for an answer. They speak in monosyllables and silence. Now that, I think, must be a terrible loneliness." Mary Bacon has her own "terrible loneliness" to remember, but it belongs to the past. Before she became a lawyer and a judge, she stayed home while her husband went to work and her children went to school. Their house was in a literal cul-de-sac. She would take her bicycle out and ride around and around the cul-de-sac. The only sounds she heard were the air conditioners humming in the other houses. "Now there," she says, "I knew what loneliness was."

The loneliness of the housewife riding around a cul-de-sac was one of many things that prompted the changes we have lived through in the past twenty years. The entry of large numbers of women into the workforce, into previously male-dominated fields and into positions of power has caused major social upheaval. Family life has reassembled behind this change. Relations between men and women have been somewhat realigned or, in some pockets of the country, radically altered. This has a great deal to do with our current loneliness. I often felt, particularly when I talked with men and women who defined loneliness as feeling unconnected to a romantic partner, that I was standing in the wake of a large ocean liner that had recently passed through. The changes had come, but the wake had not settled. Old ways were gone, but new ones had not yet come to take their place.

So I came to see loneliness as unabsorbed change, both psychologically, in individual people's lives, and culturally, in terms of how we live. An adolescent in transit from the dependency of childhood to the autonomy of adult life has not yet assimilated the change from one condition to another. A divorced person has not yet found a way of being in the world that was not "wife" or "husband" to someone. A man who wants to fall in love with a woman who will be there at the end of the day and a woman who needs a man who makes more money than she does and will be counted on to care, protect and define her have not yet come to terms with the different way we see these things now. A retired person or a widow living far from the old family circle has not found a way to adapt to those circumstances, personally new, but also culturally new.

Much of what I heard about loneliness was memory—what had been and was lost. Loneliness came to seem an emotion akin to nostalgia. Around the country, houses were being built with fake village greens and an "old-time" look to them, memories of the rural small town, as though we could create an attachment to the past this way.

Nowhere was the connection between nostalgia and loneliness more clear than in the way people talked about missing the feeling of belonging to something, the feeling of membership. Older people missed the feeling of belonging to communities and to families. Younger people missed the Sixties. A large segment of the population now has a memory of membership. Some mean simply the tribal feeling that existed among their generation in the Sixties—shared styles in clothing and culture. Some mean something more profound and more active. They remember civil rights marches and feminist actions and student protest and ending the war in Vietnam. They remember acting in concert with other people for a common goal they believed in. Their present lives have little of this feeling.

Are we lonelier, then, in this time and under these circumstances, than we have been before? It is impossible to tell. We like to think we are, which is part of our nostalgia—the golden American past of barn raisings and quilting parties, the collectivity of the frontier, the bonds of the community. We forget the isolation, days without companionship; the severe and frequent loss of loved ones; marriages and families meant as units of production, not sources of companionship.

We tend to blame machines for this pervasive loneliness. On a given day, for example, I can trot to the cash machine and do the day's business without seeing another person. The machine greets me with an ebullient message—What can I do for you today? The machine can do everything for me today. I don't need anyone. I can telephone a friend, several friends, and speak to their answering machines. I can conduct my business without encountering another living person. I can use a computer to shop or work or watch the stock market or research the American past. And I can watch television. I can read in the newspapers about "user friendly" software for my computer and, on the business page, about "friendly take-overs." What are we trying to tell ourselves?

One of the most sensible voices in the debate about technology and human values is that of Sherry Turkle, associate professor at MIT. In *The Second Self,* a study of the effect of computers on our world, she analyzes hackers—whom we would call "computer nuts," and who are among our new cultural heroes—as young men who "grew up as loners. Many of them describe a sense, as long as they can remember, of a difference between themselves and other people." She finds in the hacker culture "a flight from relationship with people to relationship with the machine—a defensive maneuver more common to men than to women. The computer that is a partner in this relationship offers a particularly seductive refuge to someone who is having trouble dealing with people. It is active, reactive, it talks back."

"The computer," she says, "offers hackers something for which many of us are hungry." By extension, as computers become more available and their use more encouraged both at work and at home, we are being offered the same thing. Turkle defines it this way: "Terrified of being alone, yet afraid of intimacy, we experience widespread feelings of emptiness, of disconnection, of the unreality of self. And here the computer, a companion without emotional demands, offers a compromise. You can be a loner, but never alone. You can interact, but need never feel vulnerable to another person."

The computer offers, as television does, the illusion that loneliness is not a problem. The machines may not cause loneliness, but they do provide a culturally acceptable way of denying it. The impulse to turn away is supported by everything that is part of normal life. The impulse to face the problem seems to belong to pathology.

The psychoanalytic approach has been to see loneliness as a neurosis or to treat it as depression, which it may resemble and can often become, but there is a kind of loneliness that plagues people like a headache does, irritating, not disabling, something you think you ought to be able to live with. Intuitive medical doctors have always known that loneliness is related to disease, that people who have adequate "social support"—a difficult thing to define—have a better chance of staying healthy or recovering from disease than people who live isolated lives. Loneliness can, indeed, make you sick. Heart disease and hypertension are now generally thought of as loneliness diseases, exacerbated by a person's sense of abandonment by the world, separation from the rest of humanity. Most addictions are also considered loneliness diseases, which the medical profession is beginning to recognize but which recovering alcoholics, drug addicts, even smokers have long been aware of. Most addicts admit that their best friends have been booze, drugs or tobacco.

There is a movement now to study loneliness. Bands of researchers sally forth to survey the population about how often they feel lonely and what they do about it. These turn out to be almost entirely white populations, usually middle class. Black family life—where marriage is less central, kin networks more important, mothers as single heads of families more prevalent—isn't adequately reflected in the surveys. When researchers on the UCLA campus studied loneliness among the students, few Chicanos participated, so it was impossible to know whether the minority status of the Chicano students left them feeling cast out or whether they formed, together, a satisfying community of their own.

It is hard to study something as essentially passive as loneliness. The most afflicted rarely seek help. A recent study of suicide concluded that only a small percentage of suicidal people called suicide hotlines. People who call therapists on radio shows also talk about their problems with other people. On the other hand, a woman I met who suffers from multiple sclerosis, confined to a wheelchair, anguished by the lack of companionship and society, confessed that she listens to the call-in shows constantly, but never calls. She is not the only one. Who, then, given the method of studying loneliness by survey, can begin to guess how acute the problem is, what forms it takes, and how it differs in different segments of society?

I drove with friends along a dark country road to a tavern standing alone in a clump of trees about four miles south of Stockbridge, Massachusetts. It was Saturday night and the parking lot was full of Chevys and Fords and pickup trucks. Inside, there were fewer people than I expected. Most of them had come alone, people who lived in the country alone. The tavern was a place to warm themselves. Women in their twenties and thirties were sitting at the bar while men of about the same age huddled around two pool tables in the back room or the pinball machine or the skittles table or the jukebox.

A few people spoke to me, only because my friends were known there:

"You have to come here for a year before you know anybody. I come here all the time, been coming for fifteen years; the people here love each other."

"Everybody knows what you're doing. If you're going with a girl, it's hard to pick up other girls here because they all know about it."

"Once, a year and a half ago, I picked up a woman here and brought her back to my place. She said, 'It looks like no one lives here,' and left right away."

"It's a good place to come if you fit. Last night, I had something on my mind and I sat at the bar alone trying to think it out, but no one would let me. People kept coming up and saying 'How ya doing? . . .'"

All night long, I watched one young man. He was blond and thin and in his early twenties. His complexion was very pale, but then, it was the dead of winter. He sat on a stool in the back room, watching the action at the pool tables. He never left to get another drink, but sipped his beer slowly. Every once in a while he stood up, put his quarter on the edge of the table and sat down to wait his turn. When he played, no one talked. In fact, he spoke to no one all night long and no one spoke to him. Around midnight, he pulled on his parka, which had been lying at the foot of his stool, and walked out into the full parking lot, the cold night and the treacherous roads.

Is he one of them?

Is he one of the people about whom Dr. Philip G. Zimbardo, a Stanford University psychologist who has been studying shyness, said: "We must do something about any circumstance in which a person can say, 'Nobody knows who I am or cares to know,' for anyone in such a predicament can turn into a vandal, an assassin or a terrorist"? Or is he like the other young man at the bar who came there to think something out, wanting to be alone? Or is he about to go off into the night and paint like Chagall, losing all sense of time and place and whether the telephone, if he has one, rings or not, forgetting to sleep or eat, falling into an unmade bed, perhaps, at daybreak, happy, connected, attached in less visible, less conventional, less acceptable ways?

And if he is one of those we must do something about, what is it we must do?

CHAPTER 2

Adolescents and Addictions

"It just feels like I'm the only person in the world"

Anice, sunny day and rather aimless. I had in mind the kind of walk you need when you've been on the road a long time, cramped into plane seats and car seats, cramped into holding your tongue and letting other people, the ones you are interviewing, talk. Along the way, though, perhaps because I find it hard to take truly aimless walks when I am working, I thought I would look for the senior citizens' center Barbara Myerhoff wrote about in her book *Number Our Days.* It was somewhere in Venice. I started out about three miles away, in Santa Monica.

It was the middle of the week in early spring and the walk above the thrashing ocean was rather empty. Ahead of me walked a man wearing beige corduroy pants and a cracked leather jacket, smoking cigarette after cigarette, walking with his head down. A drifter. A loner. His hair was unwashed.

Along the benches, people here and there were staring at the ocean. The Santa Monica Senior Citizens' Recreational Center had large windows through which I could see groups of women playing cards together. One man sat alone, outside, on the porch, staring at the ocean.

In public, the loneliness of men is more visible than the loneliness of women. There were no mothers and children along the walk, few women staring at the ocean. I passed a bar with its door open—men sitting with stools between them, looking into their drinks. Presumptuous as it is to read loneliness in the body posture of a man walking alone or in what I took to be the lonely look on anyone's face, I still felt I was making my way through the turf of the walking wounded, perhaps some of the dislocation of the economy. The younger men were unemployed, some, I felt, recently unemployed. They were marginals, people a healthy economy might have absorbed. They were staring at the ocean. The older man on the porch of the senior citizens' center was alone, in part because of statistics—women live longer, there are fewer old men—and in part because of social habit. Men make friends less easily as they grow older; women seem to continue to replace the friends they have lost. For some men, the increasing loneliness of age comes because relationships have not been central in their lives—making a living, getting ahead have been—and because relationship means romance, not friendship. Most older men lack what social scientists call the social skills for making friends with other men and have had little experience making friends with women.

Another thing that struck me on this solitary but not lonely walk was how visible Jewish attempts to solve the problem of loneliness are. The homes for the aged and the senior citizens' centers were run by Jewish agencies. The singles ads in the local newspaper had a preponderance of "White Jewish male seeks . . . ," "White Jewish female would like to meet . . ." In Houston, there is a hotline for Jewish singles listed in the telephone directory. Is this, I wonder, an outgrowth of the

Jewish social conscience, a tangent of the Jewish emphasis on family and community in the face of a perceived endless danger from "outside"? Do Jews believe more than other people that it is not right for a person to be alone, or is there simply less shame in Jews than there is in Gentiles about admitting loneliness and acting to remedy it?

I passed on to the place where the road descended, came down along the beach, through a long parking lot that became the Ocean Front Walk that ran through Venice. The loner, as I had dubbed him, was still walking along some yards in front of me and still smoking cigarette after cigarette.

We all do different things to fill the empty spaces. What is an addiction but a way of not being alone in the universe? Instead of a connection to a person, complicated and dangerous and perhaps bewildering as that may be, enough of us find connections to substances and hold to them as though life depended on our having them. It is not just the narcotizing aspect of the substances we get addicted to, their quality of blanking out the pain of loneliness, as the experts say, but a more active, more horrifying thing that happens. The substances seem alive. They provide contact, companionship, care. And they don't talk back. Food is a friend. Overeaters are lonely, seeking in food the fullness that other people find in personal connections. Few overeaters indulge themselves in public and rarely at the family table—more usually they eat when they are alone. Some plan their eating the way other people plan dates—looking forward to it, hurrying home to it, choosing favorite foods the way one chooses favorite friends, having an entire relationship with food.

Alcoholics have the same relationship with alcohol. Listen, at any meeting of Alcoholics Anonymous, to the person talking about how he or she began to drink. He never felt like anyone liked him. She was alone with no one to talk to all day. He felt shy at parties. She was traveling on business and hated the table for one in strange cities night after night. I was always lonely. I was always lonely. The form of an AA meeting, which seems contrived and Mickey Mouse to someone not hungering for what the meeting has to offer, addresses this loneliness:

"Hi. My name is Mickey and I'm an alcoholic."

"Hi, Mickey." That's the entire group, in unison.

When Mickey reports something he feels good about, the group applauds. It is the fellowship that works in AA, the feeling that you're not alone, that other people have faced the darkness you are facing, that you are not bad or weird and that they care what happens to you. The same works in Overeaters Anonymous or Gamblers Anonymous or any other group devoted to helping people sever their addictions. Fellowship heals.

We don't, as a culture, seem to understand that. Addicts may be extreme cases of a hunger we have been unable to assuage. We think of love as the antithesis of loneliness. Lonely people talk constantly of "finding someone," and if they "have" someone and still feel lonely, as so many do, they think of finding someone else. We have learned to think this way. I was thinking this way watching the man walking ahead of me smoking. That is an addiction bred of loneliness that I know well because the times I have given up cigarettes I have wandered in a world where I missed the constant touching of a warm object to my mouth, the constant live thing in my hand, the presence, the other. I have been unbearably lonely. That these "others" we choose for companions may be deadly seems, often, less urgent than the dread that without them we would be utterly and agonizingly alone.

Nowhere had I come across the senior citizens' center I had set out in search of. Now there were shops and restaurants, some boarded up, some empty, all with that desolate air of enduring after the season had gone or waiting for the season to begin. A pita sandwich shop. A pizza shop. A jeans store. A T-shirt store. An ice cream stand. Addictions board you up too, I thought, the irony being that the very substances we clutch for companionship, each in their own way, actually prevent it. The food addict hides from other people, shoveling in the comfort in a fit of shame. The alcoholic stops by his apartment on the way to a meeting, fortifies himself, arrives in a state oddly untouchable, feeling invulnerable, so fortified. I am always aware of the literal smokescreen the cigarettes create between a smoker and other people and of the rupture of conversation or interaction that occurs when I stop, break eye contact, break the connection, fish for the cigarettes, look down, light up.

I lit up at La Cantina, sitting at a sidewalk table, alone, ordering lunch. Few people I know enjoy eating alone, holding, as we do, a collective memory of the family dinner table or the collective, ancient ritual of breaking bread in community with other people. I had, at that moment, however, an identity to shield me from whatever loneliness I might have felt eating alone, to ward off the nostalgia of ancient tribal eating rituals. I was the traveler in a strange city. I was she-who-is-alone and she-who-is-working in a way that has always felt better than all right, an identity that carries its own kind of glamour and purpose and, perhaps, grandiosity, a good bulwark against loneliness.

A short, fat woman walked by, a bag of groceries in one hand, a dog on a leash in the other. A drag queen stopped to entertain the sidewalk eaters, singing "You can't always get what you want." Inside La Cantina, at a lunch counter, looking out, was a young man staring out the window and eating a sandwich. He looked like Warren Beatty. Several times, I thought he was about to wave at me, come out and speak to me, but he didn't. He finished his sandwich, came out, went to the corner, turned uphill and disappeared. I had the feeling he came here for lunch every day.

Was the man eating alone one of "them," one of Dr. Zimbardo's potential vandals, assassins or terrorists? Did he return home after lunch to companion himself with nicotine, booze, coke, hash, PCP, heroin? Or was he a working screenwriter stretching his legs after a good morning's work, going

out to breathe the air a bit and take some nourishment, returning to the work and the background of family, friends, lover,
community? I had long since given up trying to guess.

If you believe in fate, it was fate, then, that stopped me in
front of a red brick building with a sign over its white arch
showing a triangle within a circle. At each point of the triangle
was a word: Body, Mind, Spirit. In the center, the sign said:
"It's up to you." I smiled in some kind of wan, cynical sympathy
for the relentless fringiness that is Southern California, for a
naïve and sentimental predilection for the allegedly spiritual,
the weird, the counter, in which I had myself, a long time ago,
been quite immersed.

Underneath the triangle within the circle was an identification: "A Self-Help Social Rehabilitation Agency." That
sounded almost respectable. If I am interested in loneliness, I
am certainly interested in social rehabilitation. I went in, a bit
timidly.

He was sitting on a dark couch in a dark living room just to
the left of the entrance. Not sitting, actually, sprawling. The
room stank of cigarette smoke. He was smoking, half awake.
There was another young man on the other side of the room,
reading a magazine and smoking a cigarette. He gave me the
impression of a Little Lord Fauntleroy, but the one on the
couch did not. He looked like a sidelined basketball player,
long and lean, a big, bushy Afro lolling against the edge of the
couch.

"Welcome to the loneliest place in America."

Antonio Rico Harris, then twenty-one, was living in Tuum
Est, the social rehabilitation center which had formerly been
called a drug rehabilitation center. He was in the introductory
phase of the program. For nineteen days, there had been no
marijuana or cocaine or PCP in his body. And it was the
loneliest place in America.

Ellen Kaplan, the center's director, walked into the room
and invited me to her office, taking on herself the role of
narrator of this specific kind of loneliness and exercising her

prerogative as director to, I imagined, investigate me to see if continued conversation with Tony, whose life was very much out of his hands at that moment, would be beneficial to anyone. Ellen is a woman in her thirties, a transplanted Easterner, a woman of extreme competence and the kind of hardheadedness that stands well against the dangerous sentimentality I bring to these questions and to my conversations with Antonio Rico Harris, who had, at that moment, retired to a bedroom upstairs.

The change in the center's name was significant. In the twelve years that the center has been on the beach, the problem seemed to be drugs. Now, perhaps since the advent of Ellen Kaplan's directorship, the drugs appear to be a symptom and the problem to be what she calls a social disease. It's the "lack of a family unit," Ellen says, that brings people to this place, that you uncover as you listen to their stories, their lives as "junkies" and "dope fiends," as most of the residents of Tuum Est are likely to call themselves. "Even if they're in intact families," she says, "there's no relationship. These are disconnected people who don't know how to relate, who have a desire for intimacy and a fear of it. They were never taught the socialization skills to make friends."

It is not a shocking idea. "Every one of these rehabilitation places, these communes," she says, "is built on the idea of the family unit. People have a need for that family situation." So Ellen and her staff make a family. As she says "family" I look through the window over her shoulder at groups of people outside walking back and forth, some lurching glassy-eyed beside each other but clearly inhabiting different daydreams, some alone and forlorn, some huddled around benches passing joints. How magical we have made "family," how often it is uttered with profound reverence, a breathiness almost sacrosanct. Upstairs, Tony has fallen asleep on his bed, an iron bunk that reminds me of days at camp—was that a family?— fully clothed, head on his hands.

The family that inhabits Tuum Est consists of Ellen's staff, residential counselors, people who come in and out bringing various forms of help like tutoring in high school subjects and instructing in nutrition and organizing athletic outings. It is a highly structured program, very regimented, a five-phase experience that begins with figuring out where the hell you are and being unable to leave the building—that's Tony's situation at the moment—and proceeds in stages, with increasing privileges or the rescinding of privileges, with a heavy emphasis on getting a job, learning how to get along in the world, how to have a checking account and a functional life and friends. It is one of the longest and hardest rehabilitation programs in the country. Tony's physical self was absolutely at sea as he navigated his way through the second stage of withdrawal. The sickness and the heebie-jeebies began to leave, but shadows and disorientation stayed, along with the hitherto unknown emptiness of being without his "best friends."

Although the addicts used to be street people, the population of Tuum Est is increasingly made up of younger kids and richer ones. Ellen Kaplan thinks that the fact that they are seeing younger and younger addicts means "people know there's a problem and are trying to get help earlier. There is more appreciation now for the loneliness and pain they feel." Three quarters of the people who have come to Tuum Est for help are male—families, if they're involved, more often put female addicts into hospitals and many young women don't get as far as Tony did because they have, Ellen says, "a better ability to endure stress and pain."

But Tony is young and his age gives Ellen Kaplan hope. "You watch the older people here," she says sadly. "They are resigned. Most people over thirty-five say 'I've been alone all my life. I don't need anybody.' "

I am not on alien turf. There is nothing that I know about drug addicts, junkies, boozers, and dope fiends that seems different, in the essential ways that bear on loneliness, from more respectable and visible people in more recognizable situations and places. The social disease—the disconnection —infects the corporate executive traveling in a private car, private elevator, private plane, shielded from everyone who works for him by a prestigious idea of privacy. Although many people who describe their loneliness have options Tony may not have had, they don't see them. His resignation is equally familiar: I have been alone all my life. I don't need anybody.

On our way to wake Tony, we meet a counselor in the second phase of the program. A former resident who remained "sober" for nine years, he couldn't make it on the outside. He had, in those years, the magical thing called a family—he had married and fathered a child—but it hadn't been enough: "I just went to work and came home to my little family unit and that was it. First I started drinking and the next thing I knew, I was using drugs again. I started out as a pickup driver for a data processing company in Van Nuys and worked my way up to the control department. I also worked my way up from wine to heroin." He started missing work. Then he started staying home a lot. He watched the test pattern on his television set. He called the suicide prevention center just to talk to someone. None of this seems unfamiliar.

Tony's voice is hard to listen to. He swings his legs off the bed like a man underwater and quickly moves his comb through his Afro, as though he feels onstage and unprepared. His voice almost sounds drugged. He slurs. He pauses. He seems about to cry. It is a mournful sound, like the high lonesome wail of a pedal steel guitar and my adolescent memory of Hank Williams singing "I'm so lonesome I could cry" or Jimmie Rogers and the wail of a train, the wail of pain.

We move downstairs, to chairs set on the side of the small lobby, people coming and going, organizing a group to plant a garden at the side of the building, others tossing a volleyball back and forth, activity that serves as a reminder that there is a world outside those doors and Tony is not allowed into it —that's part of the first phase of the program—nor would he know what to do if he were.

Why is this the loneliest place in America?

"You see all these lonesome people wandering around. You see an expression in my eyes. People say, 'What's wrong, you look mad.' I'm not mad. It feels like I'm the only person in the world. You know that you're by yourself and I'm just terrified. Frightened. I feel like I'm loved somewhere, but where?"

Loneliness, at least in part, led Tony to make good Colombian marijuana his first good friend, then cocaine and then PCP. What he talks about now is the wall coming down on the other side—the loneliness of being without drugs. It is hard for him to talk about the past, about where he has come from, so focused is he on the present pain. There are sketchy details of that past, many of which will be filled in as I come to know him and many of which, by their distortions and omissions, will turn out to be lies. A junkie's loyalty, I will learn here, is to junk and part of the rehabilitation process is to find another object for that loyalty—other people, the world and, most crucially, one's own well-being. Tony is still close to the junk, so he tells me a story full of holes.

Tony grew up in Los Angeles and lived with his mother and brother. His parents, he says, were divorced. He started, as a teenager, by smoking Colombian grass, then smoking more, then snorting cocaine for about six months and then he was "turned on to" smoking cocaine, which was an extraordinary high. He was working at the Mattel toy company and putting his pay into the drugs, and when that wasn't enough he started selling. There was also a mysterious insurance payment that lasted quite a while and he spent it on a car, drugs, jewelry and drugs. Tony was the guy who picked up checks. "If there was any expense, it would be on me." He is talking about supposed friends, not grocery expenses at home nor, I suspect, rent. Somewhere in this hazy background, there were the people who rode around with him in the car and whose expenses he picked up, but I can't see them; they've receded into the shadows, if they were ever there. "I would go to my friends," he says, "when I was lonely, but I had drugs." As though it were self-explanatory, which it is. Drugs made sharing easier. He won't say much about this in relation to himself, but there is that ubiquitous other person: "I got a friend who's real lonely because all he has is drugs. All he has is drugs. He'll consider you a friend if you come over and smoke with him."

At Tuum Est, there are no drugs to facilitate the sharing, so what is left? At the moment, for Tony, very little. He lies awake at night on his bed thinking, just thinking, usually for an hour or two. But there are others present. Tony has two roommates. Are they awake? Are they thinking? Does he talk to them. "Oh, they're okay gentlemen. . . ."

He shrugs, as he often does at sticking points in the conversation. It's not that he doesn't know what to say, only that he is on what he can muster of his best behavior, with an odd formality in his talk—"They're okay gentlemen"—and a certain guardedness in his body. Tony, understandably, thinks he's on television or in front of a teacher and is afraid to say the wrong thing. I can't tell how much of this guardedness has to do with race, nor how much of his present estrangement has to do with being one of only a few black people in a white-run and largely white-populated institution. "There are those," he says, "who isolate themselves from me here. Which makes me lonely. Makes me think I'm a bad person, which I don't think I am." Are "those" white? Tony shrugs. There are a few other black kids and talking "to my own culture, it makes me feel a little better." But he learns a lot from "Caucasians." Good behavior. Tony gets an A for politeness.

You never remember to ask about everything. You always miss cues and walk away with tapes and notes of interviews from which it only becomes clear, much later, when you try to assemble a story, what has been left out. I didn't ask Tony, that first time, how he got to Tuum Est. That is always, if you're looking to understand people or simply looking for drama, the watershed in an addict's story—the moment of bottoming out, the decision, although it doesn't feel like a decision at the time but more like a desperate action, the only action you can think of taking—to kick it or, at the very least, to ask for help. I asked if he had been involved in crime, which seemed a natural question, and he said no and I didn't pursue it. I also didn't ask about women or sex or romance or love.

There was someone else who did want to talk about sex or romance or love. His name was Carlos, he lived in Miami and he is Cuban or was, until he came to America three years ago. He thinks of himself now as not Cuban and the ways in which he shares this with other people of his generation contributes to the kind of loneliness I heard about often in Miami. How had I found this eighteen-year-old, so full of girls and America and the good life? Again, by luck and accident and again as a deflection of my original purpose—looking into the loneliness of the aged. In that way, before the subject opened as wide as it did, I had not followed my nose, but followed stereotypes. Think loneliness = think old. It turned out, as is probably clear by now, to be a false stereotype and, in fact, one that my travels and the work of social scientists are setting on its ear: the most acute loneliness appears to be found among adolescents, not octogenarians.

But Carlos. The quirk was that I had gone to a mental health center in Miami and discovered a program there for "unaccompanied adolescents," those who had come from Cuba alone. It is one of the difficulties of the white reporter that the nonwhite world does not lend itself easily to our reporting. Access is usually formal—through an agency, a structure, an institution, which lends both our reception and our perception a different quality from what we discover talking to our friends or the friends of friends, the habitués of our circle. So Carlos came by the graces of a bureaucracy and he, too, was somewhat shy, somewhat "onstage"—the representatives of the bureaucracy were listening.

He came with an extraordinary story. Since the age of twelve, he had been thinking about leaving Cuba. Actually, the way he said it, he thought about leaving at twelve and the rest of the time was spent figuring out how to do it. He missed his first chance. When the Peruvian Embassy in Cuba opened up, allowing Cubans who wanted to leave to pass through there, Carlos was far from Havana. So he plotted. He let his hair grow long. He wore an earring. He made sure all the authorities saw him. Eventually, in his interview to begin military service, he was asked if he was homosexual and he said yes. He wasn't. A policeman consulted a committee. Wheels turned. Carlos was deported to America.

His family didn't want to leave. There were three siblings, a mother and, presumably, a father, although Carlos never mentions him. His first stop in America was Fort McCoy in Wisconsin, where he stuck close to a man who had come there with his own three sons and daughters. Eventually, Carlos arrived in south Miami, where he found many people he had known in Cuba, but they weren't the focus of his attention.

Shyly, he draws Maggie's picture from his wallet. It is a very American name, Maggie, not Teresa or Carmen, he points out. And her father was born in Cuba, but she is an American, he says. I look. Maggie has blond hair and light skin. Carlos, quite dark himself, is very proud of that too. This is the part, he says, that was hardest for him in America. The loneliness of exile is familiar not only to the entire world, but especially to Americans, whose families landed on these shores the other side of elsewhere, whose adaptation to strange languages, customs, beliefs and strange-looking people forms part of the heritage of all of us. Carlos's solution to the problem of his lonely exile—mitigated, as all the immigrants' loneliness has been, by the familiarity of the community, by attachments to a known world—was to make himself fit as quickly as possible into American life and to find, as quickly as possible, an American girl. In the beginning, the girls he met did not cooperate. He was too Cuban. They wanted American boys, for all the same reasons. Eventually, Carlos found Maggie.

He has two ties to Cuban life now. Although he has been described by the center's director as "one of the few who like to run around in American discotheques," he still plays soccer, not baseball. His other tie is his mother, whom he talks to on the telephone once a month. He doesn't feel, as Antonio Rico Harris does, that he is the only person in the world. His loneliness is a very specific longing for a lost connection. He has many ways of avoiding that longing, filling the spaces, but when they falter, he withdraws: "When I'm alone, I feel very, very bad. I miss my mother. I feel I want to cry. When I feel that way, I just stay alone."

Soledad. The word sounds different in Spanish. *Cuando me siento solo.* There is something more legitimate in the romance languages when people speak of loneliness *(soledad)* and of being alone *(solo).* The word has a rather romantic resonance and philosophical overtones. It strikes more of a romantic posture. It sounds serious, not shameful. It is soft, not a howl of pain. Nor is it shameful, in Carlos's world, to admit missing his mother. American boys of Carlos's age have long since learned to deny their mothers, to consider themselves sissies for feeling this attachment to their mothers and certainly for wanting to cry about them.

But Carlos has dreams, dreams to help him over the bad places and the times he feels so alone. He knows what he needs. He needs his mother, a career and money—he puts it in that order. He will have a big house. He will have a family. His wife and his children will not need anything. And he will design a better computer. Welcome to the American way.

"We're going to go the American way," Olivia Martinez, associate director of the clinic, says. "We're going to go on separating the generations. The children will be more independent of the family. They will go off on their own the way Americans do, which is unthinkable to a Cuban."

Also painful. Although I had turned to the adolescents, Olivia's comments reminded me of Laura, whom I had met earlier in the day. The staff of the center tried to persuade me that Laura was a special case, that she had acute psychological problems and was not typical, but I found here as elsewhere that the extremes only continued the themes at the center, writ them larger. I think the staff—with its best-face-forward attitude and its justifiable fear of distortion or insult in the gringo press, preferred Carlos's American solutions to his loneliness over Laura's desperate pain.

That morning, she had sat in a classroom with about fifty other people listening to a counselor explain the various therapies offered at the mental health center. There were more women than men there, but still quite a few men. The talk was about how to become less dependent on drugs. At the end of it, people milled about the room—as in any group, there were clusters of three and four and there were people who remained in their seats, alone. There was a raffle, with a plant and a ceramic ashtray as prizes. Then there was a macaroni meal, which, in spite of the value of the program and the intentions of its organizers, may have drawn the group there as much as anything else had.

Laura spoke, in that Latin way, of "two hundred years of unhappiness," but her particular trouble was more recent. She came to Miami from Cuba in 1963, with a husband, two daughters and a son. Her son went to Vietnam, was wounded in combat and became schizophrenic. The causal relationship is clear in her mind. In 1969, she separated from her husband. The circumstances are unclear. Laura worked. She was a maid in a Miami Beach hotel, a baker's helper and then a cook in the University of Miami cafeteria. She had a lot of friends in this time that she worked, women friends, and remembers with a smile when "the girlfriends were all together." They were *amigas*. The loneliness of separating from her husband never comes up. He seems a shadow. The children come up, vividly. Laura is crying.

Her son divorced his wife, who took their infant child and moved away. He did this, she says, because he didn't want his wife to work and his wife wanted to and the struggle between them kept precipitating what Laura calls his "big depression." Her daughters left, too. The older one lives in Coral Gables, about fifteen minutes away, but never comes to see her. Laura had stopped working. She is sixty years old. She was left at home alone.

"I had worries," she says. "I became sad. My life is very uneasy. When I am alone I am afraid something will happen to me. I feel panic." What she used to do in those moments of loneliness and panic was take Librium, a lot of Librium, and go to bed.

Someone found Laura. Or Laura found someone. It is not clear which way the rescue, partial though it is, worked. "I was told to get out of the house as much as possible." She does. She is no longer always at home alone. She has some friends at the Catholic Hispanic Center and the Meyer Senior Center, where she goes in the afternoons. And she has this place, the macaroni meal and the people to share it with.

It is easy to be romantic about other people's connections, to imagine them whole and solid and enduring and, always, better than your own. I had seen this often enough among people lying on their beds drugged with tranquilizers or staring at test patterns on the television set or particularly in the adolescents who imagined the world had gone away for the weekend and was never coming back, that they alone had been shut out of a tapestry of girlfriends and boyfriends and gangs in cars and parties and long, close talks on the telephone. But I had never seen the extent to which this happens between cultures until I listened to Anglos describe how much closer, how much better, the family and the community were in Latin cultures.

She was a former fashion consultant, very stylish, with a bit of the Grace Kelly look about her, apparently a divorcée, perhaps a widow, but a woman in her early fifties who did not have to work to support herself. She had come to one of the many social service agencies in Florida, thinking of volunteering to be on its board of directors. I met her in the agency building and when I told her what I was doing, she attributed the epidemic of loneliness in the country to the lack of large families. The world seemed to be shriveling. "You're not going to solve it in the nuclear family," she said. It was clear what this meant to her personally: "My mother lives two minutes away from me and many days she is alone and I am alone and . . . It's a shame." First she thought it was a matter of class, that the very rich and the very poor had it better than she did, but she could not explain why. One image haunted her. She had seen enough Cuban life in Miami to have formed an opinion: "Look at people from the Cuban community going shopping together," she said, her face brightening. "There are five of them to buy a pair of shoes." I did not tell her about Laura because she was rushing off to a meeting which, I thought, she imagined would provide the large family that might engage themselves in the welfare of others instead of going shopping together for a pair of shoes.

I had come far from the adolescents. They led me, always, to their families, whether they were large and went shopping for shoes together—in which case, there was always one child who felt alone in the group, who understood, unlike the fashion consultant, that mass did not equal intimacy and was often, in fact, its enemy—or whether the families were small, so the adolescents would complain of loneliness at home, proffer a wish for siblings. Their landscapes were more often not family, but school, and the hunger they felt for connection was most keenly felt in classrooms and schoolyards, on Saturday afternoons and evenings. They wanted friends. They wanted people to do things with—"lonely," to most of the adolescents I talked to, meant being excluded from the group —and they wanted to be understood.

But their landscapes were larger, still. The lonely adolescents live in a particular time and place that shapes their experience. This is where the experts come in, and they enter, bearing statistics and theories, because there is a crisis. In the past twenty-five years, the suicide rate among fifteen- to twenty-four-year-olds has gone up more than 300 percent. The suicide rate for young men has risen faster than it has for young women, and the United States now ranks among the countries in the world with the highest suicide rates among adolescent boys. In a single month, my local newspaper reported that a thirteen-year-old boy hanged himself from a tree in a city park, a fourteen-year-old boy hanged himself from a tree near his home, a nineteen-year-old boy was found in his home, shot in the head by his own hand, a seventeen-year-old boy hanged himself in his bedroom closet. Although loneliness doesn't always lead to suicide, a thread runs between them. The ghoulish stories and the alarming statistics have, however, focused a great deal of public attention on what my parents' generation worried about quietly and somewhat philosophically, believing the friends and neighbors who offered easy assurance that the misery an adolescent so clearly demonstrated would pass with the seasons, that the pains were growing pains. Except some adolescents didn't grow.

Professionals who work with troubled adolescents begin with the assumption that the specific psychological task of adolescence is grieving, mourning the loss of the omnipotent parent. It is "normal" for an adolescent to pass through a depressed, sad stage, yearning, grieving, mourning, growing away from the parents and beginning to understand the concept of death for the first time—the ultimate alone-ness. A person is more vulnerable at this stage of life to the loneliness that comes from broken attachments, from the best friend who chooses another or the boyfriend or girlfriend who moves away, to another town, to another attachment. Since girls mature more quickly than boys do, or perhaps because they are socialized, earlier, to be affiliated, they turn to boys as anodynes for their loneliness, while boys turn to teammates, other members of the band, guys in the schoolyard. Some experts think that the rise in pregnancies among teenage girls can be seen as another kind of anodyne: having a baby to take care of as protection against loneliness.

The culture sits there, waiting for blame, inviting blame. The kids don't see the culture, they only see themselves. If narcissism and self-preoccupation have any meaning, they are most visible in the adolescent stage of life and in the American kids of the Eighties who, according to the professionals who hear their troubles, have amputated the "I-thou" relationship into simply "I." And "I" is usually followed by "need" or "want."

What fills the need? What satisfied the want? Drugs, as Antonio Rico Harris had shown me. Stuff, as Carlos had shown me. I don't have anybody, but I have a flashy ring or a big house or a car or a Betamax. It is an ancient criticism of what we hold dear, but it still holds because we still hold material things more dearly than anything else. It may well be that the acute loneliness of adolescents is related not only to the painful adaptations their psyches must make, but the equally painful changes in their surroundings in the years they have already lived. The materialism of the landscape has, in a sense, increased—more "stuff" is available to more people, on credit, on the installment plan. More "stuff" is visible on television, the desire for it stimulated; it seems so within reach, all that stuff.

Adolescents do not complain of the failure of stuff to meet their hunger, they are only victimized by it, but many other people do. An actor in Los Angeles saw "loneliness" and "lack of meaning" as synonymous: "When you're involved in selling talcum powder on TV ads and talking about getting up for a role in *Knots Landing* or did you get the interview and how much did you make last year, the only salvation seems to be a warm, loving human relationship. What the hell else is there? What're you going to do—work, make millions of dollars, sit on your yacht staring into space? What have you got?"

A common strategy for coping with loneliness is shopping, stuffing stuff into the empty spaces. When the director and the woman he had been married to for seventeen years separated, the first thing he did was buy a motorcycle, which sounds like an act of exhilaration, the gesture of new-found freedom, but wasn't. When frequent fits of loneliness descend on this man, he buys accessories for the cycle, which has become his new wife, his new connection. A female professor in New York goes on shopping binges when she feels lonely and, like most women feeling desperate about stuffing something into the space, she buys clothes. If loneliness comes suddenly to these people, like a fit, so does the urge to shop, like going on a drunk or getting high. When the fit passes, the professor looks over what she has bought with a sour feeling akin to a hangover.

Stan had a hangover that looked like it was going to last a long time. Loneliness was his theme, his shadow, his companion of many years. Like a lot of people, he didn't remember being a lonely kid and up until college he was always part of something, always had friends and girlfriends; and then something funny happened when he finished graduate school. "All my friends were moving on," he says. "I felt left behind." Stan turns in his swivel chair and looks out the window at the redwoods. He is sitting very far away from me, protected by a large desk. Outside, spring is making its way through the hedges and the flowers. We are in Northern California, in a small town reputed to be one of America's drug capitals. We are not talking about ghettos here, about fast buys on street corners. We are talking about professionals, high earners, nice cars, nice houses and lots of drugs.

He describes the "garbage behavior" directly attributable, by him, to loneliness, which he calls "the ultimate bummer." Sometimes, he "chased the dragon," which means smoking heroin. Always, he snorted a lot of cocaine. Took 100 mg a day of Valium. Percodan. Halcyon, the "baby brother of the Quaalude." He had a "home pharmacy, visited regularly, all washed down with hundred-proof Smirnoff." He got Dilantin from people on social services who had extra prescriptions.

Junked up and caught up in the rock music world, Stan partied with the Grateful Dead. He'd get backstage or sit on-stage at their concerts; he'd stay up all night with the band listening to music. "My foot in the door was drugs," he says now, full of regret and nostalgia. "I had great stash. The security guys were the ones who had power. They could say 'Let this person onstage.' When you go face on face with a three-hundred-pound security guard, you can't let them smell your fear. So I turned them on to drugs." And somewhere, junked up, he managed to find a woman who moved in with him. Recently, she left. "She found it unbearable and well she should. I was totally ignoring her. If I had adequate stash, I had no need to consider anybody else's feelings."

Then, abruptly, he didn't have adequate stash anymore. He gave it up. All of it. He had lost so much weight, he tells me, his clothes were falling off and he was turning yellow. He doesn't look like that now. He actually looks robust. A trim dark mustache decorates a face that is surely not yellow. I expect Stan's account of kicking drugs to be accompanied by some measure of pride, but it isn't. "I thought that once I cleaned up," he says, "things would fall into place and they didn't. The loneliness became more and more acute." The woman didn't come back. Bob Weir, lead singer of the Grateful Dead, one of Stan's two friends, told him over and over that his backstage passes weren't dependent on drugs, but Stan doesn't believe him. He hasn't been to a concert since he gave up drugs and he can't imagine being just part of the crowd, a person with what he sees as no useful function.

Now he lives with "shallow stimulants"—newspapers, magazines and "insipid TV." Loneliness keeps him up late, postponing sleep, trying to avoid "listening to my own wheels click," warding off that "acute feeling something is absent." Social life in his town "revolves around alcohol and bars," but he is "sullen in bars. I might make idle chitchat with men. I can't imagine it with women. I'm feeling shy and afraid of rejection. The bars are full of false camaraderie and false sincerity. They have these raps and then it wears off and everybody's biting their nails. Or whatever they do.''

He reminded me of Antonio Rico Harris, another user of drugs as a bridge to the world, another person seemingly mystified by what people did without drugs, by what he would do. I went back to where I had started.

Venice had not changed. Beach Front Walk had not changed. Tuum Est was about to undergo some physical renovation. Tony had a much smaller Afro and had stopped smoking. We sat on the steps in the bright sunlight. Other residents wanted to talk this time—not only had I established my interest by coming back again (they are used to the curious and the well-wishing and the social agency people and the reporters passing through and then disappearing), but those who were well along in their recovery were beginning to see their drugged past with some definition. "When I was a junkie," they would say, "when I was a dope fiend," "when I was under the influence."

When they were junkies, dope fiends and under the influence, they were cut off. That only became clear looking back. The pill poppers disdained the cocaine sniffers, and the smokers disdained the sniffers, and the heroin addicts were separate from anyone else. There was no cliquing or running around together; it was embarrassing to be seen with the wrong kind of addict. But the detachment the kids who stopped by, as Tony and I sat on the steps, wanted to talk about was not only sad to listen to and sad for them to remember—it killed. People were too spaced out to ask for help when they needed it—food or shelter, to start with. One kid described walking away from a car accident, oblivious to the trail of blood he left in the street behind him. Another was haunted. He had been high on heroin. A girl threatened to cut her wrists right in front of him. He did nothing. She died. He didn't care.

The loneliness of the drug life. They all have stories. But Tony is distraught about the present and I find myself in the somewhat ambiguous position of having to ask permission to take him away from the building, just down the street for lunch, to find out why. I sign a form accepting responsibility.

"I have made friends. I have experienced hurt and pain." These are his first two sentences, verbatim.

We are at an outdoor restaurant bustling with life, action, movement, groups of people together, a guy passing by with a guitar who stops to sing to us. Tony seems reticent in the face of all this activity and a bit overcome by the idea of choosing from the menu. He is trying to pretend that he does this all the time—stroll around, stop for lunch—but I know that his life is controlled by the regulations at Tuum Est.

He made friends and experienced hurt and pain. Some of the friends left the program. "I've allowed myself to suffer," he says. But the pain is about one particular friend and although I know that Tony has had a shock in recent days, I have to make my way through the large salad before me and Tony has to make his way through the corned beef sandwich and the cherry soda before he will talk about it.

She was a cocaine and heroin addict who "came into the program." The program at Tuum Est is strictly monitored when it comes to couple relationships. Residents have to wait ninety days before they can become involved with someone. If a relationship breaks up, a thirty-day waiting period is imposed before a new one is allowed to begin. A relationship within the walls of Tuum Est is always a triad—the two people involved and a counselor. A couples group meets regularly and there is a couples room on the second floor, furnished with a double bed and arranged for with a counselor's permission. All this is necessary, Ellen Kaplan, the director, had explained to me, because addicts are driven by loneliness, and other people can easily become substitute drugs. Part of the social rehabilitation the program aims for is helping residents learn to build connections to other people as friends or lovers, to create families and communities. At every stage of this, they face real-life issues like frustration, mourning, things not working out, and they have to learn to face them straight. They have to learn the difference between being alone and being lonely.

Tony's problem with his girlfriend was his own violence. He couldn't listen to her. He had to dominate her. He hated it when she went out to work and left him there alone. He got violent. "When I was under the influence," he says, "I didn't have to tackle the problem. Now it's like starting from scratch, from the beginning, like grade school."

Then the problem was compounded—or suspended—because, just two days before, she ran away. In Tony's words, "She left the program this past Saturday and never came back. She split. She broke the bond we had." Tony thinks she ran away because she has a heart problem and there had been talk about her having surgery. She was scared.

"When relationships turn sour," Ellen Kaplan had said, "they go back to drugs." Is he thinking of going back? No, Tony says. In the groups at Tuum Est, people "let me know it's okay to feel this way. But I feel no one understands. There are those who say they do. There are those that care. They show it by offering to do things with me. Still, I get lonely." Besides his girlfriend, there have been other troubles.

Tony was studying for his high school equivalency test. Or trying to. He studied for a week, then he stopped and when the test came, he failed. He had been in the third phase of the program, the one with the greatest privileges, and he had to go back to the second phase. And he had been going to court for months.

I pushed the salad plate away. What was he doing in court? Well, he had forgotten to tell me this part of the story.

He was high on PCP. He needed money. There was a family in Beverly Hills he had worked for and he thought they were out of town. He drove there with a friend, who waited in the car while Tony wandered through the first floor of the house collecting jewelry, a stereo and radios, all of which he had piled in the living room when the woman of the house appeared. Tony bolted. The friend gunned the motor. The owners of the house followed and took the license number down. The friend got arrested. There was a warrant out for Tony. He surrendered himself and was sent to Tuum Est instead of to jail. These trips to court are to determine his progress and, if anything, his sentencing.

So sometimes, yes, Tony lies on his bed and a voice says, "Take it out of your mind, just get high." He doesn't. He listens to music and there are specific groups, specific albums that take him back to what he thinks of, off and on, as "a glorious time." Kool and the Gang does it. But the music also gives him "ideas I dread" and confused memories of what happened in the past. He thinks he remembers friendship and love, but he knows he doesn't, he knows what he has now is closer to the hazy, druggy intimacy of the past. He remembers Friday and Saturday nights, bars, the women stoned, the friends stoned.

He knows the lie of those memories. In the present, as we walk along the edge of the beach, in and out of groups of people, alongside someone looking drugged and out of it, Tony tells the truth. "I never really knew what a friend was, before," he says. "Those friends didn't have what I needed." And what was that? "I needed them to give time and wisdom, but the only thing we had in common was sickness. We were all dope fiends."

It's a long way from there to here. We are not talking about fairy tales and transformations. Tony is still Tony; his troubles are still his troubles. Having relationships is a messy business, full of pitfalls and brick walls. I can't say Tony has licked the problem of loneliness, only that he has learned to manage it differently. I can't call him cured, much as that would make a good story, but I can talk about change, things getting better, the loneliness still determining much of what Tony says, does and feels, but not destroying him. It ought to be enough to say Tony's life is better. Not perfect. And that where he lives may be "the loneliest place in America," but not forever. I count him among the living, which I would probably not have done in the days when drugs were his best friends.

CHAPTER 3

Male Loneliness

"My ambition is wholly personal
now. All I want to do is fall in love"

Traveling in the world of singles is like traveling in any subculture. Going from a "singles complex" in Houston to one in Westchester County is not very different from moving from an IBM office in San Jose, California, to one in Armonk, New York. The "singles world" resembles ethnic subcultures or corporate cultures. The temperature may change and the look of the land may be different, but the customs and mannerisms, the preoccupations and the language in which those preoccupations are expressed remain essentially the same.

At last count, there were over 19 million people living alone in America. Between 1950 and 1980, the numbers of such people rose 385 percent. One of the most radical changes in the way we live has been in the numbers of single men among us: 7.5 million American men now live by themselves, twice as many as there were in 1970. These men are largely the di-

vorced, separated or never-married men, many under forty-
five, whose lives are taking a very different shape from their
fathers' lives. They are a target for the marketing of products
ranging from soup for one to vacuum cleaners to magazines
showing them how to turn an ordinary dinner for two into a
seductive evening.

What do these people need? What can they be made to feel
they need? What will they buy? Almost every market that
exists has been transformed by the existence of a large number of single people with money to spend. They will buy
houses: nearly a quarter of the first-time home buyers in this
country are people buying houses for themselves. Or they will
buy condominiums, especially in "complexes" designed for
the single professional and carrying price tags well over $100,-
000. They are "above-average consumers," according to a
study by a New York advertising agency, of liquor, stereo
equipment, books, foreign cars, sporting goods and casual
apparel. They go to restaurants. They travel. They buy large
amounts of foods like curried chicken salad at $15 a pound as
well as inordinate amounts of vitamins and rennetless cheese
and fresh-ground spices. Singles neighborhoods are overrun
with gourmet food stores and health food emporiums.

Do they need companionship? It is assumed they do. An
industry whose growth has been phenomenal offers to help
people find companionship—for a price. Sometimes, the service or product is simply a mask—a singles cruise or a singles
tennis week is less about the sea or the serve than it is about
"meeting someone." Many educational operations are part of
this consentual deception—a course on contemporary film at
the New School for Social Research in New York has long
been known as "a place to meet people," as have similar
learning situations across the country. Most people who enroll
in courses on financing or yoga are less interested in balance
sheets and breathing than they are in "meeting someone." In
fact, the usual advice offered to a newly divorced or frustrat-
edly single person is to take a course somewhere.

The singles market not only buys couscous and calcium tablets; it buys magazines and newspapers. *Intro,* the first national singles magazine, claims a circulation over 100,000. Nearly every major city has newspapers and magazines for singles and pages of personals ads in general-interest magazines. You can pick up *Philadelphia* magazine or the *Washingtonian,* or *California* or *New York* magazine and turn to the personals, finding yourself instantly in a familiar world:

> Handsome successful male seeks woman to share the joys of Matisse and Malibu. . . .
>
> Warm, caring woman, tired of playing games, seeks . . .

The style of these ads is familiar, but the substance has changed. Several years ago, the sex magazines ran columns of personals ads, people seeking people, except the presentation of self in those ads was strong on sexual prowess and extraordinary body parts. The goal the supplicants sought was pleasure. This is no longer true. Everyone who wants to "meet someone" has a purpose: to close the door on being single.

Throughout the 1960s and a good part of the following decade, "single" was generally preceded by the word "swinging." There was, in the singles world, an intense, if not genuine, sense of exhilaration about being released from the bonds of marriage and family; it seemed a long time back to think of spinsters and bachelors as people who had no sex in their lives, no partners. It seemed, for some time, if you read the papers and watched television and looked only at surface behavior, that the only people who were having sex and fun in America were singles.

It didn't matter where I began: it was the same wherever I went and it was always in cities. In the past, people moved to cities for better jobs. Now they moved to find their tribes, their nations, to live with other singles. Most of the singles I met who had come from the suburbs and small towns talked of escaping the Dick and Jane worlds they left behind. Fifty years ago, an Italian coming to America from Sicily would carry with him a list of "cousins" to visit in different parts of the country; today, that confidence in far-flung connections, that expectation of finding the familiar in unfamiliar places belongs to the singles world. If you're in Chicago traveling to San Francisco, someone will tell you that the hot spot is the Safeway supermarket in Marina Park and the hot times are Wednesday and Thursday nights, preferably at the produce counter, before people have arranged their weekends. If you're in Minneapolis going to Los Angeles on business, you'll get a tip to check out the track at the Beverly Hills High School and you'll hear stories of who met whom there. If you're in Florida coming north, a veteran will steer you to Bloomingdale's computer games department, thereby eliminating the need to take a course called "lover shopping at Bloomingdale's" or to waste your time in a cinema course at the New School. I have in front of me as I write this a piece of notepaper from Brennan's Bar in Marina Del Rey and on it someone has written the itinerary for my pursuit of this subject: The Red Onion in Redondo Beach, Orville & Wilbur's in Manhattan Beach, Pancho's, also in Manhattan Beach.

The party atmosphere is gone, replaced by the sobriety and "goal orientation" of the 1980s. A lot of people who partied on this circuit are tired of it, have used it up. Some are simply afraid of sexually transmitted diseases, seeing the singles scene as a potential hotbed of infection, not pleasure: but most are worn out. Calvin Klein recently told *Playboy* that the disco scene in New York "has gotten to be a big drag" and that it was exhausting him: "I could no longer physically party all night and work the next day and do my exercises." Like the rest of us, Klein describes himself as being "in the mood for hard work" and having, in the past year, discovered that loving sex is better than anonymous sex and settled into a relationship. If the myth of the "swinging single" was built on the idea that singleness was not only acceptable, but preferable, that idea has died a fast death in most quarters, but the industry built around it hasn't. The pitch has changed. Now finding a partner and escaping singlehood is the core promise of the loneliness business.

Some of this business in conducted in San Francisco's Marina Park. At one end of the park, a parcourse (where you can run and stop at various points to exercise) stretches two miles to the Golden Gate Bridge. At the other end is a Safeway supermarket where singles shop in their athletic clothes. The clothes are expensive velours and satins, shorts, running suits, peek-a-boo shirts. It is not uncommon to overhear an advertising gentleman say to a female consultant: "Are those good crackers? I mean, really good crackers?" Local lore tells people who are "looking" to spend their time in the produce department or at the Häagen-Dazs ice cream counter. At Boys Supermarket in Marina Del Rey in Los Angeles, you hear similar lore.

Marina Green sits between the parcourse and the supermarket, facing Alcatraz. It is a permanent beach blanket filled with people pushing up, stretching, kicking soccer balls and ogling each other. Sandi Mendelson, a publicist in her late twenties, wears a thin brown mylar suit to run in. It's a cool Sunday in a closed-down town, except for the sporting clothes store a block away and the Balboa Café, a favorite singles hangout, which are both bustling.

We start out along the parcourse. The couples who pass are running with Sony Walkmans between them. Those who have just met are actually talking to each other. "On a sunny day," Sandi says, indicating the Green, "you've got four thousand beached whales out here." They're heterosexual beached whales, which makes the cruising at Marina Park different from what it is elsewhere in San Francisco. Word of this, too, has traveled along the network.

At the moment, Sandi is publicizing a book about the rise of marriage. In spite of the breakdown of the family reflected in recent statistics, marriages are increasing. Sandi knows why: "People don't have the time to get their social calendars in order. If they have one special person, they don't have to worry about it."

Efficiency. Time-saving. Return on investment. Priorities. This is the language of coupling in the Eighties. Hooked up with American technology, this businesslike attitude has led to the proliferation of video dating services. There is nothing partylike about video dating services, nor are they democratic. The promised swinging singles party of the past did not require business cards at the door, only availability. It did not require nearly as much money, either. The average fee for membership in a video dating service in a large city hovers around $500. Some cost a lot more.

The people who run video dating services see themselves in competition with places like Marina Park and with singles bars. If people can meet people free or relatively cheaply, why would they need the service? I was told why by the manager of Two's Company, one such service, in Houston. The office is in a two-story building in a complex west of the Galleria area. A young man who had come from California and worked in several other businesses before he came to Two's Company explained that people in singles bars only "play games." He assumed I understood what he meant and that I would ask, as he does, why people in their right minds in America's fastest growing city would waste their time playing games. If the bid for efficiency didn't work, there was always fear. Singles bars, he said, were dangerous places for women. The specter of Mr. Goodbar hovered over his shoulder. If game-playing and terror don't send you scuttling to a video service, the pitchman will come back to the idea of efficiency. He is selling quality. At Two's Company, you don't have to wade through the riffraff. The people have been preselected. They're able to pay the fee; therefore, they are "quality." One New York video dating service lists in its full-page *New York Times* ad the numbers of members who are presidents or vice-presidents of companies.

Frank Matticola moved to Houston three months before I met him in the Two's Company office. He chose Houston because it is a "coming place" and as he talks about the numbers that support this idea—how many billion dollars have been spent on construction, for example—he sounds like a high school kid bragging about his football team. Frank is thirty-six, twice divorced, a bit overweight or underexercised. His hairline recedes slightly. He has an open, Italian face. He has been sitting in this office for several hours on a bright Sunday afternoon leafing through the books in which women lists their likes and dislikes and "pertinent data" and he has been studiously looking at several video tapes.

Frank describes his priorities. First, he got a job as production superintendent in the oil industry. Second, he got an apartment. He lives with a friend at Tennis World, a nearby singles complex. The friend is married and planning to bring his family to Houston as soon as he gets more settled. Frank will be on his own again soon. Which brings him to his third priority. On his first day off in ten weeks, he has come to Two's Company to take care of it.

The sneer at singles bars seems obligatory: "It was just like New York. All game playing." He names the bars, but he doesn't name the games. It is clear that Frank is hesitant about his ability to stand out in a competitive situation, but instead of saying that, he blames the women he has met who were obviously not interested in him. "Females down here," he says, "are interested in either money or very good looks." What is Frank interested in?

Some men in similar situations have given me precise descriptions, shopping lists. A tall one. A short one. A nonsmoker. One who doesn't want children. A blond one. A slim one. A tennis player. Frank says, "I'm looking for someone to share my free time with, which is very little." As he talks, Frank changes. The initial sneer disappears and so does the cold language about priorities. Frank is lonely, but doesn't want anyone to know it. His second wife left him because he was "a workaholic." He finally tells me he would really like her back. He's resigned. He doesn't think that will happen. Loneliness, for Frank and for so many other people, is accompanied by a nagging feeling of failure. I can imagine his wife for a moment, not what she looks like, but how she felt that led her to call him a workaholic. I assume he spent long hours at work and felt it was necessary so that he could support his family. I wondered if there were children in his first marriage and how much money Frank is now paying for the wives and children who have gone from his life. But his wife would resent the time Frank spent away from her and feel deprived of what it meant to her to have a husband. I wondered if she had met someone else, someone more attentive, with more time to spare.

Frank's loneliness is compounded by loss. He once had what he now longs for. He makes what is clearly painful and, to him, a rather unfashionable confession. It's not just someone to go to movies with. It's not just someone to have sex with. He doesn't want to meet women; he wants to meet one woman. And he wants to marry her. "I miss being married," he says, and looks down at the floor. "You get home early and you'd like to have someone there. It's harder after you have been married."

Frank leaves to sit in an adjoining room at a small white cubicle staring at a video screen while woman after woman tells him, onscreen, who she is and what she is looking for. The manager tried to sum it up. "The men who come here," he says, "are looking for independent women. No born-again housewives." Many are divorced, some steeped in child-care payments. They don't want to pay all the bills. They don't want to pay for women on dates. On the other hand, I wonder, noting solemnly what the manager says, how many of them, like Frank, want someone there when they get home. How many, in the 1980s, are dreaming of traditional family lives?

A crossfire of expectations accounts, in large part, for the ceaseless loneliness and futile search for companionship so many of these people talk about. The women Frank might meet at Two's Company are not likely to be waiting for him if he gets home early. Not unless, as a friend of mine said, they learn to drive very fast. Those women are more likely to be working late in their own offices.

From Houston, I went to Miami, where Dr. Sol Landau described the same stalemate among an older generation, the people who frequent his Mid-Life Services Foundation. Dr. Landau, who was a practicing rabbi for seventeen years, said that the fallout can be seen in the huge number of midlife divorces. "A lot of these men," he said, "need to be mentors. They're married to women who need to throw off their mentors." The women's need, he said, came in part because women generally become more assertive in their middle years and because the feminist revolution has certainly taken root everywhere. Men can't cope with women's need to make independent lives. "The men I see," he said, "are threatened by their wives working or going to school. They haven't been able to change. They can still only function from the throne."

He threw his arms in the air, exasperated. "We get all the statistics," he says. "We see two-career families, one couple in three divorcing, so many singles, but we never really put them together and say what kind of society do we really have? We're still talking about the nuclear family as though it existed. It ain't there."

What does Frank want? What do the other men looking for women, looking for a woman, want? They certainly don't want to spend the rest of their lives asking women in posh supermarkets: "Are those good crackers? I mean, are those really good crackers?" They will say, as so many said to me, that they want someone to be close to, someone to share with, someone to love. I stood in the heavy humid air outside Dr. Landau's office, bewildered. Freud, after all, felt compelled to ask "What do women want?" as though everyone knew what men wanted. I ought to know what men want. Literature ought to tell me. Movies. Television. Men ought to tell me.

Listening to talk about loneliness, longing, the search for love, and the "intimacy crisis," you get stuck in a bubblegum of language. Shrinks on the radio are deluged with phone calls from people complaining they don't know how to relate. If you flick the dial or turn on the latest television documentary or read newspapers or magazines, this is what you hear: "relating," "relationship," "distancing," "fear of intimacy," "meeting someone," "meeting people," "narcissism," "interpersonal skills," "connecting," "finding someone," "sharing." The experts come forward with advice for what everyone agrees is a sorry state of affairs—running seminars, offering lectures to help you adjust your technique (you're looking in the wrong places, you're saying the wrong things, you're wearing the wrong colors) or to adjust your attitude (overcome shyness, learn to love, transcend fear of rejection and so on). As a child I stuck my bubblegum on the bedpost at night so I'd have it in the morning, but this bubblegum language is far less useful. It becomes a kind of litany. Eventually, the babble gets louder, the words bigger and more often repeated, the whole pink mess explodes in your face and you're left wondering where the bubble went.

There are real experiences behind this babble. In spite of the volume of words, most people seem profoundly confused about why they wake up alone or go to bed alone or spend Sundays reading and wishing someone were there. In spite of the frenzied activity of the personals ads and the video dating services and singles events, in spite of the helpful lectures, seminars, counseling services and therapies, most of the people I talked to didn't know what to do about "finding someone."

One common option was denial. Men especially were reluctant to say they needed anyone. They felt "ashamed," they felt it was "weak." Many spoke disdainfully of other people who expressed a need for companionship or love. Among middle-class men in their thirties and forties, the upheavals of the last decades about sex roles, about masculinity and femininity, had clearly left them confused about what "needing a woman" meant in the modern world. It had become socially acceptable, in some circles even desirable, to live on your own, buy your own clothes, eat in restaurants or give dinner parties. If they weren't going to have children, what were women for? They had rejected their fathers' lives—which many of them saw as wasted and exhausted by the need to be breadwinners, supporting wives and families—but they couldn't really imagine other lives to create for themselves. They saw themselves as sensitive men, people who had absorbed the language, if nothing else, of the feminist revolution. None would be barbaric enough to insist women ought to be kept barefoot and pregnant. They would ridicule the men who order wives by mail from countries like the Philippines, men who complain that they don't want women who compete with them and who glory in having brides who stay home all day, mind the children and have dinner waiting. Often, though, the men I talked to spoke as though the steam had run out of an engine that had propelled them through the years of their lives, that led up to this moment. Usually, the "push" had come from working hard, getting ahead and imagining the rewards that might bring. Suddenly, some men had seen the dreams would not come true or had accomplished enough to be less anxiously driven than they had before or had simply looked around in bewilderment.

Or fear. Or exhaustion. Stan looks back over his shoulder at a rubble of relationships. In all of them, the women were "motherly or domestic" and he got "taken care of." The last woman he was involved with got tired of taking care of him and left. I met him nearly a year after she had gone. He was the partner of a lawyer I know in Northern California and he kept shaking his head at his "condition," mocking it, being funny about it—and clearly suffering. He stays up late watching movies on television, afraid to go to bed alone, afraid to be alone with himself. He sits in bars, although he doesn't like them at all, feeling shy and afraid to speak. When he looks at his business partner, he wonders: "What would do this to him? It would have to be something financial. Would that my problems were financial. I think he doesn't feel things that acutely."

"Wonderful things," he says, "cause grief in me. I can't take a beautiful drive because it makes me feel too lonely, there's no one to share it with. Yes, I'm avoiding relationships because I'm sure they'll end. My cat got killed and that devastated me; I cried in public. I can't deal with the heartache of things dying. I gave away my houseplants because I was afraid I'd let them die."

Some men looked around in anger. I had certainly seen enough hostility to women in all aspects of our culture and, specifically, hostility toward "independent" women, "professional" women, "liberated" women, "feminists," whatever men chose to call them, everywhere. But I was surprised to hear the outburst of one of my friends, an attractive blond man who lives alone in New York and writes novels and who was feeling especially put upon one night by a woman who asked him for help with her work. "You women," he ranted, "have forgotten how to nurture. You've forgotten how to take care of men. You're just all turning into your fathers."

For Andrew, loneliness is easily equated with meaninglessness. He fixed me a cup of coffee in the kitchen of his West Hollywood apartment, not far from where Sal Mineo was stabbed. Andrew is a character actor. He has a deep voice with a rough edge on it, slightly protruding eyes and a receding hairline, a kind of tough look. He works out a lot—running around Lake Hollywood early in the morning or spending an afternoon at the gym. He's done commercials and plays and guest shots on television series. Like most people in Los Angeles, he's also writing a script and on the verge of the deal he's been waiting for and changing agents and "trying to get centered." He is a walking denial of the cliché that men are unemotional and unexpressive, but then, he is an actor.

Andrew is trying to learn to be alone. He has always had a

woman to help him over the humps. When he moved from New York to California, he brought a woman with him, but they broke up after a year. Sometimes being alone "feeds me creatively, makes me better company to be around," and then it's all right. But there are the other times, the lonely times: "I sit there staring off into space. I don't see any hope for anything. I can't make sense out of anything. I don't care if I'm gonna work or not. So I just sit there. There are eighteen things I could be doing. I sit there thinking maybe someone will call."

Men couldn't talk about loneliness without talking about their work. For some, like Andrew, the work seemed so empty and meaningless that a relationship with a woman compensated for what the work did not provide. Most men blamed their work for their loneliness. They usually thought they were talking about time—how much time their work took up, how little time was left for being with people and, especially, for "having relationships." I was astonished at how many men, now divorced, said their marriages had broken up because they were "workaholics." Usually, the women had left them.

"My problem is I'm gone so much. I was away on location for almost a year last year, on location in South Africa and London." The man with the problem is a film director. He has chugged to our meeting on his motorcycle, a short trip from Venice to Santa Monica, where we have an outdoor breakfast, his helmet draped over a chair, my tape recorder sitting among the croissants. He had been married for seventeen years and his wife had left him. Loneliness was something he said he had never known before and knew all too well now.

"Loneliness is walking into the apartment and immediately turning on the TV set and not watching it. The sound is somebody else in the room." And loneliness leads to buying things. "When we separated, I bought a cycle. I spend money on my boat. I buy myself toys."

Do the television and the toys help? Not as much as work does. "Nights are the worst," he says, "the days kind of take care of themselves because of the work." He tells me about the intimacy he feels on the set. "Our business," he says, "is easier than some others because you're dealing with emotions, it's intimate work." His kind of work has helped to give the director some skills for coping with the immense change in his life, going from "someone there" to no one there. He moved out of the house he lived in with his wife and into an apartment in Marina Del Rey. The first thing he did was go meet all his neighbors and he had little trouble doing that because "in the business I'm in, I'm used to being alone, being on location, being in strange places walking up to people and saying hello."

The men in whose offices I sat or with whom I had breakfast or drank coffee or took walks, tape recorder going, listening, asking gentle questions, urging them to share with me the experience of loneliness, about which nearly all of them felt deeply ashamed and humiliated, said they could only talk this way with a woman. The director, for example, said, almost gratefully, as I walked him to his motorcycle, that it was hard for him and hard for other men to talk to men. When I asked why, he looked genuinely perplexed, as though he had never thought about it before, as though it were just one of life's givens. "I don't know why," he said, a few steps later. "Men tend to get embarrassed at other men's problems. It's great to go out and drink, but don't get intimate." All the social science research kept coming back to me, embodied in these men made flesh, real people waiting for phones to ring or turning on television sets—that intimacy and attachment for men nearly always meant women and romance.

For women, the story was quite different. In all the surveys of how lonely we are, women said they were lonely far more often than men did. At first I thought that this reflected a greater willingness on the part of women to talk about their feelings, but there was something else to it. The quality of relationship that satisfied most of the men I talked with left women hungry. It has become a cliché, but is nonetheless true to picture a contemporary relationship this way: the woman says, "Why won't he talk to me? Why won't he tell me what he's feeling?" and the man, exasperated, wants to know what she wants, doesn't understand, is both frustrated and irritated by the force of her knocking at his door.

It was not surprising, then, that men and women coped differently with divorce. Men moved far more quickly into new romantic liaisons. Women took longer to heal—or, perhaps, to decide to re-engage, depending on friends more than men did. The director was no exception. He was "seeing a girl who lives in Corona Del Mar."

But the most surprising thing to me was how surprised these men were at finding themselves alone and lonely. The question of attachment or support or intimacy or connection had risen up like a dragon, quite suddenly and almost always precipitated by a crisis. Women tended to pay more attention to these issues, to worry or care almost constantly about their relationships with other people. Men took it for granted that there would be "someone there." It was as though, for many of them, they felt that if they did what was expected of them —namely, got good jobs and made decent livings—the rest would somehow fall into place. Often enough, it did. I had the impression, particularly with men who had been left by women, that those women had been background noise, like the television set turned on. They had been "someone there" at the end of the day.

Suddenly, the background gone, the world had looked quite different to the director, now flinging a booted foot at the kickstand of his motorcycle. He had been thinking again about the small town in the state of Washington where he had grown up. People were closer there, he said, "the numbers were easier to deal with." And he was thinking about people he knew who suddenly started going to church. It wasn't a religious revival, really, but people "looking for something to hang on to, something to belong to." What would he hang on to? He revved the cycle. "I don't have a need to attach myself

that way," he said. "I'm attached to my career." And he rode
off. *The days are taken care of.*

"My ambition is wholly personal now. All I want to do is fall
in love." The man speaking was thirty-nine years old at the
time he said this, an attractive, boyish, buoyant man who ran
most mornings in Central Park, went to his job as an executive
in a publishing house, came home and squeezed in some
hours for writing books. Somewhere in between, he also
squeezed in what seemed to me to be a lot of women.

Jasper Evian had been divorced for ten years and he was
fond of saying that as far as he was concerned, divorce by itself
was never the signal that a marriage had failed, only that it had
ended. The residue of his ended marriage, in all the time I
have known him, was a specific loneliness: he felt he had lost
his daughter. He wrote about that over and over again. His
former wife had remarried and moved, with his daughter, to
California. Jasper saw her several times a year—when he went
to California on business trips and when his daughter came
East to spend time with him alone. These visits were always
preceded by a rush of anxious preparation and they seemed
to work out well, although I only heard his side of the visits.
When his daughter left, Jasper's longing for her returned and
it remained with him, constant and dull, like a headache.

For a long time, there were many women. I lost track of
their names. He met them at parties—the publishing industry
provides many parties—and in fact his only reason for going
to parties was to meet women. He wasn't the sort of man to
boast about conquest. I'm sure, for example, that he never
talked to other men about this. He was a great disappearing
act, never spending the night with the women he bedded, but
getting up and going home. He was one of those men who
didn't call the next day, which must have driven the women
who cared for him mad, but he never promised to call, either.
He was also capable of being a genuinely good friend to a
number of women. He helped women writers quite unstint-

ingly with their work. He respected women's intellects. He lent money or his house in the country when he was asked and he was a good listener in times of trouble.

In this period of his life, what Jasper mostly wanted and needed was to be alone. I could put that another way. I could say Jasper was typical of the men women complain about, that he was the modern, uncommitted man, unable to let anyone in, unable to share himself with anyone. Perhaps he was. But Jasper was never a cold man, nor was he closed off from registering other people or allowing the world to enter his universe. He wasn't really selfish. I'd be more likely to say he was better at being alone than he was at being with anyone over an extended period of time and in this way, in spite of what he said about divorce, he might have felt that he failed at family life. His passion for solitude, however, never seemed compensatory. Jasper could have had anything. He chose solitude.

This passion for solitude began as a flirtation. He had always lived with other people and then, his last year of college, lived alone, but not very alone. It was a college dormitory and his door was never closed for long. In those days, romantically, adolescently, he thought that he was a poet, that being alone was to suffer and that "suffering converged with poetry at a point known as blank paper." He learned, that year, "that I wasn't a poet and that solitude stank. I got married three months after I graduated."

We are all haunted by unconsummated flirtations. Jasper, in the five years of his marriage before his child was born and in the two years afterward, became more and more a man "constantly looking for ways to shut a door behind him" and a man consumed by what he called a major "ambition"—were there ever enough money, he wanted to rent a room of his own somewhere. During the week, he worked in an office all day, as he still does, surrounded by people. At night, he retreated behind a closed door for several hours or, at times, he went out walking alone, browsing through village bookshops alone, "talking to no one, wanting to hear no voice but the one inside. On weekends, before the baby was born, I managed to get behind that closed door for a good part of each of the two days."

A year before his marriage broke up—he saw it coming—Jasper visited a friend in California who had been divorced. He wrote down what happened there:

> I sniffed about his large apartment as if I might discover in the corners and cracks and draperies and cupboards some key to solitary survival. One thing he said stuck with me through the rest of my marriage and saw me through the difficult early days of separation. "All you need," he said, "is two of everything." Which is pretty much what he had. Two forks, two spoons, two plates, two soup bowls, two coffee cups, two towels. . . .
>
> When I moved out of the large apartment I shared with my family and into a couple of small rooms downtown, "two of everything" became the key to my survival. I took two of everything. And that meant that I would always have something—if something very limited—to share. And it meant that I was willing to share.

Jasper lived alone and wrote about what it was like, the flirtation consummated, the passion for solitude achieved, present in his daily life so that he was in fact married to solitude, protective and jealous of his aloneness and deeply in love with it, aware of all its nuances. He found himself happier to be with other people, knowing there was a door he could shut behind him somewhere. He loved the silence. He loved the sense of being close to himself, finding himself. It led him to understand that "true loneliness has absolutely nothing to do with other people. Loneliness is entirely a condition of the self. When a person is, in a sense, deserted by his self, he is lonely."

On the page, he recorded the reactions of people who are not alone to those who are—the assumption that solitary people are unhappy, the pity, anger and envy often directed at people who are alone, the "vague feelings of discomfort elicited in groups by the man or woman eating alone in a restaurant" and the "prejudice" against unmarried people within corporations "that tends to impede their progress." He noted, also, the arrogance of some who live alone, a conviction that they are being more courageous than other people and "we love what we imagine to be the iconoclastic life we're living, which goes against the grain of everything we are taught from the time socialization begins in the crib." Jasper's notes were made several years ago, when living alone was more "iconoclastic" than it is today.

The flush of pleasure that led Jasper to call aloneness "solitude" and not "loneliness" went on for some time. The jarring notes did not get recorded. Only later did Jasper want to talk about the things in life that, to him, are meant to be shared. Like movies. When he was alone for a long weekend, he would build part of a Saturday or Sunday around going to a movie. He'd pick one out in the newspaper, check the time, figure out how long it would take to get there, walk to the movie theater, walk up to the box office and then turn around and go home. The few times he did go to a movie alone, it was "a serious movie. There's nothing worse than going to a comedy alone, without someone to slap on the thigh at the funny parts." He used to get a sick stomach if he ate alone because he ate too fast, something was missing in eating alone, the "ceremony" was missing. Jasper also has a great feeling for music and an impressive record collection, but "even when I was happy alone, there were pieces of music I wouldn't play because no one was there to hear them."

I suppose these dissatisfactions intensified. I suppose he simply changed, the appetite for solitude satiated and an appetite for something else come to take its place. I'm sure approaching forty had something to do with it. Whatever the cause, there came a night when, almost casually, over dinner, Jasper said, "My ambition is wholly personal now." I suppose we were talking about writing and publishing and the best-seller list and movie deals. We often did. "I don't understand how anyone can be after worldly success," he went on. "I'm not interested in editing or writing. I'm only interested in falling in love."

What had happened?

"I suddenly got lonely," he said.

I was interested in his use of the word "ambition." When he was married, I remembered, his ambition was to have a room of his own. His professional ambition can only be inferred from how he spent most of his time. It was something he rarely talked about. Behind the closed door in his apartment or, later, in a room of his own, those nights every evening and almost all weekend long, Jasper worked at two kinds of things. He edited other people's books and he tried to write some of his own. In the first, he was immensely successful. He rose to a high position in his publishing house and he is known among his colleagues as something of a workhorse in addition to being extremely talented. He has worked at this job for eighteen years; for twelve of those years he took no vacation. He is one of the few book editors with seniority who actually sit, pencil in hand, and comment line by line on what they are reading. He works and reworks books with their authors. Even at this dinner, denouncing worldly ambition, he spoke with immense pleasure and pride of how he had suggested a new opening scene to a novelist and then changed the personality of one of the characters and how the novelist took notes. His own books did less well. They came less easily. They had a harder time finding their way into the world. They accumulated fewer laurels. Still, he kept writing and I know from experience that ambition, however disguised, is part of what keeps a person alone at a typewriter with the door closed.

He elaborated: "There isn't anything I do in my professional life that really makes me very happy. There's no success that I have that lasts. My name's in the *New York Times* this Sunday. I have a new book coming out next month. I have another new book coming out. I don't feel any pleasure from those things at all. I don't even relate to them. There isn't any pocket of joy that I can build up and accumulate." It was not a tick of dissatisfaction or a passing depression.

He had no "pocket of joy" with friends, either. Rather, he had "contacts." "My Rolodex is as large as the phone books of some cities," he said. "I probably know several thousand people, but I hardly know them at all. As soon as I leave the office, that Rolodex seems to have disappearing ink. Not that I don't like these people. I've always worked so hard in my job that I've never developed that skein of friendship so many people in my business have." By friends, I discover, he means men. "I've longed all my life for a close male friend," he says, almost sheepishly. He knows he is not alone in this, but somehow it doesn't translate into having a male friend. "The men I know," he adds, "are almost leechlike in their desire for friends. They like male rituals like sports events and having fantasies of screwing the same woman together." I know that Jasper likes sports events and I'm sure his fantasy life is as rich as anyone else's; still, he insists that this is because of lack of time: "If you deal in the course of the day with fifty people in different capacities and if your work day lasts twelve to eighteen hours, there isn't time to have a friend in the midst of that."

But there was time for love. Jasper turned out to be as good at exercising his "ambition" to fall in love as he had been at getting a room of his own and making a career. Not long after he told me about his ambition, he was riding a train from Philadelphia to New York and struck up a conversation with the woman riding beside him. This is not a usual thing for him to do. The rest is a love story that takes place in the modern world, but is full of very traditional elements. The woman was much younger. She told him she had a boyfriend, but that, it developed, was simply her way of protecting herself against a stranger. She lived in his neighborhood and Jasper's first plan was—since he is "honorable" and doesn't intrude on women with boyfriends—that she might come over to his apartment one or two nights a week and "sit and read with me." He would have companionship and retain the silence he loved and still get his work done. She came over and "hopped into bed." He was then having "six or ten affairs, the usual," but he "knew if I was ever going to live with anybody else, it would be somebody new." This new person seemed a potential buddy, and Jasper found her, over the months to come, a "remarkable companion," but she was hard to win. Real estate was the determining factor. She had to move out of her parents' house, where she was living, and she had no place to live and no money. He went away on a trip and left her the keys to his apartment. One day, he called and she was there and he "knew I had her." She moved in. She got pregnant. They got married. They had a son.

"I don't think about solitude anymore," Jasper says. "My love for it definitely went away. I had enough. My fear of being married again was not only fear of giving up women, which is hard enough to do, but giving up being alone. I changed. I come home and somebody's gonna be there."

Jasper's "somebody" was, obviously, not just whoever had been sitting in the seat beside him on the train from Philadelphia. She is a "remarkable companion." She suits his rhythm. Unlike other couples, he says, "we don't make a plan in order to fill our time. Because she's there and I like being with her, I don't worry about weekends. When I got lonely, I started to worry about what I was going to do if I was all alone from Friday to Monday." His description of the "fit" between them, the rhythm, the companionship and ease tells me again why her, why not someone else. "I always used to say to the women I was with, 'Are you okay? Are you happy?' I never say that to her. It never occurs to me to ask. She exists as part of the natural world. She moves in and becomes a tree, a piece of nature. I'm one tree and she's another. With someone else, I'd be a tree and she'd be a stone."

In Jasper's memory, there is a specific moment crystallizing what felt like a tree and what felt like a stone. He had been having a long conversation with a woman about narrative methods. The woman was not his "girlfriend," but he had a girlfriend. He had a great feeling of "elation" about the narrative methods discussion and a great feeling of "despair that I could never talk about that with my girlfriend. She wouldn't understand why I was excited about having that conversation with somebody else. I wondered when in my life am I going to have a passionate physical relationship with someone with whom I can discuss narrative methods? But I realized I don't really want to discuss narrative methods at home."

The heart has its reasons. I was happy that Jasper, whose period of loneliness left him sleepless and distraught, had "found someone" and returned to being a jovial, charming fellow who could discuss wine, tennis and narrative methods, as he had before. In many ways, his choice went against the grain: he did not share male resentment about supporting women. It was a "traditional" choice, although I might expect that the woman he married will, when the child is older, pursue a career. He still works twelve hours on an average day. When Jasper's wife went into labor, she was lying on a couch in his office late at night while he did his work.

CHAPTER 4

Female Loneliness

"I've become a workaholic because
I'm so lonely"

She had taken work home and had been sitting there for
several hours after dinner going over the reports, alone, the
only sound in the Manhattan apartment the pages as they
turned and the drone of the television set in the other room.
No one was watching the television set, but the noise com-
forted her and she kept it on when she was home and alone,
which she was often enough. The woman was in her late
thirties. She had been married young and stayed married for
twelve years, then come to New York, divorced, had a decent
job and a slew of rotten men. Mario, whom she had once lived
with, came on occasion to sleep with her and returned to the
woman he was now living with. She said she'd take what she
could get, that Mario was an addiction she'd one day kick.
That night, she worked until a little after eleven and then went
out for a walk.

A lot of people think about food when they feel lonely; she was one of them. It appears that women move more readily than men do to the idea of food, the sensation of food when they crave warmth, touch, companionship, closeness, nurture, whatever they may call the opposite of the droning television and the echo of turning pages, the hollowness of those sounds, the persistence of thinking, every once in a while, that a soft peck on the back of the neck would make going back to the pages easier.

It is hard to know what to say about the work she was doing that night, whether she needed to be doing it at a time of day when others were snuggled in communal meals or arguing with their lovers or whiling away the evening on the telephone. It is hard to know how much the long hours at work are necessary, and in what ways necessary, or how easily the work would be abandoned were there something better to do. I am talking here about work beyond what is required to pay one's bills, although what is required is often, also, not clear. These were the things I wondered about as I went from woman to woman, women who lived by themselves and worked at careers, not jobs, what the magazines would call the new woman, the one with no children to support, the one often envied by friends for her freedom and independence, the one whose parents still worry about the way she lives.

My friend was walking along the street and thinking about food. If you asked her to tell you what the least lonely experience in recent memory was, she'd tell you about her sister in California, what it's like to sit in her sister's house in the middle of a king-size bed, the kids running around, food all around them, the phone ringing, activity, a sense of being in the middle of life. In fact, she has been thinking for a while that she might move to California, to be closer to her sister, for what she calls a community.

I might say here what's missing from these thoughts. She can't say "if I only had a man." There are many reasons for that, for this woman, for other women. They know better.

Many have had a man and although the fairy tale says women don't feel lonely when they have Prince Charming, they do. They sit across from lovers or husbands at dinner tables with nothing to say, feeling nothing in common, wishing there were someone to talk to. It is worse, this loneliness with a man, than the loneliness of being alone. Many divorced women have said they felt so much less lonely when they left their marriages. So my friend walking along the street was not just then thinking about a man, although, like many of us, that's the first thought when loneliness begins to bore into you, the visceral thought, what the gut cries out for. She was thinking about food.

There are a lot of horror stories I might tell at this point. I have heard them from friends, read them, lived through a few of them myself. A woman is feeling lonely and walking along a street and thinking about food and she might, if it were a horror story, buy first one pastry here and another there and a third a little way along the avenue or she might have wolfed down an entire pizza by the time the next streetlight turned red, but this isn't one of those stories; the dimension of this woman, her loneliness and food is far more quotidian.

She came to a McDonald's and, in fact, that was what she had been thinking about all along—some texture of the bun and the burger that seemed what she was hungry for. In she walked. Up she stepped to the counter, but not before she looked around. It was late. There were people sitting at tables, not derelicts, exactly, but not what you would call the glitterati. And each of them was sitting alone at a table. Losers. She ordered: "Two Big Macs and a cup of coffee." She stumbled. "No, two coffees, one light, one black." She had never drunk a cup of black coffee in her life and she was not on an eating binge either. The second burger order was not for herself, was, literally, for no one. It was her cover. It was meant to silence the voice that she heard, although no one in the place paid attention to her and the person taking her order was surely more interested in what time he'd get off his feet than in how many burgers this lady wanted.

The voice said: "You're alone. You're a loser. Don't let anyone know."

The same voice led her to call out, on other occasions, when the delivery from the Chinese restaurant arrived in the evening, for example—"Hey, Joe, the food's here," although there was no Joe. It led a friend of hers to wear a wedding ring as she went about Manhattan, a fraud, a protection and some odd solace. The protective part of pretending to have a man waiting for his burger or his fried dumplings or his woman is not to be discounted. A woman alone is vulnerable, emotionally and physically, and does well, of necessity, at times, to pretend she is not alone. Surely a woman in her apartment may not want the delivery man to know she is there by herself. Surely a woman in a bar pretends to wait for a man for security reasons, realistic ones. Still, the truth is harsher and more full of contradiction, a truth about loneliness, the need for denial, the price of denial, that has something to do with history.

We live in an extraordinary historical moment, with its own versions of the ideal woman, its own models for female behavior and its own atmosphere of expectation on the part of women—and its own set of prohibitions. That all these things are radically different from what they were a generation ago has become, perhaps, a cliché of our time. We are not living our mothers' lives. Although most of the goals of the women's liberation movement have not, in actual fact, been accomplished—the right to abortion may be withdrawn, the lack of economic parity between men and women remains stubborn —it's a different world for women and men. The basest popular culture—television sitcoms, for example—show women making their own way in the world, unprotected by a husband's paycheck, undistracted by diapers. The middle-class single career woman is a stock figure on the stage of life as we see it in movies, on television, in advertisements for everything from credit cards to banking services to makeup and hairspray. Linoleum wax and oven cleaners seem these days to be pitched mostly at men. This woman responsible for herself is also a stock figure in real life and particularly in my own. There were no far-flung journeys necessary for me to report on questions of loneliness and intimacy among single women. I could simply pick up the telephone or visit a friend or remember the life around me.

Statistics show the change, point out who I am talking about. The increase in the single female population in this country has been dramatic. There are 37 million never-married, divorced or widowed women of all ages. The percentage of never-married women between the ages of twenty-five and thirty-four in the population has more than doubled in the last ten years. In the last national survey of women business owners, 73 percent were unmarried. In a survey of executives on the Fortune 1000 list, the executive search firm of Korn Ferry found that 48 percent of the women were married and 39 percent had children; 95 percent of the men in this group were married—86 percent of them to spouses who did not work outside the home—and 97 percent had children.

Those are the numbers. Set them beside the ideology. "A woman needs a man like a fish needs a bicycle." I remember seeing that slogan on bumper stickers everywhere in the 1970s. The modern woman's epic, as it was created in the 1970s, goes like this: Woman grows up conventional in a conventional world and marries nice boy who can hunt food for the table or perhaps provide a swimming pool, has babies, mothers and mothers and then CLICK! she realizes life is passing her by, her energies go to serving other people's needs, she's an invisible doormat to whom nobody listens and whom nobody really knows. So CLICK! becomes SPLIT and off she goes to be herself or find herself or love herself or create herself. I hardly mean to disparage these issues, which are real, only to magnify them so we can see where we have come from and what has weaseled its way into our thinking about how we live, how we should live. All right. In *A Doll's House,* Ibsen left us at the point where Nora slammed the door. I always suspected, given the kind of world Nora lived in, that she wouldn't do very well on the other side of the door. But here we are in the 1980s and I have a different idea about Nora's possibilities.

She could go to law school if she wanted to, if she could find the money. She could get a corporate job if she had the credentials and rise and rise and not be stopped until, as *Fortune* magazine recently put it, "the $75,000 to $100,000 level," where "the trouble begins . . . and seems to get worse the higher one looks." She could go into politics, become, perhaps, like New York City Council President Carol Bellamy, whose average day was recently described in the *New York Times:* walked across the Brooklyn Bridge at six in the morning, worked in her office, campaigned at a subway stop for a fellow politician, went to a hearing, a rally, back to her office, to meetings, an event at Lincoln Center, a speech at a Jewish temple, the Liberal Party dinner, then to a call-in program at 11:30 P.M. and then home, where she lives alone.

Nora would feel like neither freak nor anomaly. On television, she would see women driving their own cars into the driveway of houses they had paid for themselves. She would, most likely, be a woman with many friends. Unlike her mother, she would have men as friends as well as women and the quality of those friendships would, equally likely, go beyond the usual evening at the theater or outing at the Olympics. They would be intimate friendships, relationships in which she and her friends confided in one another, helped one another, came to one another's aid when it was necessary.

Because I have transplanted her, in my mind, to America, I will add one more thing Nora now has: she values independence above everything else. The learned helplessness of all our mothers hardly ever crackles in her. She doesn't get depressed and lie in bed in the afternoons. She doesn't go crazy. When she fears she might turn into one of those women, when the remnants of the historical past well up in her, she works harder, makes more money, decorates her apartment. What soothes and comforts her, even inspires her, is the exhilaration that at last she has won the freedom and independence for herself that has been the province of men all along. She too can be the Lone Ranger. She can ride into town alone and fearless. She can survive in the jungle.

So it comes as no surprise that admitting loneliness into her own consciousness, much less to a listening ear, feels like compromise and failure, a regression to the "old-time stuff" she has so earnestly worked her way out of. Her life provides sufficient avenues through which she can avoid—not assuage —loneliness. She can go to business meetings all day and in the evening too. Alone at home, she can work.

There is comfort and reward in professional work. Unlike housework and mothering, this work receives recognition in the world, this work makes a person feel like "somebody." You feel in charge of your work at this level more often than the traditional work of women in the home, with the necessity of being responsive to other people's needs, ever allowed. This work, unlike housework, has parameters and definitions, and although many professional women feel their work is never done, that sensation hardly compares to the endlessness and formlessness housewives and mothers complain of. And there are economic rewards.

The woman who walked along Second Avenue in search of a hamburger for her hunger and lied to the takeout clerk at McDonald's is of the world I am describing here. She lives in a large apartment on the Upper East Side in Manhattan in a high-rise building with a well-appointed lobby overseen by a doorman. "Make sure," a friend advised her when she was looking for an apartment in the city, "that you get an apartment where you have to ride an elevator." She did, but riding an elevator is hardly a guarantee that one's comings and goings will be attended by interaction with other people. Those riding together in elevators in this building, in other buildings and in other cities, rarely speak. My friend describes the "great distance" people keep in the elevator—"they stay in their bell jars"—and what is to her the style of this city: "People are more guarded about protecting their privacy." When she thinks of "the dance of loneliness, it is pedestrians pouring out of office buildings along Fifth Avenue at rush hour."

Still, my friend has her own contradictions on this subject, like the rest of us. The woman who lives across the hall has tried to befriend her—invited her for coffee, dropped by at odd hours of the day, broken the silence in the elevator. What one allegedly wants, a kind of neighborliness whose lack is so often complained of by people who come to New York from places where the daily style is otherwise. But this woman across the hall is an engulfing kind of person, too needy, too anxious, too suffocating. And so my friend, in her words, "iced her out."

It's not a lonely life; it's a life with pits of loneliness, like holes in the ground. Sometimes loneliness means exhaustion, the weariness of doing everything for herself, taking care of everything and why isn't there someone there to share the burdens? Sometimes loneliness means comparison with other people and an awful sensation that there's something wrong with her. Most of this woman's friends have "significant others" in their lives and "you go out with a couple, you all talk about how come you're alone, you kiss each of them goodnight on the sidewalk and go upstairs alone." The answer to "how come you're alone?" moves, at times, to self-denigration and the "anorexic mentality takes over. I think it all has to do with my looks. I make lists of how much weight I'm going to lose in the next eighteen years. I think about having a nose job."

Now I have to tell you, because I have been sitting in this woman's living room all evening, that she is talking about distortion. She is not fat. She is also not alone in focusing her sense of what is wrong on fat. The female propensity for obsessing about weight and fantasizing the waves of change that might occur if only one lost a few pounds—these have been analyzed by Kim Chernin, among others, as symptomatic of a psychological and social crisis among women that belongs to our time as much as conflict about sexuality and hysteria as its symptom belonged to Freud's. For Chernin, the epidemic of anorexia among young women occurs in a social context— women are conflicted about power and confused about identity, uneasy about "taking up too much space," and about the implications of having a truly developed female body or female self. I think Chernin would see, immediately, that my friend who fantasizes that losing a few pounds would end her loneliness shares common ground with other women of her generation.

I can come to this question from another direction. Here is a woman in her thirties who has lived for some time in an intimate relationship with a man, who has sufficient closeness to other people in her life and who, when I asked about loneliness, talked only about her professional life.

Hers is the loneliness of the hidden self—nobody really knows who I am or cares to know. It is the loneliness of the immigrant experience—I find myself in a strange land with strange customs I cannot fathom, unable to feel part of things, unable to fit. This is the loneliness of being discriminated against, of being iced out, refused intimacy, friendship, camaraderie even, at times, an understanding word.

The promise of the 1970s was that sex discrimination had been done away with and that gender would no longer be a barrier to women in their professional lives. Most women now in their thirties went to graduate school or law school in an atmosphere that encouraged women to enter professions from which they were previously excluded or in which their progress was severely limited. They expected to encounter little discrimination; hard work and merit, they believed, would carry them along. This rather astonishing innocence— or denial—quickly dissipated.

San Francisco psychologist Elizabeth Milwid interviewed women who had been working in professional careers for five years, with a view toward discovering the psychological realities of day-to-day work life in male-dominated fields. She spoke with bankers, lawyers and architects. Among the things her interviewees said were these:

Being ignored is like feeling you're a gnat; you ask a question and you get brushed off.

One of the hardest things I've had to learn is to withstand what's called the rejection game. If you can't play it, they blow you right out of the water. They more or less insult you. It's like hard-assing. You can see it between men all the time. You have to be able to take it. It's really like an arm wrestling contest.

I feel like red flags are waving, but you can't let it get to you. If you show that you feel hurt and excluded, they will continue to do the same old thing to you. Don't make jokes about it and don't acknowledge it, because if you do then you're trying to break into the inner sanctum. The ranks will close immediately in front of you.

Most of the women Dr. Milwid interviewed discover that, having proved their technical competence at work, they run smack into unstated but nonetheless intransigent obstacles to progress—the "informal" aspects of their organizational structures, the male-dominated company cultures. It is difficult, although some say it is getting easier, to establish friendships with men at work, to become part of informal networks. Men standing around the water cooler grow silent when a woman passes. Dinner conversations in a group of men leave her out. A woman who works for an oil company once told me that the sport-obsessed company culture never bothered her because she had been interested in sports all her life and could talk about it with the best of them. She discovered, though, that whatever observation she made about a game score or a player's performance, she was either ignored or she would be asked what she thought of women reporters in male locker rooms. She was never allowed to forget that she was a woman, she was different, she was an outsider. Friendship with female peers was rarely mentioned by the women I have spoken with. Often, they have few female peers. Usually, they are pitted against other women at their professional level—for promotions, for recognition—and never seem to rearrange their female–female relations differently.

Isolation in the corporation is a clear derailment of the fast track, a sure barrier to progress. Most women working in strongly masculine cultures know that decisions are made in ways to which they have no access, that the Old Boys' Network is real and impenetrable. This is a sure cause for frustration about one's ability to progress, but is it a cause for loneliness? Most of the women I know who find themselves in this situation are confused about what they want or need from other people at work. Some feel, as a banker said, "These guys don't know how to be human with each other. I'm glad we're in there." Some feel comfortable with their relationships with male peers but uncomfortable about relationships with older men, the men with real power. That may frustrate success, but it doesn't make anyone feel lonely.

Men have been socialized to compartmentalize their relationships at work and their relationships outside of work. They don't come to the office expecting closeness with other people—their attention focuses elsewhere, on mastering the work, achieving recognition, making money, getting ahead. A male friend was recently entirely overwhelmed by the intensity of emotion he experienced at the end of a project he worked on with another man. He nearly cried at the pride he felt for both of them and the tremendous closeness of having worked hard side by side on something that turned out well. I only remember his comments on this subject because he seemed so surprised. Closeness wasn't on his list of things he wanted or needed at work.

Women are less clear about this subject. My friend's astonishment at having a deeply personal reaction to a working experience is met, at the other end, by the accusation and concomitant confession by women that they do take things that occur in their work lives "too personally." Experience in the office is personal experience for women. They find it harder than men do to detach and compartmentalize; they were socialized more forcefully than men were to attend to relationships, to be nice and to be liked. A coldness, an impersonality, then, might have a different effect on a woman. It might make her feel lonely.

So we come to Maggie, who goes to and from her office in elegant business suits, who leaves early in the morning and comes back late at night and spends parts of all weekends working. Unlike the woman who dreamed of a hamburger, Maggie lives with a man, and unlike a lot of women who live with men from whom they feel compelled to hide their sense of accomplishment in the world, Maggie lives with a man who has a penchant for ambitious, high-achieving women; she cannot say, as many successful, lonely women say, that men are too threatened by her to move closer. Maggie is thin and earnest, brunette and lively. Her description of life at the large corporate law firm in Manhattan is harrowing:

"The people who are rewarded are the sickest ones," she says. "The distorted personalities, men unwilling to feel anything. Work provides them with an excuse not to feel anything. They never have to be full human beings, never have to develop. It's amazing that people could survive on so little, without emotional sustenance. They're out of touch with pleasure; in fact, they have no respect for pleasure. They could run concentration camps."

You'd think Maggie had been unable to succeed at the firm, that her words sound like sore-loser words, but in fact, she is doing well. Still, she sees what she sees: "There's rarely unguarded closeness in the office. The atmosphere is so dominated by male sensibility and is so competitive. You feel it's important to know everything all the time. You pretend it to

your colleagues. You always have the feeling of no one to turn
to; you can't depend on people to learn things from. And you
can't reveal anything about yourself because you know it will
be used against you. Women especially have to watch themselves, constantly reassure men that we are not dangerous,
we're not going to provoke them, not going to cry or have fits.
Men can say 'tell the sonofabitch to go fuck himself,' but the
women have to be Goody Two-Shoes. A woman can't forget
her place. Most of the women at my firm are out of it; they
don't know the code or they just don't care. They're more into
real life."

I ask what she means by real life and part of Maggie's answer
is about the need for real, personal connections. "Men are
more focused on Him, the boss. Women," she says, "will
make connections elsewhere—with secretaries, with office
mates. The secretaries at my firm," Maggie says, enviously,
"have much more camaraderie than the lawyers do. They talk
to each other, have great loyalty to each other and have lunch
together."

Maybe lunch is part of real life too. The lawyers at Maggie's
firm don't go out for lunch; they eat at their desks. There is
too much work to do. The break at lunchtime—to walk
around, to see someone outside the firm—is less important
than the pressure to get the work done. Maggie violates the
norm on this—she insists on going out to lunch and insists
that doing that keeps her sane.

But Maggie is changing. She has a new secretary and, contrary to what she has done in the past, Maggie just wants her
secretary to do her job. "I don't want the responsibility of a
relationship," she says. "I need so desperately for her to perform. I don't want to be involved in her life." She looks
ashamed. Is that awful? Is that wrong? Have masculine values
overtaken her? She reminds me of a judge I know, another
hard-working woman, this one a mother as well, who came
home exhausted one night and sat down to dinner with a
troublesome adolescent daughter. "What I really felt," she

told me, "was dammit, I put the bread on this table. I keep you in good clothes. Isn't that enough? What right do you have to ask anything else of me? And I felt I was turning into my father."

Maggie stays because the work challenges her, uses her talents, and because she likes the money she earns. Other women she has known have left the firm—this is part, in Maggie's words, of their preference for real life—to have babies. These are women who can afford to do without a second income in the family, although most of them intend to return to work when their children are out of diapers. In their exodus from corporate life, women leaving to pursue family life are accompanied by women leaving to pursue careers on their own. Dr. Milwid found that most of the women in her study felt they had "topped out" in their careers—they weren't going to get any further or higher—and were seriously considering "the entrepreneurial option."

First, Susan has to cancel our appointment because *Vogue* magazine is coming to photograph her office. Then I have to cancel because another professional commitment interferes. This is the atmosphere in which we all move—an atmosphere of so little time. Walking in the woods is a luxury. So are baking bread, spending an entire day with a friend who has no connection to one's profession, lying in bed reading, doing nothing or even being depressed. The demands are great. The anxiety is high. We share a general anxiety about money, about keeping up in an expensive city, paying the rent. With a sideways looks at the future, we are preparing, financially, as all the books about women and money advise us to do, for old age. Maggie is saving to make a real estate investment. My friend on Second Avenue wants some good clothes for a vacation abroad. These are worried pursuits of an elusive economic security: If we are driven women, we are driven, in part, by necessity. Susan and I, of equal necessity, find time to meet only on a holiday afternoon.

I come back to the question of work as I walk down the corridor to her midtown office. Do we need to spend all this time working? Are we truly workaholics, people whose pleasure is intimately tied to the mastery and control implicit in the work we do, the sense of fixed boundaries and achievable goals so elusive in relationships? Is our sense of self now bound to recognition for the work, bank balances, real estate investments, credit lines, the joy of a deal well made, a negotiation well handled instead of less concrete, less "productive" pleasures? Are we hiding in our work, as men have done? Are we using work to fill a void that actually cries out for other people? Why are Susan and I meeting on a holiday afternoon?

The morning before I went to meet Susan, I had been talking on the telephone with a friend in California who is negotiating for a book contract. What did they say? What did the others say? If you say this, what will they do? I stopped. "You know," I said, "we sound like some Eighties version of *Modern Romance.* 'What did he say? If you insisted, would he marry you?' " It had that sound, but the drama and excitement here was about work and what it meant to us. I wasn't sure whether what I heard was funny or not.

Susan's office is crammed with drawing boards and its walls are covered with designs for her projects, which include an art gallery and the apartment of a famous designer. She is short, wispy, with blondish hair, and sweet. She is the kind of woman about whom some people might say in astonishment, "My, has a little girl like you done all that?" "All that" includes teaching modern dance, designing women's dresses until "some people wanted to turn it into a big business and I said no," going to the Parson's School of Design, working for a year in an architect's firm where all she got to do was "sharpen pencils," deciding she needed a degree, "but I'd never be taken seriously if I didn't go to a place that had rigor and so I went to MIT," then a job with a prestigious firm and now out on her own for two years and still shy of forty.

"I was always interested in doing things on my own," Susan

says, pulling a three-legged stool up to the table. Her grandfather, father and stepfather all owned their own businesses, but if she was imbued with the entrepreneurial spirit in her family, she hasn't been aware of it until I ask. In fact, she was encouraged, if that is the right word, in the other direction—" 'Why don't you be a telephone operator?' my family used to say. 'Then you can get a job in any city.' " Susan has an orphan air about her and as she talks about her family life, I begin to see why. When she decided to go to MIT, her family refused to cosign a loan, an act, she says, of "aggressive nonsupport."

I have seen the same orphan air in the other women with whom I have discussed the subject of loneliness. Surely the experience of loneliness itself is the essence of feeling an orphan in the world, but these women shared something less general. Their families had committed "aggressive acts of nonsupport" in relation to these women's careers. Each of them had told me the same story, one way or another—they were meant to marry instead of have careers; work was something to "tide them over" until they found husbands; it was never meant to be the focus of their lives.

Susan learned, as other women have, to support herself, both economically and psychologically. Her work in the architectural firm was "a network of relationships," what she calls "the coffee shop buzz" of the large office. And there was a mentor. And a series of "unavailable men I've had a work connection with." When she speaks of the "mental, intellectual, creative bond" with a man who is a "soulmate" about work, her eyes light up as though she is remembering a childhood pleasure. We will come to the men in a moment, but we are still talking about the work.

She did well at the firm. "I was jumping in terms of the hierarchy," she says. The trial period was grueling, but short. "After the initial head cracking, where you have to prove you know what you're doing, they love a woman in the field." But Susan was not "a company person" and everything she learned at the firm was preparation for being on her own.

When she left, she had one important client.

"I didn't realize how awful it would be without that atmosphere, those four hundred people, that buzz." For six months, Susan was alone in her apartment, day and night, working on the job for her client, who became "my only relationship. It was awful," she says. "I never knew day from night and was panicked throughout. I had no way to judge the progress I should have been making. The job took much longer to do than it should have." The only person she stayed in touch with was her former mentor, but "he can't quite understand because he's always worked for a large firm."

Eventually, Susan hired a woman to work with her, then another architect, male. She thought of him as a "soulmate in terms of work," but he "doesn't help me at all. I've been doing all the work. I hate that. He's a cynic and bitter and introverted, so I have become his mother. I protect him from the world and I do all the work myself." She is about to fire him.

Susan says she has friends, but her friends can't share the burdens of her work. "Do I have to do this all myself?" she says. In fact, she is turning over the idea of joining a firm again: "I've got to have a more vital environment." Although Susan has no desire to have children, she craves "a full emotional life, a context outside the work. I don't want to be involved with work and have no emotional life. The more a woman works," she says, "the more she needs someone at home. You want a place you feel safe."

So the target becomes a task and the task becomes a second job. Where are the men, a woman may wonder, for women like us? You can see part of the problem just by reading the personals ads in *New York* magazine. The men looking to meet women all describe themselves as successful. Many say they are workaholics who have awakened to the fact that there's more to life than work; they seem to be looking for women to humanize them—as movie cowboys were looking for "good" women to civilize them. There was one ad recently from a man who said he was tired of being lonely, and the ad stuck out like a black spot in a sea of bright neon—everyone else seemed so up, so energized, so wrapped up in marketing themselves. I doubt he got many responses. And there was another who I'm sure was deluged with responses—he described himself as "a thinking woman's man." Most of the men advertising themselves are quite specific about what they want—usually, a woman ten years younger, sometimes, even more specifically, a "model-type" or a blonde. Women are businesslike about this search, workmanlike, looking for the right kind of man, with shopping lists of their own: an intellectual equal, a financial equal, someone who is not a workaholic, someone able to make a relationship, capable of commitment, not afraid of intimacy—whatever cultural cliché comes to mind as the mind tries to shape itself around a clear idea of what one does not want: a series of one-night stands, a tide of disappointment, an intolerable distancing.

I might stop to point out how far these feelings are from the alleged sexual revolution. Nobody here wants to sleep around anymore. For one thing, most women have passed through a period of promiscuity, been, perhaps, adventurers, and been, too, in their own words "hurt" or "exploited" by men whose only interest in them was sexual. The fear of herpes or of other venereal disease may have something to do with this turn away from carefree sex, but less, I think, than an awareness that women fall in love with men they sleep with, that the "purely sexual" encounter leaves women wanting. ("Why is it," one woman said, "that every time I meet someone I'm attracted to, I want to move my dolls and dishes into their house?") Perhaps the most pressing deterrent to casual sex, however, is time. Who has time for it? These are pressured, high-powered lives in which every minute means something. What's the return on investment for spending a night with someone who's moving on in the morning? What's the risk? What's the strategy?

Still, behind the cold talk is an even more chilling experience. Some women say their mouths hurt from never being kissed. Some say they think they will go crazy because no one ever touches them. Most are somewhat in a state of shock. Our mythology tells us that men are eager for sex, in pursuit of sexual encounter, and most of these women are stunned, somewhat bewildered and then bitter to discover that the men who slide into the periphery of their vision as possible partners are either not attracted to women, afraid of impotence or are actually impotent, or are intimidated by women who make their passions known.

Not everyone wants to move her dolls and dishes into someone's house. Women may be lonely for sexual intimacy and exhausted or appalled by a professional life that involves being out every night on business and almost never home, and yet still not be interested in marriage or even living with a man. Making peace with living alone, with seeing oneself as alone in the world as opposed to coupled, has been the consistent theme of women's literature in recent years and pops up in popular magazines all the time. Some find their own solutions:

Sandi Mendelson runs. "Madison Avenue makes you feel lonely," she says. "In every piece of advertising, every movie, every book, you see the love relationship. If you weren't fed that all the time, you wouldn't feel that you're missing something." Sally doesn't feel she's missing anything. "When I feel lonely," she says, "I go out and run. I feel nature is my friend."

I wonder, as we jog along toward the Golden Gate Bridge, whether the women in New York who feel their loneliness so keenly are reacting not only to the conditions of their lives, but to the life of the city. Although this life offers enormous distractions from loneliness—you can surround yourself with people, drown yourself in activity—it is hardly a place where the environment makes intimacy easy. New Yorkers live overwhelmed by the feeling that there isn't enough time for everything, that social life must be scheduled well in advance; friends see each other less often, I suspect, than they would if they lived elsewhere. Few people drop by unannounced to borrow sugar or take a spontaneous walk in the streets. Nature, of course, is hard to remember.

Sandi and I come to the end of our run. "Friends can see you through," she says, as we make our way to her car. "But when all your friends start dropping like flies and having babies, then you can feel lonely."

Professional women have various levels of connection to other women that provide, for them, what men rarely provide for one another. One level is what has come to be called the network. It's part of every woman's survival kit. There are organized networks—Women in Communications, Eastern Women's Business Association, things like that—and informal networks—sometimes just a list of contacts in your own field. The impulse behind networking is compensatory—to provide women, who are immigrants into the professions, with that association, access and acquaintanceship that men, who have been at home in these worlds all along, take as their birthright. The assumption, of course, is that women with similar interests will help one another. The masculine assumption, I might point out, is that powerful men will "bring along" less powerful men—in other words, the support among men in terms of work usually falls into place as a father/son relationship. Until recently, women have had few mothers in the workplace and even fewer daughters. The outstanding women who have moved ahead in their fields have, as often as not, been unreceptive to helping other women along. Many of them have shrunk from the feminist wave and insisted that if they could make it alone, other women could too. Not so the current generation, who see one another as sisters and, ideologically at least, are committed to the kinds of activities that help a woman feel less alone in making decisions about her career or confronting the Old Boys' Network or finding an accountant or a stockbroker. None of this is friendship, but it is a connectedness that can feel like companionship, provide a feeling of community, make a woman feel less alone.

Nikki Von Hightower moved to Houston, a place that, with its corporate transfers in and out, feels transient. "Moving here," she said, sitting behind the desk of the Houston Women's Center, where she is the director, "was the first time I felt real loneliness." She had come with her husband, who worked for a large corporation and who "just went right into business. It's no different here than in Atlanta or Tampa for him. You just gotta learn the street names." Her first job provided much less feeling of community. "I had been involved in the women's movement in New York and I sensed what community involvement was," she says, "what it meant for your life, what a severing that was to lose it." So she went to meetings of the National Organization for Women in Houston and "although I didn't feel terribly welcomed, I persisted." After a while, she had "the feeling of belonging again. It provides a kind of security. I know I can go anywhere in the women's movement in the country."

Other women feel less mobile, less able to go anywhere and find a sense of belonging. Ellie Chaikind, a Houston psychotherapist, says her practice has a good share of women who have come to Houston because of their jobs and find themselves engulfed by loneliness. "I hear over and over," she says, "the longing to go back—to where they came from, to the sense of community and friends they've left to move here." One of the things Chaikind asks these women is what they do on Sundays. I've asked the same question all over the country because it became clear very early on that people with active professional lives are occupied and involved throughout the week and have somehow made Saturday a day for doing domestic chores and catching up, but that Sunday looms like a nightmare in the week. Chaikind's patients don't do much with their Sundays. Some find a library. Others find a bookstore. One went to a video dating service, which is where I met her.

JoAnn was filling out her application. The manager had

allowed me to look through the loose-leaf binder full of applications—people describing themselves and trying to articulate what they were looking for. The men, as I have said earlier, were looking for some odd and impossible combination of independent women—i.e., women they would not have to support financially—and women who would be home when they arrived at the end of a long working day. The women here, at least in terms of what they were willing to write on an application form, had different requirements. The most consistent thing women said they were looking for in men was a sense of humor.

As I turned the pages of the book full of wants, it was clear that women didn't need men to take care of them financially or to provide them with identities or give them a life or any of the things previous generations of women were dependent on men for. They needed fun. They needed a good giggle at the end of a day at the corporation. They needed relief from the sobriety, no-nonsense fast-track Eighties. Men with a sense of humor, I thought, stood at the opposite pole from the vague and mysterious "stress" all the working women I had met complained of in their lives.

JoAnn is thirty-three, with springy blond curls and a half-giggle, whatever she is saying, but these subjects—loneliness, men, stress and work—make her very nervous. A few weeks before this bright Sunday afternoon, JoAnn moved to Houston from Oklahoma, where she was a sales rep. "I didn't know one person," she says, "and I traveled the whole state. I'd come back into Oklahoma City on Friday night and I'd be in my apartment, throwing myself on the floor sobbing, until Monday morning, when I left to go back out on the road." She asked for a transfer. Now, "all the guys I work with are old and married. I just want somebody else to be part of my life. I've thought of adopting as a single parent. I do want more than I have now, whether it be a child or a husband."

She thinks she knows what kind of man would make her feel less alone: "a nice guy with a sense of humor, someone sensitive." Other women's questionnaires also talk about "sensitivity," "being able to express his feelings," and "warmth" as important qualities in a man.

"But JoAnn," her friend Barbara, who has also come to enroll, interrupts, "you would never date a man who makes less than you, would you?"

"No."

The crossfire of expectations between the sexes comes back at me. Men and women are equally confused about what intimacy is, or love or marriage, what one might reasonably expect from a partner. We're in the middle here, all of us, beyond something clear and defined about relationships between men and women, beyond traditional structures that have shaped how we think about all these things, into a time without definition or clarity, with few structures or images indicating how to live differently. No wonder then that this aspect of personal life overwhelms so many and that work, which appears less transformed than private life does, seems simpler. No wonder the working world, with its attendant mystifications, codes, networks that ice women out, seems something one might well master—with the support of other women, with networks and information and books and conferences—as opposed to the world of love and attachment, about which so many women I know have only the smallest glimmer of hope for happiness.

The job may be a woman's lover as well, might be what she marries. For all the strictures on female behavior in corporate life, many women feel that what the job asks of them is what they ask of themselves. One of the women who works between seventy and eighty hours a week told me how resentful men she knows become when she explains that she has evening hours after nine available and perhaps the whole night. The corporation isn't resentful of such strictures but is, in fact, encouraging.

And the job may be the place a young professional woman

looks to for community, although in this respect she might be more frustrated. As I sat in the office of the video dating service in Houston, it became clear that Nikki Von Hightower's immersion in the women's movement, the instincts that told her to go to a meeting of the National Organization for Women as an anchor in a new city, were irrelevant to JoAnn and Barbara. At least they saw it that way. Eight years made a big difference. The urgency of the women's movement appeared to be gone. Both JoAnn and Barbara felt the battles had been won. The urgency about getting and keeping a good job, about economic survival, was far greater in these women than their need for membership in a community of women. They didn't need membership; they needed men.

No romantic attachment. A workplace dominated by older, married men. No feeling of membership, no community at hand. What's a woman to do? What do you do on Sunday?

"I can find a project if I want to, to fill up every moment of my time. I used to read all weekend long to avoid loneliness. I have so much work to do. It forces you not to think about being lonely." Sally is talking to me. We are sitting in a bar in Los Angeles, in Century City: the table is glossy and black, the din around us almost impossible to talk over. It is the end of the working day. Sally is blond, glamorous, competent, overworked and just past thirty. She is an agent in the film industry.

"Sunday nights are the worst," she says. "Sunday's a family day. Saturday's a day when the stores are open and errands get run. But Sunday . . ."

Her voice trails off. Sundays. Families. I think Sally knows how much she idealizes the family, how much she has absorbed the stigma of singleness in a coupled world. The idealization is easy enough to understand—in fits of loneliness, it seems the rest of the world is hooked up and only the lonely person is floating free. Like a true modern heroine, Sally has proceeded with her single life with a certain kind of determi-

nation to make it a good life, not to lie around waiting for a
man or a family to make "real life" begin. She has bought a
house for herself—"there are times you wish you wouldn't
come home to your own house with no one there except you
and your dog"—and she has traveled alone.

"Last summer," she says, "I went on a trip to Wyoming. I
spent one entire week alone in the mountains with my car and
a map. Do you know what it's like being in Yellowstone National Park in July and being the only single person in the
park? At night, you go into the dining room at the lodge for
dinner. You sit down at a table by yourself. You don't have
anybody to talk to."

It won't help to remind Sally that each of us and a lot of
other people have experienced sitting at a table somewhere
on a vacation feeling estranged, adrift from the others there,
feeling alone, feeling lonely. Nor will it help to point out the
possibility that alone in Yellowstone Park can be an occasion
for deep spiritual experience. She knows those things. She was
lonely there.

"Loneliness is a feeling that's not really reflective of what's
around you," she says, nodding to a client who passes by,
shaking hands with another agent who stops at our table. "It's
about not having continuity; there's a sameness to it, but
there's nothing that sustains you when you feel lonely. You
have nothing to look forward to. A lot of successful women I
know have focused on their careers because they've had a hard
time in relationships. But they really have a problem, too.
They intimidate a lot of men. We're really still in transition
about relationships, how you're supposed to feel about things
and how you really feel about things."

At the table in Yellowstone, she was supposed to feel exhilarated, independent. She felt bereft. Night after night, at
drinks, dinner, on the town, working, being with people,
which is, after all, the essence of her working life, she is supposed to feel on top of the world. Instead, "I can go out every
single night, I do go out every single night, and still not feel

I've communicated with anyone or related to anyone. We contribute to our own loneliness. I think it's really an unwillingness to be involved with anybody else."

Sally is attacking her own unwillingness, chipping away at the idea of relationship as though it were a block of marble and the statue within would, with enough chipping, reveal itself. Chip. Loneliness extends back to childhood: "In Denver, we lived in an apartment building where there was only one other child. I remember not having anything to do. I remember the boredom that was really loneliness." Chip chip. "My attitude has changed about what's important to me. I'm really just working my way into relationships. I haven't had a boyfriend in years and years." Chip. "How come the men I know seem to manage? Well, those aren't relationships they have. I don't think they're involved with the women they go out with. And the women have very low expectations about what they need from someone." Chip. Chip again.

The bar is emptying. Sally is going to a business dinner and I'm going to the airport. I'm on my way back to New York where, Sally thinks, relationships are easier because people are geographically closer—but where, another friend says, people live in bell jars, the piling up of bodies forcing them to keep greater distance. I know location is the least of our worries.

I don't feel depressed by these encounters partly because the women I have met are not depressed. They haven't been lying on their beds crying or going to pieces, but struggling, with a considerable amount of self-respect, to find an appropriate distance or closeness to the rest of the world. Chip. I buckle my seat belt. The lights go down for takeoff. Across the aisle, a woman flips open her attaché case and pulls out what look to be reports. She doesn't look down at the ground at all.

CHAPTER 5

Family Life

"Between being a happy family and getting a divorce is a whole world of isolation"

F amily" is a romantic word in our current vocabulary. People exhale when they say it, sighing the way one sighs over the word "love." "The Family" is seen as a protection against loneliness, an assurance of connection. A person alone on a crowded shopping street at holiday time falls prey easily to the fantasy that the mom and kids lugging brightly wrapped packages are part of a happy family, en route to home and shared bliss with still more family members—the father, perhaps the grandparents, cousins, uncles. Sunday is the loneliest day of the week because we think of it as a family day. The fantasy of always having someone around, always having someone to talk to, of being permanently "related" is the ghost that haunts Sundays—the family out for a stroll in the park, the family in front of the television set, the family sitting down to the Sunday dinner—which is synonymous with family meal.

"Haven in a heartless world" is the image, historically, most often conjured up as description or hope about what a family is. The force of this idea faded in recent American history and has recently returned doubled. We have few images in popular culture now about the liberation of breaking away from the family, little music or art or thinking or talking about inventing tribes or communities or other ways of connecting ourselves to one another that don't revolve around the idea of a family. The return of the idea of the family, sanctified and romanticized, is present in all our political rhetoric, in the debate about abortion, in the cultural shift that makes single less appealing than it was in the last decade and more a target for industries that promise to make singles double and establish a family.

In some ways, we never really devalued family life; alternative life styles were a fringe and most people preferred what they hoped was the security of family life. Our emphasis on "resurrecting" families is, in part, a code for the backlash against the women's movement. There is a punitive aspect to our collective worry about the quality of family life and our sense of its importance—from latchkey kids to teenage suicides. The punishment is aimed at women for working, for being at the office instead of at the kitchen table waiting with milk and cookies.

I got an inkling of why the idea of "family" had become so important now, so magical, while I was traveling in the steel-mill towns of Pennsylvania. There, amid a general despair and destruction, in the midst of massive unemployment and hopelessness about the future, a woman said: "I was brought up to believe in three things—the church, the union and the Democratic party." Each of these institutions had failed her; that is, she felt none were true advocates of her interests, none really "cared" what happened to her, none had the power to shelter or sustain. What, then, was left? The family. Naïve though the thinking may be, many people feel betrayed by things they had been brought up to believe in, feel cast aside and disillusioned by church, labor union, political party, company—institutions they once imagined themselves attached to. Such people turn inward instead, to the American tradition that fosters self-reliance as a goal. If there are any other presences in that place where one can trust, they are members of one's family. The same sinking feeling that there is nothing "out there" to hang on to fosters our uncertainty and terror about nuclear annihilation and contributes to a massive desire to hold the family close.

But some families won't hold close. In most, the sensation of being alone, left out, misunderstood, not wanted—whatever refinement one wants to make on "feeling lonely"—comes and goes. A woman told me about an extreme situation. Her father had committed suicide while her mother was pregnant. Her mother found him dead in the garage. "I was born," she said, "into difficult and lonely circumstances. The family lied to me about what happened to my father; everybody in town knew it except me. On top of that, my mother was very ashamed of what happened and then, to make me a triple outsider, I was a Jew in a Christian town."

A lot flowed from that beginning, almost all of it related to loneliness. Not only was loneliness "mainlined into me," but she took it on—"I bought it." When, well into her adult life, she fell in love with someone who returned her love and they lived together, "I knew then how lonely I had been. I had my first experience of the absence of loneliness. I can't describe the joy of not being lonely. I enjoyed every minute, feeling deeply, profoundly relieved. It was like slaking a thirst you didn't know you had."

Loneliness "drained" her. Always, she said, she was on the lookout for companionship or love. She was only half there in terms of what she was doing. Her concentration was interrupted, her work suffered and her perception of herself was always off "because of my loneliness. That's why I drank. You know, I only discovered lately that I didn't drink to get energy or any of that, as I had thought. I picked up the drink when

I was about to confront loneliness. When I was with people, I was all right, I didn't drink." Now, with the help of Alcoholics Anonymous, she is a recovering alcoholic and "battling loneliness means facing it down without any drugs, without any bevel."

The thirst you didn't know you had exists in all families, but most experts say there are aspects of the way we live now that contribute to greater loneliness in family life—or, at best, that family life offers little bulwark against loneliness. In some cases—the bizarre circumstances that the woman I had been speaking with had so vividly drawn, for example—the child comes into a family with little chance of feeling related and is bound to grow up lonely. Children rarely held or touched "fail to thrive," and that goes far beyond the biological facts. Children of alcoholics, when they come to understand the course of their lives and the origins in the family of many kinds of distress, always talk about a particular kind of loneliness—an alcoholic parent who has trouble relating to anyone, whose trouble is exacerbated by drinking, whose presence is always unstable and not to be counted on, whose children almost always grow up feeling alone in the world, distant from other people and given to being secretive about life in the family and life altogether. The same is true of incest victims and those abused as children—all of whom learned to withdraw and mistrust other people.

But loneliness can be passed on in families in less pathological ways, in patterns that follow those of alcoholism or other substance abuse, but seem rather more ordinary. Many people have described a family life in which the parents clung tightly to one another and shut out both the world and the child. The parents had no friends; there were no models in the home of what it meant to have friends. There was a sense of being stranded, both shut out from the clinging marriage and alone in the rest of the world. Nobody ever came to dinner. Nobody called or went to the movies. Nobody confided in anyone. The family seems, to people who talk this way, the most antisocial unit imaginable, less a haven than a dungeon. Some children growing up in families like these become compensatory— filling their lives with other people, looking for other families to "adopt" themselves into, marrying young. Others repeat the patterns they learned at home, isolating themselves, walling themselves off from intimate connections, ignoring the thirst.

Almost every woman I met who had lived a traditional family life as an adult responded to my questions about loneliness by speaking first and without hesitation of her days as a young mother at home with a child. I sat around a large table in the living room of a house where a crew of women had just been scraping the ceiling of an upstairs bedroom. This group, in a suburb outside New York City, meets weekly to help each other with chores like the ceiling or weeding the garden or plastering a column on the porch. They are all in their thirties and forties, most of them still married, all of them with long experience raising families, which is what brought them to this suburb. After the work chores are done, the food comes out and the talking begins.

"I don't really make friends at work now. I did when I was a teacher because there was no competition among us. Now, we don't trust each other. There's an atmosphere at this job in which you never admit you've made a mistake and the only thing you say to the people who work with you is 'Good morning.' "

Someone poured the wine.

"Well," another woman said, "I have a good friend at work and she's leaving and I'm glad. It's difficult to balance. I don't want intimate relationships at work, even though the people may be marvelous. The distance is freeing."

Someone sent the basket of bread around the table.

A songwriter said she liked to work alone, loved being home alone all day, and the woman to her right interrupted her, "Until nobody's there. . . ."

We had planned to talk about loneliness at work. The group had been eager to hear what I had to say and to tell me about themselves, but the conversation never jelled because these were women who never invested much desire for intimacy in their work lives. Closeness and connection belonged in the family. Then, after the casseroles had been dished out and the salad served, a woman with an open face and intelligent eyes, wearing jeans splattered with paint and a checked shirt rolled at the sleeves, paused, with her fork in midair, and said all this talk about loneliness reminded her of a part of her life she had nearly forgotten:

"The loneliest time in my life was when my son was an infant. We lived in Queens and my husband went to work every day. I had nobody to talk to. I couldn't tell my mother about it because this was supposed to be great, being home and having a child, and I couldn't tell my husband about it because he was working so hard and I didn't want to burden him. So I took the carriage out every day and walked and walked. But then winter came and the streets weren't clear and I couldn't go out. The only thing that made this better was when my husband quit his job and started doing free-lance work at home and then, well, it got better."

A memory. Many women have the same memory, some of being stuck at home with the children and some of being stuck at home while the children are gone. I heard these memories all over the country and each of them came in answer to my asking what the problems of loneliness had been in people's lives and what they had done about them.

Crystal Lugo grew up in East Los Angeles. In high school, she "couldn't get into it. I would rather be with my friends. We'd go to someone's house and we'd get high." She dropped out of school for a year, came back and went on to junior college. At eighteen, she married a man who had a good job as a dental technician, and after a while there was enough money to move from the old neighborhood to something better. Upward mobility, it would be called, carried Crystal

Lugo to a new place where "all my neighbors were retired. I didn't have anyone I could relate to. The telephone was my only communication" and she used the telephone to talk to her mother every day and to the friends in the old neighborhood who had kids, stayed home and collected welfare. Going anywhere was difficult because her husband took the car in the morning and there was little public transportation.

But she had Jeanine Michele, eight months old at the time Crystal and I talked. By then, however, life had gone off in a different direction. She had been home with the child all day, cut off, spending her time cleaning the house and watching the Spanish soap operas on television, waiting for her husband to get home, starting dinner much earlier than she needed to. Then there was trouble in the marriage, followed by a separation. Crystal didn't drift away or onto welfare, as other women have done in these circumstances. She found a program for displaced homemakers administered by a social service agency and began getting training in office work.

There are thirty-five women and one man in the program, all of them single parents. They are learning not only the skills of office work but, as Crystal says, "how to be with people." Most of them don't know. Crystal was so used to staying home and so scared about being with other people, as though "being with people" was not something other people did unselfconsciously, like breathing. Crystal was learning, but she was still afraid. The program was in danger of being cut. If that happened, what would she do? She hesitated. "I don't know." She hesitated again. "I guess I would end up being a waitress or I'd go on welfare." More hesitation. "Maybe I'd go back to my husband." And the soaps? And the isolation?

A tall, dark-haired woman, in a suburb of New York City, is talking in much the same way about the empty house, the presences that once filled it emptied out. This time, however, it's about divorce. Mornings are the worst time. There is something about waking up in an empty house that had not always been empty that is hard to overcome. Her talk reminds me of single people remembering the bustle of the house in the morning in their childhoods—the bathroom door slamming, pans being rattled, the radio giving the traffic report. This woman remembers words. "Now nobody says 'Good morning' or 'What's for dinner?' " Her husband has left; her son is at college. She turns on the television set. *Good Morning, America* keeps her company. Or she goes out on the country roads and jogs.

The rhythm of the day takes over; the loneliness recedes. Although she is qualified for different kinds of work, she chose to take a job in a local hardware store because "it's a family-owned business and there's a sense of family there." As with most people, her own sense of loneliness fades in the face of other people's. "I feel awful about the old ladies who come into the store. They seem to be saying 'please talk to me' or 'please touch me.' There's nothing more reassuring than hands-on contact. Skin on skin. Touching someone makes a big difference."

Yet the past cannot be falsified. Although divorce is sometimes considered the greatest source of loneliness in contemporary life, I have met inordinate numbers of divorced people who say they were more lonely in their marriages than they are after divorce. Many, especially the women, say they got divorced because they felt the people they were married to were strangers, offered no intimacy, lacked any communication. Nights spent lying back to back in bed, not touching. Feeling unseen, unheard, shut out, denied—whatever the phrasing, the feeling is the same.

The pathological version of loneliness in marriage was brought home to me in the living room of a white clapboard house in Houston. This was no one's home, although it was made to look like a home, a casual scattering of chairs, a coffee-maker brewing, rugs on the floor for a person who wanted to sprawl. The place was the Houston Area Women's

Center, which acts as a clearing house for problems women have in the Houston area and supports a shelter for battered women, one of the major problems. Three women sat in the living room. Jean was a counselor at the shelter and herself a formerly battered woman. Cindy and Katy had moved out of the shelter after some time there and were sharing an apartment.

Now we are in the world of headlines, cover stories in national magazines, specials on television. One cobweb of family life has emerged into the limelight, partly through the efforts of places like this one, which not only recognize the need for shelters for battered women and make known that they are available, but are equally attuned to the kind of psychological rehabilitation process that will leave a woman who has allowed herself to be battered aware of the road she traveled to that violent place, alert to the pitfalls that would lead her there again.

The experience of being battered within a marriage is a nightmare bracketed by loneliness on both sides. Loneliness and isolation—on the part of each spouse—precedes the batterings, and loneliness and isolation follow it. The women's side is easier to know because women—these three sitting patiently in what looks like a living room—want to talk about it; talking about it, like talking about your drinking in AA, is part of the cure. And they are messianic in their desire to pass this story along to other women, let them know they are not alone, that there is a way out. The pattern of abuse in these three lives is the same—he hit her once, maybe again; she tried to pacify him; sometimes he was drunk; the pacifying didn't work for long. The individual details are lurid and terrifying —knife gashes, hair torn out at the roots, abdominal scars, broken legs. I think of violent childhood acts perpetrated on my dolls. These women, unlike my dolls, have blood, flesh, muscle and vein in the places where they have been torn apart.

The isolation to start with. For Cindy and Katy, there was the isolation of place—they had left behind the familiar world

of family, friends, neighbors, networks, to come to the place
where the streets were paved with gold. Nikki Von Hightower,
director of the center, had told me this was a common story;
a couple uprooted, a man often frustrated by the lack of gold
in the streets, and the woman easy victim to his frustration.
But there was a deeper kind of isolation to start with, one that
preceded the marriage.

They were lonely children, these recovering women now so
obvious in their camaraderie and care for one another, so
aware of each other's stories and where each of them still
hurts. Before, they were alone in their families and they speak
particularly about feeling estranged from their mothers. Jean,
who has been married three times, twice to men who battered
her, seems more bitter about her relationship with her mother
than with either of the men:

"I went to my mother after I'd left him and she said I
shouldn't stay there too long because he might be coming
over. And this is *my* mother. If I called my mother today,
immediately after saying hello she would tell me what I'm
doing wrong with my life. If you don't have the support of
your mother, that's a void. I'm beginning to wonder about
this. Most of the women I've worked with at the shelter had
bad relationships with their mothers. I think these things
started out with a loneliness within a family."

None of these women ever mentioned a father. Although
they blamed a persistent loneliness throughout their childhoods on mothers who hardly listened or cared, they seemed
not to have noticed the lack of participation of fathers in
family life. This, though, is understandable, given what they
told me about their expectations of men, their idealization of
men and the ways they worked themselves into states of total
dependency that ended in knife-wielding horrors. I'm not saying they blame themselves, because they don't; they do see
their own contributions to what happened and they see how
to change.

"I love you." Is it loneliness, then, to have spent your childhood and adolescence looking for someone who will say "I love you"? Jean says that was her attitude and throughout one of her marriages, she begged her husband to say it and he never would. When he became violent, she told him he had to "seek help," but he "would not seek help because he thinks there's nothing wrong with him. So I left. That was fine until I started dating someone else. Then he came by to tell me he loved me." She doesn't stop. The next sentence comes at the same pace, with the same sensible inflection of the rest of the story she has been telling. "I could have killed him."

I love you. A lonely child, particularly a lonely woman, the women told me, grows up dreaming of the man who will love her and compensate for the loneliness of her family life. She craves closeness; fears distance. She believes the popular songs. "We're going to the chapel and we're gonna get married and we'll never be lonely anymore." That one echoes from my adolescence; these women have theirs. Who are the men who batter them? We know less about them than we do about the women, but they, too, appear to come from lonely families, to have been socially isolated, to need the women as much, perhaps more, than the women need them. Recent, very preliminary studies of batterers describe them as uncommonly isolated people, often virtually friendless. Experts believe that most forms of abuse—incest, alcohol, drugs, battery—are mood-altering experiences that provide temporary escape from feelings of loneliness and inadequacy.

Somehow the panic of loneliness and the pain of feeling unloved turns the forlorn into victim and victimized and shifts the ground of the exchange from loving to controlling. Each woman described the progressive control her husband took over her life. He didn't want her to see her friends. He picked up the phone when she was talking to a friend and told her to get off or threatened the friend if the connection wasn't immediately broken. He never left her alone, went to the mailbox or the laundry or the cleaners with her, took her with him when he went to get the car repaired. All of these men are described by the women they hurt as "con men" or "Dr. Jekyll and Mr. Hyde," men who managed to charm the families of these women so thoroughly that their reports of battering were disbelieved. Since the women came from families where they felt little sympathy or support to begin with, their experience of telling a family member about being battered and hearing that it was their own fault seemed logical to them. Most of the time, they told no one, out of shame, feeling they must be nuts, blaming themselves, adding to the isolation.

Jean talks about the loneliness on the other side of the bracket with as much intensity as she has described being cut off from friends and family, being a terrified prisoner tiptoeing around her house. She had gotten out of the relationship and had some serious counseling. It was a Saturday afternoon. She was alone. She had what she calls "a double loneliness" because her children were grown and gone and she was truly alone "for the first time in twenty-something years. Part of me sat down and cried for a while. We seem to be programmed to have someone take care of us as we're growing up so when we get out of these relationships, a big fear is of being alone and having to take care of yourself. So part of me cried. At the same time, I was overjoyed at being able to turn on the educational TV station and watch how people lived in Japan. I didn't give a damn how people lived in Japan, but I was ecstatic to turn on whatever channel I wanted."

The haven became a dungeon. The dungeon was, after much struggle, escaped. For Jean and for many other battered women who begin to believe in their own capacity to get help and change their lives, the women's shelters offer havens based on commonality, not the desire to be taken care of; interdependence, not the dependence of a wife whose husband tells her to hang up the telephone; companionship, not the terror of leaving someone and being bewilderingly on your own. "You go to the shelter," she told me, "and there are forty-five women and children there, all colors, all races. I never thought I was prejudiced or biased or anything, but in there I got a good chance to examine what I was. The bonding that happens in there goes across everything—economics, education, race, religion—it doesn't matter. I've seen Nigerians, Iranians, Orientals, Spanish people—all these women in one room just extremely caring of one another. We have group meetings where we explain the cycle of violence and battery —we basically confirm what the woman already knows. The best groups happen after the staff cuts out, after nine o'clock when the kids go to bed. You sit from then till four in the morning and you tell what yours did to you. You take turns crying and laughing. You can't explain it to someone who hasn't been through it. A special friendship happens there."

And afterward. First, there are the scars that stay with you. "If a man comes up to me and moves his hand and starts talking real loudly I feel totally petrified," Jean says. And there is the rebuilding of a life, readjusting ways of relating to men. Jean has married again but this marriage, she says, has much more independence and mutuality between the partners—"he feels as much responsibility for the relationship as I do. I don't think I could ever be dependent again—financially or emotionally. If I find myself falling back into traditional roles or into submissiveness, I have to stop myself. For me, it's very important that I can look at my husband and say 'I want you and I love you, but I don't need you.'"

Cindy and Katy watched Jean, listening to her with a kind of awe, as though she were a graduate student and they were freshmen. They are only recently out of the shelter, out on their own, looking back. Much of what they say fits the pattern Jean laid down. Cindy is twenty-four and blond, and she has an awful scar on her leg because her husband slashed her with a knife and tried to kill her.

She had been living on her own since she was eighteen. She thought of herself as a competent person, worked, had friends. She had been raised in a foster home, never had contact with her real mother and, at seventeen, "more or less adopted" another couple as parents, but "I don't like to call

them and say, 'Hey, my life's a mess,' " so when she started
getting into trouble with her husband, they were on the list of
people she couldn't tell. The man she married was someone
she had known for two months. He'd been married twice
before. She didn't know then, but does now, that both those
marriages ended with battering.

There were signs he was a batterer, but she "didn't pick up
on them." Her friends said marrying him was the best thing
ever to happen to her. Another Jekyll and Hyde. More signs.
"He told me if I touched the door to the truck he'd break my
hand. Now we have this attitude that men are real macho.
When he talked that way, I thought, 'Oh, my god, he really
does care about me. He would break my hand rather than have
me open the door. He's such a gentleman.' "

Four days after their marriage, he got "thrown in jail for
thirty days." A year before, he'd been arrested for driving
while intoxicated and put on probation and then, right after
the wedding, he got picked up for a felony arson. He told her
he hadn't done it. She believed him. He went to jail. When he
came out, he was "like a total stranger to me."

While he was in jail, "I sat home and just moped. I could
have gotten a job, but I didn't. I didn't know what to do with
myself. It was like once he got put in jail, my whole life fell
apart. I couldn't believe that I went—"and she snaps her
fingers, hard, like the sound of someone cracking—"just like
that."

At the end of his thirty-day sentence, her husband came
home to a life where "you're married to that person, but you
have absolutely nothing in common. The run of the conversation is: what do you want for dinner? That's it. This man had
me believing that I was the problem. Before we got married,
we talked about having kids and we both agreed we'd do it in
two years. Then, all of a sudden, he wants to get me pregnant
right away and I said no. He didn't want me to take birth
control pills because he didn't want me having any side effects.
They're good at knowing what you want to hear.

"I was chained to him, really, because I wanted to make my marriage work. I worked four days and I got fired because of all the shit that he started, calling on the phone, coming to the place where I worked. The manager said, 'We really like you, but people here are real nervous about having you here. We're gonna end up being hurt because you're here.' "

Unlike many women in similar situations, she left at the first violence. He came after her with a knife. She shows the scar again. Uh oh, she said. There had been minor instances before and she'd stayed home because she didn't want anyone to see the bruises, but the night he picked up the knife and slashed her and she went screaming to a neighbor who wouldn't help and then dashing down the street and eventually the police came, that was the night she stopped making excuses for him, stopped believing it was all her fault, stopped thinking a person had to live this way to have somebody, stopped thinking the world didn't care just because her family said she had the responsibility of making her marriage work. She went to the shelter and now, her "sanity saved," she's trying to figure out what's next.

Katy is very thin, with short, cropped hair, wearing jeans and shifting around in her chair as though somewhere it holds a nook of comfort. Her pain, which is real and physical, is not the result of battering, but of an ectopic pregnancy, which she is just recovering from and which she overcame to come talk with us.

"We almost lost her," Cindy says.

But we didn't. Katy is much older than the woebegone teenager she appears to be. "I was thirty-four when I got married," she says. "I'd dated, had my share of affairs with married men and that is lonely. You want to talk to somebody and you can't get to them. You can't call them. I told my girlfriend, the first man I meet that's single and wants to marry me, I'm gonna marry. All my life, I think all I ever really wanted to be was a housewife." Like Cindy, Katy had decided that if only she had a man of her own and a family of her own, she'd never be lonely again.

So she was in a bar and a band was playing and there was a guy she passed on the way to the ladies' room. When she came out, he was still there. He followed her back to the table and within five minutes, asked her to marry him. You know she did because she had told her girlfriend she'd marry the next man who asked her. I don't think she knew a lot about him at the time—he had a job as a brickmason, wore nice clothes and had been saved and was a Christian, that's about it. The signs, always ignored by women who end up in battery situations, were there the first night.

"He wanted to take me home. I had to wait for my girlfriend because she didn't know how to get home from there. He said it was just around the corner. So I went. He took me up twenty thousand million roads and twenty thousand million turns and I didn't know how to get back from there. He had decided I belonged to him, I was his."

She was his. He beat her. She stayed. "I blamed it on alcohol. I blamed it on insanity. I blamed it on his childhood. I believed him that he was hostile and bitter because everybody had taken advantage of him all his life. I was social worker number one."

Eventually, Katy made her way to the shelter, then to the apartment with Cindy and to a liaison with another man she won't talk much about. Three women; three stories overlapping and echoing each other; three narratives of loneliness, dependency, terror, battery, withdrawal, and the horrible prospect of facing life alone, mitigated by the friends and the care each woman received from those who understand. These are stories about working-class women. The jobs they work at and look for are in factories, offices and coffee shops. Their men work with their hands. But the story is not very different, only more hidden, when the women stay home overseeing the gardener and the maid and the men work with their minds, managing corporations. The pattern is the same, the stigma is the same. The woman is met with perhaps greater disbelief by friends or family because the man in question is a pillar of the community. As I write this, the newspapers are clucking their tongues over the battery of Charlotte Fedders by her husband, the top enforcement official of the Securities and Exchange Commission. John M. Fedders has resigned his job. Mrs. Fedders did not go to a shelter, as the women in Houston did. Most do not. The gruesome story came out in a divorce hearing. She testified that her husband struck her in the abdomen when she was pregnant—a common occasion for battery. He blackened her eyes, wrenched her neck. Through his attorney, Fedders blamed his troubles on business-related problems.

The corporate wife tells me how her husband comes home from work, eats a fast meal and disappears into the study to continue working. This is a happy family. There are no arguments, no overt tension. The children understand. The wife understands. In some families, it is the wife who walks into the study and closes the door. Those are people in the managerial class, but the problem is not confined to them. A woman working in the city government in a steel town in Pennsylvania said she had so little time for friends, so little time for relationships, because she worked so hard and so long. A family life was out of the question. Would an analyst probe to discover that this woman works hard and long to avoid intimacy? If so, something would be overlooked. The job she does now was, in the past, done by two people. Cost-cutting, across the nation, has had similar results, particularly in blue-collar families —a person must work longer hours, harder, to sustain the family that is then neglected.

A neglected family, in which people feel unloved, unattended to, detached, disconnected, is related to economic reality as well as to attitude. A friend employed by a "workaholic" organization, where a premium is set on working long hours beyond any realistic need, where the heroes are those who stay at the office until after midnight, was stymied one night. There was actual work to be done beyond ordinary business hours. He had promised his wife that he would go to a lecture with her. He spoke to his boss, explaining he had an obligation to the wife and the lecture, but that he would return to work that night by ten. The boss agreed to let him go, but added an admonition—"Don't encourage her." What sort of marriage and, by extension, family life can thrive in a context where the company discourages and resents time spent with the family? Yet this is more than a problem with corporate life. I wonder what might have happened had the boss been a woman. It seems that corporate hostility to family life—which exists despite all efforts to include families in company outings and other empty rituals—has something to do with male hostility to women, men's desire to spend their time together playing baseball or taking over companies or making hit records—without the interference of women and children. I tend to believe that Yoko Ono was telling the truth when she described how the Beatles resented her relationship with John Lennon and accused her of being responsible for the group's eventual breakup.

Humor tells you where the trouble is. Among executives, I have heard endless tasteless jokes about demanding wives, nasty jokes not only about women, but about family demands and the threat they seem to pose to corporate progress. A wife, for example, was preparing her child for a visit from the child's grandmother. "Guess who's going to spend next week with us?" she said. "It's someone you haven't seen in a long time." The child answered, "Daddy?"

The current debate over "quality time" is unresolved and probably always will be. Although many people blame the loneliness in their family lives on an absent parent—the suicide father, the working mother, the obsessed male executive, the faraway grandparents, the distracted parents—it is not clear, here, as elsewhere, how much closeness, intimacy and attachment have to do with the actual presence of other people, how much with their ability to communicate when they are present. It is clear, however, that one generation of men now looks at its sons and sees choices being made that are very different from its own. These men see their sons spending time with wives and children, sometimes at the expense of their careers, sometimes not. Mike Wallace is among them. In his autobiography, *Close Encounters,* he talks about the different road taken by his son:

> When Chris and his wife, Elizabeth, began to raise a family, they resolved that their children, Peter and Megan, would not be brought up in a home from which their father was gone much of the time. Having watched his old man lapse into the life of an ambitious, driven itinerant, Chris was determined to avoid that fate. And so, to his everlasting credit, he has made career concessions that keep him in Washington most of the time, close to Elizabeth and their children.

Changing family life was the subject of a conversation at a kitchen table in the country. I sat munching sandwiches with doctors Paul and Frances Lippmann one long, stark winter afternoon in the Berkshires. The ice in the driveway had been so bad that I had parked down below on the road. A friend who planned to join us called to say the roads were nearly impassable. In the continual, circular debate about whether city living or country living was more lonely, we participated. The Lippmanns are city transplants. In the city, Paul said, he was taken up with the communication network, the people, the media, the beat. In the country, nature replaced those things. We sipped more coffee. Both Paul and Frances think it is easier to live as a divorced person in the city, that the availability of casual relationships and casual sex is greater. The loneliness of that casualness is not known to this couple, whose world is peopled mostly by families, ice on the roads or not.

Fran Lippmann talks about the children. "I see more children who come from families that are not tuned into them because they're tuned into other difficulties, other troubles. I see many kids who come because mother has decided she doesn't want to be mother anymore. These children often feel they are an interference to their parent's careers, that they're not wanted." And yet. And yet. "The old way wasn't necessarily better, because there were a lot of mommies who never should have been home, who needed to go to work. There are children of working mothers who feel a sense of pride and accomplishment in what their mothers are doing, particularly the daughters. In working-class families, the culture is usually set up better, there is usually a grandmother to look after the children."

Paul Lippmann hangs back from the conversation. As the first cups of coffee were poured, he had offered an observation: "People sometimes achieve interesting things because of that absence of personal contact. Schizoid people, whom we think of as suffering great loneliness, deeply detached people, those are the ones with the most extraordinarily intricate inner lives." Neither his wife nor I had taken him up on what he said. We had gone on to talk raptly about families, about the devaluation of motherhood, and the children lacking milk and cookies when they came home from school. We had talked about aloneness in childhood, how we had been punished by being made to go alone to our rooms, how children are left alone in separate beds, given separate rooms if the family can afford to do that, how privacy became a virtue teetering on the edge of loneliness. Fran had spoken again and again of how the single women she sees in her practice still feel a deep loneliness about "meeting somebody," no matter how successful they are. When we were silent and the snow had begun to fall around the house, the sky grown gray, someone going to answer the telephone or wrap a sandwich and put it back in the refrigerator, it seemed that what we had been talking about was the real stuff of life, was how it ought to be—mom, dad, cookies, cold roads, warm kitchen, food, nurture, good talk, good friends.

The extraordinarily intricate inner lives of the deeply lonely. I remembered what I knew about this man. Somewhere in his forties, with no preparation and no foresight, he had picked up a pen and started to draw. Miracles poured forth—in pen and ink, crayon, on paper, canvas. He produced image after image with passionate Jewish content—rabbis, visionaries, seers, victims, martyrs. On many of his images, he scribbled words or fragments of words in Yiddish. It was astonishingly beautiful work, reminiscent of Chagall's. No one was more surprised than himself, more elated, mystified, perhaps frightened and perhaps, equally, exhilarated. He knew whereof he spoke when he mentioned the interesting things that come from such deep detachment. And the kitchen table had little part in it. Nor did his wife. Nor did I.

I tell this story lest I lose sight of how complex the issue of loneliness is, how ambivalent we are about the spaces between us. I tell it because it is the other side of the coin that has the lonesome cowboy on the front. Alongside the sterility of absolute independence, of the literal and spiritual death that can come from lack of meaningful connectedness, are the virtues of loneliness, which are little comfort to people in deep anguish, wandering, lost, in a world that seems to have no definition, no color and no end.

Paul Lippmann returned to the conversation at the kitchen table to speak not of his own visions, but, in a way, on behalf of men. Or of the men he has come to know in his consulting room. The loneliness of these men, he said, was related to cataclysmic changes in family life. Divorced fathers, for example, suffered terrible loneliness for the children they were not raising, and he had listened as these fathers tried to trick themselves into not feeling that pain. As women went back to work or to school, the lives of married men changed in ways that led to loneliness. Now, he said, a man can't go out for Thursday night beer and bowling with his men friends because his wife is in school and he has to be with the baby.

Is it lonely to be with the baby? Women, as I have said, often remember their early years with children and without work as the loneliest of their lives. Men in larger numbers than ever in history are beginning to have the experience of being alone with the baby. Some are with the baby while the wife works. Some are with the baby when the wife is gone. After *Kramer vs. Kramer* appeared, a film about a father raising his son after his wife has abandoned them, family therapy centers around the country reported an increase in referrals. The film legitimatized a problem. Fathers crawled out of the woodwork, seeking help. At the same time, fathers raising children alone began to discover some aspects of such living that were not the least lonely, chief among them the pleasures of nurture and companionship to be had with children. And, many single fathers said, they didn't feel the isolation women reported as keenly as the women had because they were actually less isolated. When they took their children to the playground, mothers swooped down on them, offering help. Single fathers were usually richer than single mothers and could afford to hire help, create support systems and even find their experiences reflected in popular culture, not devalued—as motherhood had been for the women who felt so lonely—but praised, admired, considered a great adventure, sometimes even an act of heroism.

For all the destruction bemoaned by those who speak of the end of the family, the disintegration of family ties, the breakup of the alleged haven in a heartless world, there is a tremendous amount of construction going on at the moment. Social worker Constance Ahrons is credited with coining the term that describes one such construction—"the binuclear family." We know what that means, although it hardly existed twenty years ago—divorce does not end a family. Although the disappearing father who must be hounded for support payments and whose emotional support is negligible is still a figure in American life—joined by the disappearing mother, in far smaller numbers and usually for reasons not unlike those portrayed in *Kramer vs. Kramer*—something called the family survives. Parents live separately, very often with new husbands or wives; the children may shuttle between them and they may mourn the loss of the original home, but I have heard many stories of children whose lives have been doubled by this new arrangement—they have two homes, not one, and they often have several sets of grandparents, aunts, uncles, stepbrothers and stepsisters. Most of the studies of children of divorce that have so horrified the advocates of family life at all cost were done in the 1960s among adults whose parents had been divorced. Those people grew up marginal in a world of what appeared to be solid nuclear families. Today's children of divorce inhabit a different universe. Their friends are likely to be children of divorce also. Or children of second marriages. Or third marriages. Although loneliness is certainly a factor in their lives, it can hardly be said that their homes have been broken or that they are the castaways they might once have been.

I think, in this context, about attitudes toward family life portrayed in the Moynihan report, issued in the mid-Sixties, which warned the nation that black family life was "a tangle of pathology." One of the most outspoken critics of that report was sociologist Herbert Gans, whose observations are extremely relevant to the question of family loneliness. Families break up, Gans pointed out, for many reasons "and removing one member—e.g., an angry, unemployed black father—may be a healthy and realistic move." The same might well be said of families where abuse—wife-beating, child molesting—is the cause of loneliness, and the breakup of that particular family may be the first step in allowing its members to find satisfying, as well as safe, attachments in other forms.

Gans also pointed out that matriarchal families, which are typical of black life in the United States, are not intrinsically pathological because of the "kinship system" of black females, which he found "surprisingly stable." This kinship system involves not only blood relatives—sisters, aunts, cousins—but neighbors who look after one another's children, move around the neighborhood or the city in groups, pass on survival information, aid and comfort one another, provide emotional support and understanding.

Moynihan shook his finger at illegitimacy, yet Gans says that "bastard" and "promiscuous woman" are the vocabulary of the white middle-class observer. Having any child, he says, "for black girls often means becoming an adult and playing the important role of mother over the family." It also, as counselors who work with teenage mothers assert, is seen as a hedge against loneliness and often functions as exactly that.

Two young women at a Harlem school where they are preparing for high school equivalency diplomas told me about this. Actually, they wrote it down as part of a school exercise. One described a lonely day:

> My lonely day is when I'm on the subway train on my way to school no friends or relatives around just thinking about my children on the subway with many strangers who I dont know, no one to talk to, people just staring and looking like something is wrong and I've come from another planet.

Another woman wrote some advice about how to make a lonely day better, pointing out not only the companionship of being with the child, but the "kinship system" among mothers in her neighborhood:

> I would go to the park with my daughter. Play around with her. Take her to the store. Once she got sleepy I would take her upstairs, wash her up, put her pajamas on her. And then I will go back out to the game room and play a couple of videos or maybe I will go to a friends house and listen to some records or watch television or maybe just go sit in the park and talk. I would ask my friend for her opinion on my baby. Would I be doing the right thing? What kind of medicine should I give her.

What would I do if she gets sick. Because she knows all about babies.

So the absence of loneliness appears as "family feeling" in places where a traditional world view would lead you to least expect it. One final example, as untraditional as you can imagine. In Berkeley, California, a lesbian woman lived alone with her teenaged daughter. She had had many affairs, but no permanent attachment. The daugher was difficult in understandable ways—the family she had been born into was alcoholic, her mother was living through a period of intense loneliness herself, wanting a partner and substituting political work for intimacy. The daughter seemed friendless or, at least, she never had friends call her at home and her mother never met any of them. Then her mother fell in love with another woman and, after a while, the lover moved into the house. Suddenly, the daughter began giving parties. She had friends stay the night. "It's odd," the mother said, "you would have thought she felt a great sense of stigma about my living with another woman. But she didn't. Suddenly she felt she had a family. It didn't matter what kind it was or how unconventional it may appear to anyone else. She felt, at last, that we were a family."

CHAPTER 6

Widows and Widowers

"You can't ever find a place for yourself on Sunday"

Each of us has places that remind us of loneliness just below our own surfaces or elicit our fear of a loneliness to come: a desolate house in a winter landscape; a living room hung with photographs of people who have died or moved away; a crowded subway car. My places are that walk from Santa Monica down through Venice and the stretch of civilization, the land of the retired, from Miami's South Beach up through, say, Pompano.

The people sitting on the porches of small residential hotels in South Beach are mostly old women. Plastic and aluminum chairs are set in rows as in a movie theater, but the lights don't go down and the show never comes up. My grandmother sat here. She lived alone. Her daughters lived nearly an hour to the north and came once or twice a week to visit, to do the shopping, to bring food, to sit on the chairs and be anxious to leave. Their husbands came too—perhaps more anxious to leave, lacking the bond of guilt that held the daughters. My grandmother loved to sit on those chairs as she had loved to sit on the benches in the middle of the Grand Concourse in the Bronx, because she loved to watch the world. The world she watched was growing more dangerous. In the Bronx, no one sat on benches in the 1970's or 1980's. There had been too many robberies, purse-snatchings and assaults. In Florida, she was afraid of the Cubans. At night, sometimes, gangs of kids would drive by in cars and throw beer bottles at the porch she sat on, at her, but her love of watching the world was greater than her sense of its danger.

Actually, to say she lived alone is not quite accurate. There were other people like herself in that hotel and a woman who owned the place, much younger, who kept watch on the old people. She was a cheery, stable fixture in their lives. And there was my grandmother's sister, who lived just down the hall. Katie ate her meals with my grandmother—in my grandmother's room, at a small table covered with a checkered cloth that stood by the window. My grandmother's daughters were upset about this arrangement, feeling Katie was taking advantage of my grandmother, freeloading. They were more upset to discover that the two old women were sleeping in the same bed every night. My grandmother's bed.

It went on this way for several years. My grandmother grew impatient with Katie's senility—she asked the same questions over and over, she hardly knew who anyone was, she could not keep track of money. My grandmother grew feeble. Her daughters began taking her to stay in their homes. Each daughter lived better than the mother and their condominiums looked out on more serene settings than the streets of South Beach. One "sun room" fronted a lagoon; another, a landscaped green expanse and a swimming pool. My grandmother hated these views and was, until she was less able to care for herself, anxious to leave. She would look at the houses in the distance from each sun room and wonder aloud about the lives she could see silhouetted in lit windows: What were they doing? Was this one the husband? Were the children fighting? She missed her porch and her street and being able to watch an active, bustling world. Less than a week after they "put her," as her daughters said, in a nursing home—she needed full-time care—my grandmother died.

Just north of my grandmother's hotel is a place ostensibly richer. In Hallandale, the big beachfront condominiums have marble and crystal in the lobbies, doormen and concierges to watch the comings and goings of visitors and to protect the property. The old women here sit inside, not outside, on chairs upholstered in dark, rich fabrics, not plastic and aluminum. Most of them sit alone. They are well dressed. Their jewelry sparkles in the dim, indoor light. They have made their faces up and had their hair done by hairdressers.

The doctors know these women better than anyone else does. Up and down the boulevard in Hallandale are the medical offices, particularly the offices of cardiologists, where the women spend much of their time. Some are not ill at all, only lonely. Others are ill and their illness is exacerbated by loneliness.

Dr. Stanley Bernstein is a cardiologist who has practiced in Hallandale for years. He has seen everything. Frantic phone calls from women saying "My husband looks funny, what should I do?" Continually. The same women. Less often, the husbands. Women who come to Florida with husbands hover and flutter over them, fearful they will grow ill and die, fearful of being left alone. They know the statistics; they know their husbands will die before they do; and they know that the lobbies of their condominiums are full of well-dressed women sitting alone. Some of their anxiety comes not from what they know, but from what they do not know. Dr. Bernstein says most retired couples have never known each other—they have lived conventionally divided lives; his life was work and hers was home and family. They have actually spent little time alone together. Each wince or twinge or mood or fetish is, then, strange to the spouse and cause for panic. Call the doctor.

The doctor sees, too, the second, third and fourth marriages of people whose spouses have died. The men, he says, are impotent, but they marry anyway. The women, he says, are impotent, too. "They don't get aroused. They think all the men are terrible. They're comparing them to the men they married sixty years ago." Within these marriages, illness interferes, life becomes even lonelier. One of Dr. Bernstein's patients has had a stroke. Her husband has hired two home care nurses. He spends his day sitting and watching her. He only leaves the apartment to carry her daily urine specimen to the doctor. This could, tragic though it is, be a story of deep connectedness. What people fear most is dying alone. Here is a woman dying with an attentive, bound husband, yet the story, in Dr. Bernstein's version, has none of the comfort people hope for when they project themselves into sad scenes like this one, only loneliness.

The married people in Dr. Bernstein's practice are not only cut off from each other, but equally cut off from the families they have left in their move to Florida. They track those of us left behind with the passion an obsessed lover has for the loved one. None of us knows quite how to behave. Parents leaving the children is a recent phenomenon, reversing the ancient village pattern of children striking off on their own, parents and grandparents remaining relatively rooted, growing old in familiar circumstances. Here is an older generation striking into the wilderness themselves, severing familial bonds themselves, faced with the task of living longer than previous generations, rooting themselves in new places, imagining lives unimaginable to their own parents.

The doctor sees their resentment. The grandchildren come to visit, they tell him, and all they want to do is go to the beach. The children keep in touch with them, but at a distance, because, after all, the children have lives of their own. But when "something happens"—a common euphemism in retirement communities—"the children are here in ten minutes. They call in 450 consultants. And they're angry at the doctor."

He talks a lot about anger. One eighty-two-year-old woman has had three or four husbands and outlived them all. She has two sets of children, but "they don't want to have anything to do with her. Her kids are always described as the brightest, they're married to such influential people, they make so much money, but she actually hates their guts because they've left her alone." What does the woman do with her anger at being alone? She calls the doctor. "She says, 'I'm dying. Put me in the hospital.'

"Don't misunderstand me," the doctor says, "these people have legitimate symptoms. The aging process produces medical problems, but they're magnified so much by loneliness. The doctor is seen much more frequently than he should be. And the doctors make them sicker. What bothers me is the inability of the people around to help them. We don't know how to treat loneliness. Neither do the psychiatrists. We give them drugs."

They give them drugs. The doctors distance them, calling them "these people." And the doctors have their own anger to contend with. "In overcoming the isolation of living alone," Dr. Bernstein says, "they become murderers. They're murdering me." And the doctors to whom people turn for succor and assurance are full of bewilderment and despair. Dr. Bernstein's father, in his late eighties, lives with him and complains all the time that he is lonely and has nobody to talk to. "I think you ought to warn everybody," he says, his arm making a sweeping gesture toward the window, taking in the luxury buildings, the warm sun, the expensive cars being driven slowly up and down, "that this is only going to get worse."

So I issue the warning, although I will come, later, to cheer some of the extraordinary measures the elderly are taking to combat loneliness. For the moment, I am among the lonely, especially the women.

Four widows assemble for conversation in the apartment of one of them, who decides she cares not to discuss the matter and spends her time serving coffee. We are in a condominium complex near Pompano Beach, which sports an enormous clubhouse where lectures and dances and classes and other social events take place, manicured landscape, swimming pools, guards at the gate. I have been instructed to be punctual in our arriving and in departing because each of the four women will leave to make herself dinner at six and then go off to a card game or a mah-jongg game. Life in their retirement, at least weekday life, is very structured.

"We ran away. We ran away here."

Each has moved to Florida after her husband died. Each came alone, knowing no one and each had to learn, among other things, to make a life for herself. "Here is where you pick up your life," one of them says, but she is the only one who feels she has done that. Gloria Winnetsky shifts on the floral couch. She likes to read. She enjoys her own company. She is hardly lonely and she thinks that is because she was less dependent on her husband when he was alive than her friends were on theirs.

Shirley Moses is an energetic, dark-haired woman. "I used to enjoy my own company," she says, "but now I don't." She turns to Gloria. "You can't ever find a place for yourself on Sunday here," she says. "This Sunday, I ironed, I sewed. I called my kids. I couldn't call you, you had your grandson." She turns to me, unable to say "I," "You feel you're shut up inside." Inside herself, inside her house. But it is not, in fact, physical isolation that plagues these women. Shirley says she plays cards, as she is about to that evening, with eight other people and "none of them give a damn about me." Who gives a damn, then? I expect, for a moment, an indictment of the children, the faraway children busy with their own lives, but Shirley says no, "your children don't take away your loneliness, only your contemporaries."

Honey Albert is well tailored, well coiffed, her hair a ginger pageboy that makes her look younger than her sixty-seven years. She is the most recent arrival in southern Florida and the most recently widowed. If the others are capable of talking about loneliness and describing their situations clearly, Honey seems a jumble. She is grieving. She is depressed and lost. The loneliness weaves in and out of her general distress, barely separable as a thing-in-itself.

She has not picked up her life; she has lost it. "I was one of the most secure people in the world, but now I vacillate. Perhaps—"acknowledging Gloria's comment about dependency on her husband—"perhaps Phil ran my life in a way that made me feel secure." Yes, I will learn later, he did, and yes, the extent to which a woman has managed for herself in her marriage has some bearing on how she will manage as a widow. "I walk into the apartment," Honey says, bringing us to the present, "close the door, and something happens to me. I feel nauseous. It's not because I don't have friends. I can be with you all day," she tells Gloria, "and I'm still lonely."

"Alone should be a stone." It is a Yiddish expression and every woman in this room knows it.

But Honey Albert is not as full of self-pity as she sounds. There is more. There is resolution: "When I got here, I thought, 'I'm not going to spend the rest of my life alone in my apartment.'" She went to the swimming pool and walked around it, introducing herself to everyone there. Now, she says, she is thinking about going on a cruise, but "I can't go alone. I have even offered girls to pay their way to go, but . . ."

One of the women laughs, interrupting her. Didn't she put up signs, too, in the laundry room, inviting anyone who cared to come by for coffee to drop in some afternoon? She says she didn't. The others say she did. The ridicule rises in volume and Honey seems to shrink. The laughter is not quite contagious, because it doesn't affect me. I might be the daughter of one of these women and I know well the standards of behavior in the culture from which they come. I know why

they are laughing, although I cannot sympathize. How dis-
couraging it is, I am thinking, to find your attempts to break
out of loneliness met with no support, with ridicule instead,
and how much simpler it might seem to resign yourself to a
life alone in your apartment.

The impulse is to turn away. That is the first thing that lies
behind this ridicule. The woman who invited us to her apartment to discuss loneliness has refused to participate because,
I imagine, the shame of it is too great, her own impulse is to
turn away and she imagines it to be the impulse of others who
might read what she says. An open admission of need—Honey
walking around the pool or putting up, if she did, the sign in
the laundry room—is rarely met with a generous response.
But in the middle-class Jewish culture in which these women
have spent their lives, there is a specific prohibition against
"being pushy." It is a prohibition that exists perhaps in an
effort to protect against the stereotype of the "pushy Jew," but
it is applied especially severely to the behavior of women. Or
it has been, in the generation that now sits laughing at Honey.
If you need the beginning of an answer to the question of why
companionship fails so badly among people so desperately in
need of it, the answer is in the laughter and in the unstated
vision Honey's friends have of how pushy and pathetic her
first efforts to break out of her loneliness were.

In fact, the options for these women, as they see them, given
their own constraints and the constraints of their culture, are
severely limited. Couples, for example, are off-limits. They
hardly ever socialize with couples and they stay away from
most activities at the clubhouse which attract couples. Shirley
says, "If you want to know about loneliness, go out with couples. You feel part of you is missing. There's a line drawn.
You're not part of the group." But the problem of couples is
not entirely self-inflicted. Every woman I talked to in the world
of these widows and every couple, too, said—always, of
course, about their neighbors—that married women don't
want them around. They are guarding their husbands.

So we come to men. No woman here thinks of male friends when she contemplates loneliness and considers connections. They see the social disadvantage of their gender—single men are not shunned by couples; in fact, single men are pursued for dinner parties and theater parties and nights at the movies. "Men have no problems," Gloria says, "a man is always very palatable." Men are not only palatable, but scarce. One man for every twenty women, they say. So men are valued and women are not. More than valued, the men are idealized. Women chase after them. Somehow, in pursuit of a marriage, it may be all right to be pushy, but the women in this room remove themselves from the chase:

"You've got to be the type of woman who can push. I'm not."

"You have to get a man right after he's widowed."

"The men are looking for very rich widows with cars."

Some women, I am told, scan the obituaries eagerly, waiting for wives to die so they can go after the men. The women show up at the bereaved man's house, always bearing food. Men, some say, have developed the "pot roast" test to decide which of the waiting women they will favor with their company.

It is hard to dismantle the aura of desirability about older men that hangs in the south Florida air, but most recent research plays havoc with this idealized vision. Before I found myself in this living room, the hour growing late, the women growing fidgety about their card games, I had visited Dr. Anne Peplau at UCLA, a psychologist who has been studying loneliness and aging.

"One of the myths we have been debunking," she said, "is that the people you really need to worry about are lonely old ladies, that men somehow do better. The evidence comes out overwhelmingly opposite—women seem to be better able to adjust to old age and widowhood than men do, especially if the men are not married. Through most of men's lives, marriage seems to provide a social buffer for them. If their wives die before they do, men are in trouble in terms of their physical health and their mental health.

"There is pretty good evidence," she went on, "that women are likely to keep making friends throughout the life cycle. If women lose friends, if their friends die or move away, they replace them. Men don't. I don't know if it's that men can't make friends or that they don't think it's important." In conventional marriages, women learn what social scientists call "social skills" because, Dr. Peplau says, "they tend to be the social secretaries." They also learn the survival skills that you need as you grow older: they know how to eat properly, when to go to the doctor, how to manage on a budget. The skills that men have acquired in their work lives are probably less useful to them in old age."

This is how it has been. For men, intimacy means a woman, a wife or girlfriend. For women, intimacy means both a romantic relationship and a reliance on friends. Dr. Peplau didn't know, nor do I, what will happen forty years from now, whether the generation that will then be the elderly will evidence the same patterns. If younger men seem to be expanding their definitions of intimacy—into relations with male friends or female friends or more intimate relations with their children—and younger women are refusing to nurture men as a single, life-long occupation, then perhaps loneliness among the aging, and particularly among widows, will have a different shape in the future. The women in Pompano Beach are accustomed to being needed in ways that my generation will probably not be. This may help us. But I have not given up on the older generation, struggling to make for themselves a peopled world. How could I? The next time I saw Honey Albert, nearly a year later, her life had changed.

She looked different. Her hair was much shorter—the pageboy was gone and the color, I think, was more muted. She looked as though she were straining less to appear younger. Instead of the rather dressed-up costume and jewelry she had worn at our first meeting, she had on a pair of pants and a loose overblouse. In fact, she looked like most of the women

who live in that condominium—they have discarded their
northern city clothes for casual Florida attire and cut their hair
short perhaps to eliminate the bother or expense of hairdressers, but surely for convenience, too. So she looked like everyone else and yet, in a curious way, she looked as though she
had settled into herself.

All afternoon, she had been trying to get a plane reservation
so she could attend a friend's funeral up north. She'd fly to
Newark. No reservations available. And she had no warm coat
any more; what would she do about that? She'd fly to Philadelphia, then, and take a train. No reservations. And what about
the coat? She had taken a Valium. A friend had called.

"I'm not very good today. A dear friend died."

"Well, I'm hanging up. I don't want to hear about your
problems."

That is how the conversation went, according to Honey, and
I have no reason not to believe her for I have seen other
citizens of Honey's world turn from each other's pain in similar ways. They are not cruel people; they are frightened. They
live constantly with the fear of death and they watch the fear
become reality for people around them. This is what happens
in communities made up only of older people—they watch
each other die. The presence of death and the denial of death
permeate their conversations with each other and their moments alone. The ambulances come and go. The emergency
button in each apartment, connected to a central medical
office, sits there, waiting. It is both a comfort and a threat, as
the isolated roadside bars in rural New England represented
both friendliness and danger.

Friends die. Living friends turn away. Honey has heard that
Myrtle comes twice a year to Florida, but she never calls.
Honey wonders why and then a friend tells her: "Myrtle is very
superstitious. Her husband is still alive. She sees you and
thinks she may be the next one. So she doesn't see you."

Still, all is not misery and rejection and although Honey says
first that I have come at a very bad time, we keep talking, we

sit at the kitchen table, we have a cup of tea and the talk changes. In spite of the upset of this particular day, Honey is happier, her life is less lonely. She has made a peace of sorts with the condition that, the first time we met, had her in the throes of panic, depression and despair: "Aloneness is an actuality," she says. "Loneliness is a state of mind."

The friends I had met her with before were not friends as she would use the word today, but the first people she had latched on to. Or who had latched on to her. She cannot remember having chosen them, but she is aware now of choosing others. As she describes the old friends and the new friends, two things are clear: she is talking about the false self she adopted to fit in when she first moved to Florida and she is talking about class.

We go back to the beginning, to life before her husband died. They lived in a suburb of Trenton, New Jersey. Phil, her husband, owned a rubber mill machinery business. They had a six-bedroom Tudor mansion and "four in help" all the time, including a gardener and a man to look after the swimming pool. Honey hesitates. She thinks I won't believe her, so she leaves the room and returns with a box of photographs, which she proffers with a mixture of shyness and pride. The Tudor mansion. The immense living room. The gardens. Her children had all the privileges of upper-middle-class life—lessons and schools and money to spend. Honey and Phil entertained, went to the theater and to concerts, traveled. Phil's father died. Then Phil's brother died. He was left alone in the business, which had grown big and thriving. She shows me a full-page magazine ad for the business, as though she still expects that I see her as a woman full of fantasy and illusion.

On June 4, 1979, she was getting ready for bed. Phil said, "Aren't you going to kiss me good-night?" She went to kiss him and he fell over. The massive coronary killed him instantly. For the first month after that, Honey says, "I didn't know day from night." The attorneys sifted through Phil's business papers. Honey, like most women of her age and class, knew nothing about how the business ran nor what it was worth. The attorneys discovered that Phil had enormous debts and that he had been borrowing heavily on his life insurance policy to keep the business going. He was in financial trouble not because he had managed his business badly, but because he could not control nature. The mill sat at the edge of the Delaware River and its frequent flooding was ruining the business. The attorneys suggested that Honey sell the business. She agreed. A buyer was found. She was only beginning to know night from day. She followed the negotiations in a daze. The buyer asked to think the deal over during the long July 4th weekend. On July 6th, the Delaware River rose eighteen feet above the building.

Honey tells the details of how she "came down a few pegs" with extraordinary precision. She stayed in her house for a year after Phil died, trying to sell it, but a Tudor mansion turned out to be a white elephant. In the end, the selling price was $57,000. She chose the condominium development she now lives in because she could afford it. Before she left the mansion, she held a two-day sale of her belongings. She moved to Florida with "the leftovers."

The leftovers are beautiful. Honey shows me her living room: soft gray velvet, bright lacquered red and black Chinoiserie, a mirror, a chandelier. Her den is furnished with pieces that came from the maid's room in her house, but she won't show it to me. There is a drawing of Phil hanging in the hallway: a dapper man wearing a hat at a somewhat rakish angle, a nice, warm smile. I begin to miss him too.

The need for a false self, as Honey perceived it, arose almost as soon as she settled into her new home. She was at the swimming pool. In response to a remark one of the other women made, Honey said, "Really? I wasn't cognizant of that."

"Cognizant? What's cognizant?"

Honey felt exposed. She wasn't being pretentious; that was the way she talked. But the other women didn't have vocabularies like hers and they mocked her when she used words unfamiliar to them. After a while, she started minding her tongue. And minding what she said about her past. Although she felt she had tumbled, financially, she noticed that she had a bit more than the other women did. She was always aware of resentment lying like a snake about to spring and of touchiness about having or not having. If she offered to pick up the check for a cup of coffee, another woman would refuse. If she bought something "a little costly," she learned not to tell anyone. She put the pictures of her former home away in a drawer. And she started to write a book about her past, a way of confining the secret language and the secret life to a hidden place in which it can still be kept alive. Externally, Honey began to look, talk and act like the other women. She fit into the group.

The loneliness of the self in exile from other people is a common theme in this book. Many people mentioned not being able to "be themselves" with others as their definitions of loneliness. Some, like the homosexuals I talked with, eagerly sought communities in which they could "be themselves." Others were less clear about what aspect of themselves they felt they had to hide. I was struck, always, by the extent to which people will go to become and remain members of a group, by the ferocious energy people put into distorting how they feel and what they believe in, to keep a connection they fear will be ruptured by such disclosures. But I was most struck by the terrible loneliness of false connections and this, after a while, is what struck Honey.

"They weren't really my cup of tea," she says about the first friends she made in Florida. They were, although she doesn't put it this way, lifesavers. They were very much like the television sets that lonely people become so attached to—the comforting noise of human talk in the background, the comforting sight of faces, gestures on the small screen. The other women must have known this about Honey because the rupture came when one of them said to her, about the ubiquitous card games that are the backbone of social life among widows in the condominium, "The girls don't want to play with you anymore."

"It was the best thing to happen," she says, moving to her kitchen stove to put some fish in a pan and begin preparing her dinner. Soon after the "girls" rejected her, a woman called who had been sent by someone from Honey's old life. They became friends. Then there were others, women closer to a word Honey stumbles over and I eventually supply—"closer to your own class?" Yes. "There's a whole new type of woman here now. They seem to have come from a different strata, wives of doctors, attorneys, engineers."

That a woman is defined, to herself and to others, by her husband's profession and the class to which he belongs because of it, is a perfectly natural way for Honey and other women of her generation to see the world. So is the next thing Honey tells me, the second way in which her life has changed.

There are two men. About one, she tells me nothing except "He's not young. He's close to eighty." And that he comes every Sunday. This matters a lot, the regularity and the fact that it is Sunday when he comes. Honey has found a place for herself on Sunday. She has found a friendship with this man, but the friendship has an edge to it.

"Do you think," she asks, "that men are only interested in sex?"

She has turned the fish over in the pan on the stove. Even the word "sex" charges the atmosphere in the kitchen. "Sex" is a dangerous word. Honey is a woman of my mother's generation and the subject raises, for a moment, old ghosts—the mother's control of her daughter's sexuality, the daughter's curiosity and shame, an ancient struggle. But we are not mother and daughter, Honey and I, we are women together talking about men and intimacy.

No, I don't think that men are only interested in sex. I actually think that men are terrified of sex, of deeply connected, passionate sex, of the sex that moves beyond conquest, the kind of sex women dream about when they complain about loneliness. But I don't know Honey's friend and I have no idea what he is interested in; I have answered about men of my generation. I know that one of the theories offered for the social control of women is man's terror of female sexuality, a woman's biologically limitless capacity for orgasm.

Honey grows timid. "I wouldn't know what to do," she says about sex. I have a sense, as we talk, of the longing, the enormity of the sexual longing and the ferocity with which that longing must be repressed in the kind of world Honey lives in, where women spend their time with each other and play cards and never mention it, where the hope of finding a man seems against the odds. I have been told by other women Honey's age of the way sexual longing breaks through these generally successful attempts at repression, aided and abetted as they are by larger cultural attitudes in which aging women are not seen as sexually desirable and post-menopausal women, incapable of turning sex into procreation, are instructed to be beyond desire. The breaking through of this desire, usually wrapped in memories, is awful. One woman told me she passed her television screen and saw characters on a soap opera kissing. She sat on her couch weeping. Honey says the only time this memory and desire comes over her is when she is reading a novel with a very sexy scene in it.

The second man in Honey's life, is, perhaps, a possible connection for this passion. This one came to visit his brother, met Honey and invited her to a dance at the clubhouse. "I haven't danced in years," she says, and she danced. Then he asked her out for New Year's Eve. But then "something happened"—that ubiquitous euphemism—up north and he had to leave. But he called her. In fact, he called her on a Sunday, while the other man was there.

We are back in a familiar world. It is the world of girlhood. He called me. He must like me. And I have several suitors now. Am I part of the group? Do my friends like me? Will he call again? Are men only interested in sex? I have the oddest feeling that Honey, in picking up the threads of her adolescence and facing, again, the same issues she faced in her adolescence, is taking up a life that, for the forty-odd years in which she married and raised a family, somehow stopped. It is as though there was no authentic life between then and now. And this, I think, is the problem many widows face.

The grief a woman feels at the loss of someone she loved, was intimate with and who was part of her daily life for decades is acute and nearly unbearable, but it does lessen with time. The widows who continue to be lonely suffer at least in part at the hands of culture. They have not been schooled in independence; they were not encouraged to lead lives of their own; they do not know the ways of the world. Faced with loneliness, I have seen many widows revert to the dreams of their adolescence and imagine that the solution to loneliness is popularity, as it was when they were teenagers.

They cannot be friends to each other, this generation of widows, because they grew up in a world where women saw each other as competitors, threats, dangers. They did not have the balance of the other side, as my generation has had, the comradeship among women, the sense of a shared enterprise, the common focus of energy on activities like doing our own work, advocating the ERA or the legalization of abortion, going to law school or business school. Widows who suffer often have in common their mistrust of other women. Honey has said that the "girls" are vicious and hostile and that she, herself, can "talk to a man much better." So they find themselves alone with each other, unable to connect to other women in meaningful ways, being lonely, needing each other, despising each other, sister victims in a cold and deadly world.

Honey is happy. Because she suffers from night blindness and cannot drive, friends are coming to pick her up and drive to a movie theater. Of such details of daily life is the conquest of loneliness made. I feel, as I leave her getting ready for the evening, that the changes of the present bode well for the lives of those of us who will be widows in the future.

We may not have to wait that long. Like buds popping up in the garden, some nourished, some withering before they have even had a chance, I have seen people later in life breaking out of the constraints of their pasts—their personal pasts and their cultural pasts—to form alliances that sustain them. This is especially true among older women who have led traditional lives, whose idea of companionship, enforced by the cultural values around them, has been a husband and children. The first such bud I found was a small tract house off a main highway in Van Nuys, California.

Mildred was close to seventy. She had been married several times and the husbands were divorced or dead. Most of her life, she had not relied on men and the marriages were conspicuously absent from her life story. Mildred was an Oklahoma "Oakie" who moved to Glendale, California, in 1928, one of ten children. Now she has three sons, ten grandchildren and three great-grandchildren, so as you listen to Mildred, you can conjure how populated her life is, kids calling up, toddlers going in and out of rooms, a life like that. Her first marriage lasted five years, leaving her to support the sons and with apparently little rancor. "Why carry bitterness?" she says. She worked as a waitress and "a nice neighbor" watched the children. Obviously, there was not much money, but Mildred's story sounds like Loretta Lynn's songs—a life of poverty with a good share of loving and close family feeling. She remembers, for example, that Wednesdays were "leftover" days at the restaurant and dinner was made up of whatever she brought home. "If we all wanted a hot dog," she says, smiling (really, she is smiling), "we'd cut it up four ways." Friday night was family night.

With a collapsed sense of time passing, Mildred tells me how the children grew and got married and she went to work for the Santa Fe Corporation managing a department and when she was sixty-three, "it came time to retire." She sold her house and bought a mobile home. "Now, there was freedom. You didn't have to pack your clothes or anything. I was so tired of getting dressed. I did nothing but wear jeans the first year." And travel with a neighbor. But the newness wore off and she found herself worrying about what would happen if "something happened" to her and so she settled down.

Mildred parked her trailer "on my son's land" and lived there for some time. When she described it, I imagined rolling hills and the trailer sitting off in the wilderness, but when we went to have a look at Mildred's former home, I found myself on a suburban street in Sherman Oaks. The trailer had been hooked into the utility lines and stayed in the street. She wasn't happy there, so she started looking for another place to live.

This is where Gene Mallory comes in. Gene is Mildred's contemporary, but he is from Iowa and a more strait-laced background. He had moved to California in 1950 to work in the aerospace industry on what he calls "the outer fringe of technology." He describes himself as "an intellectual, brought up on Greene's *History of England* and Parkman and my mother was the head of a group that studied ancient history." Gene's wife had diabetes and over the course of ten years became progressively more ill. She lost her job at the savings and loan association, but not because of illness. In a curious way, it had to do with other people's loneliness.

He said, "They put her out. Probably blacklisted her because after that she couldn't get another job. Why? Because you know a lot of old people don't have social contacts and they like to talk to people at the bank. She had a lot of old women who were her personal customers. Then they changed the system and you had to get on those lines and go to any teller they told you. They'd line them up and the women would say, 'No, I'll wait for Mrs. Mallory.' These were old women she was looking after. And the Savings & Loan fired her."

Gene cared for his invalid wife, went to work and looked after the house. The house means a lot to him, so looking after it involved keeping it clean, repairing and puttering, hauling wood for the fireplace and stacking it out back, patching the roof—things he does to this day. When his wife died and Gene went about his days alone, he wilted, as many widowers do, and people who cared about him kept prompting him to find someone to live with. For a while, he resisted. "I put up with it," he says. "Seems my whole life has been putting up with things I don't like." After a while, he decided to take a trip back to Iowa and thought it would be a good idea to find someone to live in the house and look after the two dogs who had been his companions for years.

Here is the point of intersection. Mildred was thinking about changing her life and a few people had made suggestions. She thought she ought to live with another woman, but the few she went to see about that "wanted to be served." Gene thought he ought to live with a man, talked to one who "kept me dangling for a while." Besides, he always got along better with women because "I never was an athlete or sportsman. Generally, when I find something breathing I like to leave it that way." The local senior citizens' center started sending some women over to see if that would work, but Gene, partly still the Iowa farmboy and partly the man who had spent ten years caring for an ailing woman, was sensitive on the subject of responsibility and carrying one's own share of the load. "None of them"—the women—"wanted to do anything, any work"—so he sent them away.

Then came Mildred. Although Mildred is more daring than Gene is, more flexible and adventurous, a woman who bounced around in a trailer, for example, and raised her children without the steady support of a man and although Mildred is, in most ways, a freer person, open to unconventional ideas and able to move in and out of various ways of thinking, still, what happened between these two people is extraordinary. Each was quite lonely and each recognized the need for companionship. But of what kind? With whom? Under what conditions? Neither wanted to live with the children. Each valued independence, wanted to go his or her own way a lot of the time, but, still, needed someone.

The road had not been marked when Mildred and Gene decided to live together as roommates. Most of the people they knew lived in marriages or lived alone or moved into their children's homes or found themselves in institutions of one kind or another, removed from the neighborhoods they had known and the people they had been connected to for years. The solution Mildred and Gene invented—economically equitable, designed for companionship, then highly unconventional—has become more common in the 1980s. Organizations have evolved whose sole purpose is to match senior citizens with one another, whatever their gender, for live-in companionship. It is an interesting turn because it does not look to the family to provide this companionship. The pride that has kept older people from allowing as how they might just need someone around has not disappeared, but the movement to put people together, to build communal housing for senior citizens, has overridden it.

That first day, Gene showed Mildred around the place. It would not have taken long. There is a large living room with a flagstone fireplace at one end of the house, looking out on a yard and some trees, a narrow corridor containing a serviceable but not spacious kitchen, a hallway opening onto Gene's bedroom and then Mildred's. She has two smallish rooms in the front of the house, the bedroom and a room meant to be a sitting room.

Gene is out somewhere. So Mildred is showing me the house. Her hair is bright white and she is dressed in blue slacks, a striped jersey and a bright red blazer. She keeps tugging at the waistband of her pants, complaining that she has gained weight. At seventy, Mildred has stopped smoking because she didn't like the way cigarettes smelled up her car. She has started exercising to bring the weight down, but, still, she is touchy on the subject, although I hardly find her fat. What I like best are Mildred's eyeglasses—harlequin shaped and sparkling blue, kind of tarty—and, of course, her manner.

"The first night," she says, opening the door to her bedroom, "I was a little worried. I lay there staring at the bedroom door. I knew he was clean, but I didn't know if he was a moral person."

The decision to live together as housemates was an edgy one. Mildred asked her three sons for their permission, which they appear to have given readily. Gene asked no one. He just did it, but there are members of his family who do not quite approve.

So there they were. Mildred's bedroom has an afghan and family pictures. Her sitting room is filled with huge quantities of knitting work—afghans, Dutch-boy hats and scarves. I am reminded of Rumpelstiltskin. All this knitting is meant for holiday presents for her family and friends. She is also involved with a Meals to the Homebound program, visiting sixteen people a day, bringing food and, perhaps of equal importance, other kinds of nourishment. Several of the people she visits are former showgirls and one is a famous retired actor—all this she relates to me with some pleasure at being close to glamour, however faded. And with pleasure at being of use to people.

"Pray that your loneliness may spur you into finding something to live for, great enough to die for," Dag Hammarskjöld wrote in his diaries. Perhaps what Mildred has found is less grandiose but nonetheless in the same category—a way out of loneliness by involving herself with other people, being useful, being needed. She finds it hard, now, settled in with Gene for about two years, to remember the loneliness. All she will say about it is, "I thought I had loneliness licked by the tail, living on my son's property in my trailer, but I didn't. All my friends had died off or I just lost touch with them."

She is well aware of the contrast between her life and some of the lonely lives around her. The homebound to whom she brings meals are among them but so, too, are healthy, active people who seem somehow to have lost not only their friends and their families, but their own capacity to move around in the world, forging new relationships. "One of my friends is so lonely," she says, "that she's at the senior citizens' center all day long. I'm always in and out of there."

Out of there. That is important to her. Her relationship with Gene works because "we have complete freedom. No explanations. It's more like brother and sister. No ties whatsoever." (The contradiction here is passed over without comment.) The important thing is: "I don't feel like I have to ask him when I go out."

The difference between marriage and friendship or between marriage and the brother–sister relationship or whatever Mildred and Gene choose to call their arrangement is discussed often in the course of my visit. There are ties, mutual dependencies, some admitted, others buried. They often go out to dinner together, Dutch treat, but in the house, Mildred says, "I just stepped into the female role. I took it over," by which she means that she does the cooking and cleans up. They spend most holidays together. "All you need to do to make a relationship work," she says, "is recognize where your boundaries are." The same might be true of marriage, but Mildred sees herself freed, almost relieved that this is not a marriage—"I'm a rather dominant person, bossy. If we were married, I'd want to make changes. I think age has something to do with it. Your demands are not as great when you're older."

Gene comes home. He stirs the fire, showing me, proudly, the stack of ash wood in the yard and explaining that most people don't think ash burns well, but it does. The dogs bound through the living room, are banished outside and then reprieved. Gene, too, is quite emphatic about how his relationship with Mildred is different from marriage. "We keep out of each other's hair," he says. "We're good friends. If we were romantically involved, I'd be aggravated by her absences. But we're independent entities, not parts of a single entity."

They know, both of them, that their arrangement is a pioneering one. I remember the late Barbara Myerhoff, an anthropologist and writer who had been chronicling the lives of senior citizens in Southern California, telling me that older people in this country are now the true pioneers, that it is they who are evolving new forms of living, making new kinds of coalitions. Did Mildred and Gene feel heroic? Gene said he's "always been ahead of the general way of doing things." Yes, some people still snicker at their relationship. Then he pooh-poohs the innovative nature of their arrangement—"most decent people can get along."

From Gene's point of view, they get along by being careful to avoid conflict. "She has her TV," he says, "I have mine. Commercial programming turns me off. The programs stink bad enough to drive a slaughterhouse cat off the gut wagon." Gene is not only more reticent than Mildred is, but, I discover quite soon, more worried. He avoids conflict with her because "I'm afraid it would be the end if I didn't. I hope it will last," he says, "that neither of us gets sick or unable to cope." It doesn't occur to him that there might be any other kind of rupture. This seems to be it, permanently, and he tells me later that "this is more or less my last stand. We're both dependent on each other."

It's not a perfect alliance from Mildred's side. As we sat around the table, Gene in his red wool shirt and his gray wool cardigan, his pale glasses perched somewhat professorially on the end of his nose, Mildred bringing tea from the kitchen and a tin of biscuits, setting out the plates, she remarked that she had no idea how long Gene's wife had been dead. Funny, with a woman friend you would know something like that. Her only other objection to Gene is that he does get "lost in the past" and she kids him a lot about that. No matter. But as she sees me to my car, Mildred says maybe living with Gene is working for now but, unlike him, she has little feeling of permanence about it. Nor does she want permanence. Maybe she'll build a small place of her own on her son's property. What about Gene? She doesn't know.

Some senior citizens, then, are pioneers. They have few role models because their parents did not live as long as they have lived. What they know of the past is that the elderly moved in with the younger generation and that was the end of the story. The idea of making alliances in a new place among strangers is not part of the history of people who are, as we so cruelly say, past their prime. So they are beginning to experiment and to invent. Some show the way. Others falter.

It is a common illusion that the presence of another person will protect us from death. A friend riding on the subway in Manhattan—an experience fraught enough to make one think of death—suddenly hallucinated that all the passengers were wearing green surgical masks and dress and that he was in an operating room about to die. And he felt not only frightened but horribly lonely. He missed his wife and three children. It was the fear of dying alone, he said afterward, that prompted him, in part, to have and to value his family. Many people have spoken to me about the connection between loneliness and fear and dying. Loneliness does feel, at times, like death, the death, at least, of a part of oneself. But the fear spoken of more often is quite literal—alone, unprotected by another person, I could easily die. People who live alone worry about this often. Daily, the newspaper tells us of someone who fell, passed out and died because there was no one to summon assistance. The elderly, who are, in fact, more vulnerable to illness and accident, connect loneliness and death more frequently and, at least in part, with good reason.

I went to a place where care was assured and still, not surprisingly, the problem of loneliness was a plague. The "home," as it is so ironically called, is in Manhattan and as you pass along the street from the outside, it is impossible to imagine the loneliness within. This is a good home: the floors and walls are spanking clean, there are paintings and—at the time I visited—Valentines and colored pictures hanging along the corridors. The staff seemed cheerful. People live here because they can no longer care for themselves. Many are ill. About half the population suffers from what professionals call "cognitive impairment," which ranges from severe dementia to the kind of startling impairment I saw in one woman who carried on an entirely lucid conversation with me, talked about a book she had been reading and went over to her bulletin board to show me the photographs hanging there, then stumbled, perplexed, because she couldn't remember who all the people were. They were her children.

Much has been provided for purposes of socializing. There is a beautiful auditorium for theatrical events; a well-stocked library that was recently the cause of scandal when it started subscribing to *Playboy* magazine; a lovely garden; many common rooms. Yet many of these rooms were empty. They reminded me of the singles housing complexes in Houston, with built-in recreational rooms, meeting grounds, similarly unpeopled. Why? The residents of the home are not all so ill that they cannot participate in the events that are scheduled or find a piano to play or get themselves to the library to browse. Why?

The psychiatrist in charge asks the same question and puzzles over the answer. "Why don't these people relate to each other?" he says. They are together when there is "a formal reason—like meal times," but otherwise, in his experience, "they depart to their rooms. They don't become buddies or visit each other to talk. They don't form social bonds. They seem to choose not to socialize. Why?"

Most of the rooms are double occupancy, although the psychiatrist thinks there ought to be more single rooms because privacy is as important to a person's life as sociability is. In one room, a man nearing the age of one hundred, entirely lucid, is resting on the bed. His roommate is out in the dayroom. He has no friends here, he says. Each person I talked with claimed to have nothing in common with anyone else. Yet the psychiatrist tells me that these two men who share a room have music in common. One is a former violinist who played with the NBC orchestra and the other is an aficionado who listens to music all day long. Do they ever speak about music? No. Why not?

In the dayroom, a woman plays cards at a table and smokes cigarettes. She is, for this place, young, not past sixty-five, and when I ask her if medical advice following her two strokes did not involve giving up cigarettes, she says, "Cigarettes are my only friends." Many of the people in the home cling to me, literally. The touch of baby-soft skin clutching at my hand stays with me the rest of the day. One woman touches me with her left hand; the right has been paralyzed by a stroke. She is lonely, she says, because she can no longer play the piano and make the music that has been her life's companion.

All the television sets are turned on early in the day and no one is sure that they are turned off again at night. They provide the background, some semblance of living going on, but no one watches the programs. No one talks to anyone else, except, of course, to visitors—myself, causing a stir because I am a new face—and family members who come between eleven in the morning and seven in the evening.

In part, staff members are attentive to the loneliness of the residents. The psychiatrist is always aware of how much he touches the patients, how much they need to be touched, how touching can communicate what cannot be communicated verbally. This is especially true of people in advanced stages of dementia—"the contact is valuable, even when it's impersonal contact, when it could be anyone touching them. There's a simple scarcity of human touch here, although the nurses are more intuitive to all that. The doctors are terrible at it." Older people who are not touched, exactly like infants who are not touched, develop a "failure to thrive" syndrome.

On the other hand, the institution of the nursing home, by its very nature, works against relatedness and creates a situation in which people are bound to feel lonely. I don't mean the particular institution I visited, which seemed better than most, but simply any place that thrives on routines sacredly enforced and in which individuals have little personal authority or even personal life. A person in an institution, especially a nursing home, is essentially helpless and dependent. In this one, the greatest opportunity for relationship comes not from the doctors—largely foreign born and trained, their English poor, their ability to communicate with patients hampered; their vision of this job as a way station on a career path to somewhere else—nor from the "more intuitive" nursing staff, paid for giving care and out the door at the end of the day. Those who help most in terms of loneliness are volunteers, who come sometimes daily to feed people who cannot feed themselves, to sit in silence, to provide companionship. These volunteers are usually women and they usually live alone, finding, in the act of providing companionship for someone else, solace for themselves.

There are attitudes within the institution that contribute to a specific kind of loneliness among the women. Dr. Stanley Cath, a Boston psychiatrist with extensive experience among the aged and within institutions, finds considerable differences there in the way male and female patients are treated. "Ninety percent of the people in nursing homes are women," he says. "And ninety-nine percent of the staff is female. The staff not only welcomes men, but treats them like princes. The women are socially neglected. Male patients have the attention of the staff more quickly and more frequently and this shows up in questions like who will be walked? who will be exercised? All this depends on the vagaries of human connectedness."

Dr. Cath sees tremendous differences between men and women among the aged in institutions in terms of what intimacy means, how it is achieved, why it is avoided. Women, partly because they are so neglected, form what he calls "the 'Bobbsey Twin' syndrome—protective of each other, dressing each other, being involved in activities that have little purpose except bonding with each other." I have known this to be true outside institutions—older women riding buses together, chattering away in what seems to me aimless talk but has a serious purpose, walking the streets with their arms linked.

"In male friendships," Dr. Cath says, "the medium of exchange is outside the relationship. Usually, the only friendships men have are over sports. Male patients are worried about having their freedom curtailed. This kind of male denial leads to loneliness. Men value freedom; women value contact. And for paranoid men, the nursing home situation—being cared for by women—puts them back in a childhood situation. Sometimes, their feelings of fatherlessness are intolerable."

The dayroom on the fourth floor was spanking clean. The television was going. The sun streamed in. There were only two patients in the room, each in a wheelchair. The woman slumped in her chair. Her hair was dull; I could hardly see her face. She rolled her chair toward where I sat on a couch talking with the psychiatrist, stopped, looked us over, turned and wheeled away. The man, who, I was told, was over a hundred years old, was dressed in a blue polka-dot shirt and gray pants. Nurses came in to check on him from time to time, touching his shoulder, adjusting the wheelchair. He didn't come near us. From afar, he tapped out a rhythm with his hand on the arm of the chair. Every once in a while, he let out a sound. At first, I thought he was whining. Did he feel fatherless? Was his freedom unbearably curtailed? Not this man. He had been kissed and stroked and fussed over. "Loneliness," Dr. Cath had said, "has to do with an individual's failure to create an inner, soothing presence." This man, for whatever reasons, had not failed. He was not whining. As I came closer, I heard, distinctly, the rhythm and pitch. He was singing.

CHAPTER 7

The Work Connection

"You can't reveal your hand to anyone"

Ⅰhe man's wife had left him. In Silicon Valley, where this particular wife left this particular man, more than half the married couples who arrive together continue alone. The spouse who leaves is most often the wife, for reasons that came clear during my stay there. To start, I was hearing about one of the men whose wives had left. In his distress, he had sought a therapist. Her office was bright and windowed, the second floor of a two-story building in a complex that also housed real estate offices, dentists, a travel agency and some clothing stores.

The therapist asked the man she talked to about what was going on in his life and, particularly, the current pain. He said no one. Pragmatic, the therapist issued an assignment: before he left, the man would have to think of one person he could, as they say in California, share his feelings with. He sat and thought. The room was silent. The therapist waited.

I don't know what went through the man's mind, but I assume, because of the way he eventually answered, that he thought about the people he knew at work. He would have had to think about them, because almost all the people he knew worked in the electronics industry, if not for his company, then they had passed through it on their way to another one. He spent more than the usual number of hours in a day somewhere near those people, in some way involved with them. In Silicon Valley, an average work week is seventy to eighty hours long. It is hard to get away from the work, from the computer industry that has made the Valley the site of America's new gold rush. It's not quite a company town, in the way the country is dotted with company towns—Bartlesville, Oklahoma, in the shadow of the Phillips Petroleum Company; Fort Wayne, Indiana, in the shambles left by the closing of the Harvester plant. It is an industry town. Whether you work for Atari or Apple or an upstart company just getting off the ground or one about to fold, the people you see, the things you hear about, the language in which you hear them—they're monolithic, they're hi-tech, they're computer. The technology dominates, not the company.

In Silicon Valley, when you're done with your seventy- or eighty-hour work week, you're not done with an obsession with information and technology nor with the mode of competitiveness in which everyone operates. For recreation, you might go to a park in San Jose where, on weekends, you can play live "war games"—not video games—dashing through the woods, capturing enemies, shooting them with a yellow dye that means they're dead. You can go to The Bull and Bear, a restaurant and bar owned by Nolan Bushnell, founder of Atari Computers, and, during the week, watch a running electronic ticker tape keeping track of your company's doings on the stock exchange on the East Coast. If you look around the restaurant, you'll see groups of men talking about the computer business—usually men in threes, two company men and a visitor, likely an overseas visitor. The men at the bar are alone.

Silicon Valley is a place of shifting sands. Its residents are nearly all displaced persons—people who grew up elsewhere, went to school elsewhere, have family ties elsewhere. Although such transplanting is common in American life—we go where the work is, we go where the work takes us, we go where there is better work—Silicon Valley has more of it than most other places. In Houston, another center of much coming and going at the behest of the job, I remember a business leader giving a dinner for some newcomers. He thought Houston a lonely place in this particular way, with its arriving and leaving of executives on the way to somewhere else, but he himself was relatively exempt. "I went to Rice," he told me, referring to Houston's university. "My wife went to Rice. It's very different for us." There can be few Silicon Valley counterparts of this genial host, with a strong sense of his place in Houston's own version of shifting sands. Twenty years ago, the Valley was a thirty-by-ten-mile strip between San Jose and San Francisco only beginning to shed its distinction as the prune growing capital of America. It wasn't called Silicon Valley until 1971.

But the man sitting in the therapist's office trying to think of somebody else to talk to was not a new arrival. He had worked for his company for twenty-five years, an anomaly in a place where not only are many people new arrivals, but there is also fast turnover, of "cowboys," as a lot of people who work in the semiconductor industry and those who watch and analyze how it works call them. The cowboys are people with easily transferable skills, engineers and scientists moving from one company to another, selling their skills to the highest bidder, working the spring roundup and moving on. But this man had stayed in place. Nor was his an isolated place. Although I was to hear many stories of people who worked alone, whose only companionship in the course of a day was a machine, this man was not one of them. He supervised twenty managers.

He had sat silently for some time. Then he snapped his fingers. "Back seven years ago," he said, "at a Christmas party at work, when my son was on drugs, a man I work with came up to me, put his arms on my shoulders and said he was sorry to hear we were having trouble with the kid. I'll find him."

In Silicon Valley, more than anywhere else, I began to get a sense of traveling through concentric circles. Literally, of course, I did not ride on beltways, but up and down straight highways, turning into Mountain View or Cupertino, sliding into the afternoon traffic heading out of Palo Alto. Structurally, though, in terms of what I was looking at, there were the circles—a person at work here, usually a scientist or engineer or an entrepreneur, himself a man with a technical background who had parlayed a product into millions or had failed to do so or was waiting to do so. Then, around this person or sometimes an extension of him, was the organization, the company, and surrounding that a circle of onlookers, kibitzers at the card game, management consultants and organizational experts, therapists of every possible kind, whose work was to watch the industry and the companies and the people and come to some understanding of what was happening and why. At the center of these circles, I ought to add, was the silicon chip, which often seemed to glow like the embers of a campfire. Except, the fire was not dying, but roaring.

Jean Hollands watches the people. She doesn't have to find them; they come to her office for therapy. The office is warm and comfortable and Mrs. Hollands is a warm, ebullient person with a strong entrepreneurial spirit of her own. She has a press brochure ready—laminated cover, bright green binding. She is the director of the Good Life Clinic in Mountain View, which actually *sounds* bright green. The brochure lists the companies she has worked with as a Human Systems Analyst, the television and radio shows that have featured her, a page of testimonials and clips of articles about her from local newspapers and from *People* magazine.

Hollands's specialty is what she calls "the Silicon Syndrome," which consists of the frustration, chagrin, misery and isolation of women married to what she calls "the sci-tech man." The majority of couples she sees in her practice, which is full of "couple loneliness," consists of "humanist-social" wives and that nonhumanist, nonsocial phenomenon, the "sci-tech man." Among other things, the sci-tech man works solo at home and at work, loves structure, planning and rules, lacks humor and "people skills." Given the kinds of personalities involved, the nature of the work people in Silicon Valley do, these problematic issues lend themselves to catchy headlines—The Computer Is "The Other Woman"—and to good anecdotes. One woman almost turned back from a vacation trip when she discovered her husband's personal computer secreted in the car trunk. Another talked of how hers slept with the computer terminal beside the bed. A man said that since his wife had left him, he'd be able to spend more time with his personal computer.

With, I would think, some irony and some eye on the lingo of her audience, Jean Hollands wrote a book about "the Silicon Syndrome" aimed at women, telling them how to "reframe" their man's behavior, find the button that gets him started, recognize the overload button. In person, she didn't talk that way at all.

The place, she says, fosters loneliness because of the unique combination of the sci-tech personality type, the culture built around it and the "Gold Rush syndrome," everyone busy getting the gold, thinking of little else. Women deny their emotional needs, inhibit their complaints about alienation from their husbands. "Why should I be complaining?" they say. "Look how he provides for me." "These people don't have best friends," Hollands says, "neither the men nor the women. It's not a drop-in kind of life. The men are antisocial. The closest to a best friend in their lives is their secretary. It's more satisfying to be at work than it is to be at home and the companies foster that mentality. The companies avoid families. They hold retreats for employees and leave out the families. It's the really progressive companies that include them."

Tom Peters, who had been spending his time going from company to company as a member of the McKinsey consulting firm, trying to figure out what worked and what didn't, sat in his office, wearing running shoes and a tweed jacket, swiveling back and forth, talking out the ideas that would soon appear in his book, *In Search of Excellence,* co-authored with Robert Waterman.

In the gospel according to Peters, the small number of American companies that are well managed treat people as a family. They use the language of family. "The chairman of 3M said it someplace," Peters told me. "For a few American companies, the company has taken the place of the church in the community. He's right. A large part of the magic of some of those places is they have provided a sense of community."

Tupperware is his first example. None of this magic is arcane; all of it, Peters said, is "hokey, cornball stuff. At Tupperware, they take a bunch of modestly disoriented, middle-aged American women. Usually it's a first job experience for them. They put them in a five-person cell, show them how to put on a Tupperware party. They make it absolutely impossible for them to screw the first one up. Then, every Monday night, every one of the Tupperware distributorships all around the world meets. The people march up on stage according to their sales of the last week. They walk up in the reverse order to the prior week's sales—but it's to applause. Unless you were stealing and didn't go to work all week, you get a badge."

And IBM. No badges there, not literally, but equivalents. "For a hundred-person IBM branch outside of Manhattan, the sales manager rents the Meadowlands. The salesmen run into the stadium through their players' entrance. Their names flash on the scoreboard in electronic lights, ninety-nine feet high. To become an IBM salesperson, you go through eighteen months of armylike bootcamp. You all sing the songs together. IBM puts on a huge effort to create community wherever you go. There's such esprit associated with the institution. They probably give them more community within the corporate environment than most of us have outside where we work. There are IBM day-care centers, country clubs, recreational areas. You move from IBM in San Jose, California, to IBM in Armonk, New York, and you probably don't know you've moved, except for the temperature difference."

Tokens of belonging. I think of the pennants and mugs of college days. In one of Peters's classes, a student wore a belt buckle from the Lonely Mallard Hunting Club, acquired at one of the recreational activities administered by Hewlett-Packard. The "deep-felt need to be a part of something" doesn't discriminate too severely about which "thing" one becomes part of. The Mickey Mouse hokey hoopla Peters describes reminds me of organizing techniques used by the Moral Majority, the recruitment posters now abandoned by the army (Uncle Sam Wants You) and the seduction practiced by cults of all fringes. Peters agrees. Business, he says, is now showing an explicit acknowledgment of the absence of community.

"Community" seems to stand, in Peters's mind, at the other end of the scale from "hierarchy." "The first thing I see among the better-run companies," he says, "is very much related to a sense of community. You ain't got the corporate fortress with twenty-seven Rothkos and the best of Bauhaus in the corporate furniture. They don't differentiate between the peons and the heroes. That's where it starts. I get sick when I go to Manhattan and see these executives in their suits and the last time they've been to the line is four years ago. At a Hewlett-Packard facility in Colorado Springs, one of the better-run companies, there are two thousand people working. I walk in. I want to see the general manager. Where the hell's his office? It's on the plant floor. Most companies that have two thousand people working for them, the manager is in a separate building guarded by nineteen secretaries."

Peters was awash with an indignation mostly muted in his book. "I'm disgusted," he says, "with the degree to which most management doesn't understand this stuff. They sit in splendid isolation on Park Avenue and talk about the Japanese threat and go lobby in Washington to get it fixed. They treat their people like dogs. It sickens me. I see it in ninety-eight percent of the places where I spend my time."

We talked in a small office on the fifth floor of an airy building on the Stanford campus, the chair swiveling, the tape recorder going; we talked at the height of the recession, when unemployment figures hit a post-Depression high. Lonely as it might be to work in a context where management sat hundreds of miles away surrounded by Rothkos and secretaries and not "caring," it would surely be more lonely to have none of these things. This led Peters to middle management.

"I think the loneliness and isolation in the middle-management suites comes from the fact that middle management has no job. There are five layers between the first lineworker and the chairman at Toyota and there are seventeen at Ford. Now, what do you think those other twelve layers are doing? They're trying to figure out how to get up to the next layer and they're designing reports which harass the people below them just to keep themselves busy. They have nothing to do except design bigger reports. The economy is so bad that, for the first time, there are a whole bunch of middle managers under the gun who may lose their jobs. I see a much greater willingness to cut the middle-management fat out during this recession than I've seen before."

If there was a national mood that day, those months, edged by fear, anxiety and depression, Peters had caught it. But he called it loneliness. "I'm lonely as hell a lot of the time," he said. "Lonely in general. The whole mess that we're part of, the unrelieved depression. So what the hell am I supposed to do? Go around and do consulting to big companies that I'm not going to make any difference for? There are eighty-five million books on the shelf. Who wants to write the eighty-five-million-and-first?" And he wasn't so happy about where he was living, either. He spoke of the "California loneliness, the frenetic narcissism. The search for infinite variations on stimuli has got to be one of the loneliest pursuits of all."

What, then, did he imagine? Was there an IBM in the sky that would create a community for Tom Peters, who seemed —discounting the self-servingness of his talk and the general edginess and uncertainty that must have accompanied the months before *In Search of Excellence* was in print, sold millions of copies, moved him out of that office into bigger ones, sent him traveling as one of America's highest-paid speakers on the lecture circuit—who seemed genuinely adrift? If he wanted to call it loneliness, I'd leave that up to him. The absence of loneliness was something he could imagine. The absence of loneliness was to be "richly involved in daily life."

But daily life for many people, including those who work for "excellent" companies, includes the experience of having no one to talk to, no one to feel close to, no one who cares. This is especially true of the "outcasts" at companies with strong cultures and values, like IBM. Those who don't fit the community leave, as one programmer did who "felt like an outsider" in the company and its family. "They were WASPs from Pennsylvania or Ohio," he said, and this New York Jew "didn't fit in." At the investment firm of Merrill Lynch, he again "didn't fit in." For human contact, he said, he and the only friend he had at the company smoked marijuana and rode up and down the elevators barefoot. Eventually, this man faced his difficulty with organizations, with structure and authority. He set himself up at home as a consultant. When he feels lonely there, he is plugged into a whole community through his computer or he picks up the telephone and talks to someone, makes a visit to a friend in an office.

"You can only create a sense of community with some strata of the population," Tom Peters had said. "There have got to be some crazy folks who enjoy independence." Peters numbered himself among the crazy folks. He couldn't work for any of the "excellent companies."

The "crazy folks who enjoy independence" stand squarely in the American tradition. This is where the Lone Ranger rides in again, kicking up dust. The American hero is the man who goes it alone—Johnny Appleseed, Paul Bunyan, Henry David Thoreau, the mythical cowboy on the range. This is what we think of as the spirit that made America great, the frontier image, the soul of the pioneer. In fact, such mythology often obscures the connections American heroes, real or fantasized, actually had. There were women and families on the wagon trains; there was a community of cowboys at home on the range. The presence of Tonto in the Lone Ranger story gives lie to the myth that the man rode alone. Tonto was an Indian and therefore didn't "count." Though, time after time, he saved the "masked man's" life, he was not a partner but a shadow. The "crazy folks who enjoy independence" may want to stand alone, but still know there is a Tonto lurking behind a rock, ready to step in when things get tough and willing to ride off into the sunset without much credit. For a male executive, the corporation provides a Tonto—in the form of his secretary.

Nowhere does the idea of the man who struggles to the top without aid or comfort, the man who takes on all comers alone, exert more force than in American business. It is the dream of most men to own their own businesses, be their own bosses, a dream now shared by enough American women to alter the shape of work in this country. Nowhere does the tension between individualism and membership, between the conflicting needs to be free and to belong, manifest itself as clearly as it does when we think, choose, change or worry about our work.

The fellow riding the elevators at Merrill Lynch, feeling out of touch with the organization, not part of its family or its community, grew up, in fact, in the American tradition where a man could work for himself and, in the blessed land of opportunity, survive and prosper on his own. This man's father owned a candy store. His father had several opportunities to "better himself" in the course of his work life, but spurned them all because they would have meant working for other people. He had to be his own boss. He let his children know that he was a Lone Ranger. To work in an organization, be a "subordinate" to anyone, was a chilling, deathly alternative. His son and daughter both worked best alone. They, too, were Lone Rangers.

Roger Gregory spends 60 percent of the sales season peddling books to accounts in Michigan and northern Ohio. "If you've never had the experience of counting the flowers on the curtains in Howard Johnson's to see if they're the same as last time," he tells me, "then you don't know what loneliness is."

It hits him late at night. The paperwork's done. You've seen "the seventeenth rerun of *Gilligan's Island.*" You've read every magazine, from *Glamour* to *Mechanics Illustrated.* You're not a drinker, so "you're not in the bar telling road stories and hitting on the waitress." You look out into a parking lot full of salesmen's cars, mostly Chevys. You know that in the morning, it's going to be "like the drunk waking up and having to pick up a matchbook to find out where he is." The phone book tells Gregory where he is.

The loneliness of the road makes you vulnerable. "If anybody shows me the slightest kindness, I overreact," Gregory says. He has gotten somewhat hardened to this, but he remembers that when he started "the second account I called on, they invited me to sleep on their couch and I did." Every night, he calls his wife, who is at home with their young child. "My wife accuses me of having a ball on the road," he says. "But I'm mainly selling my product. There are no deep relationships. Maybe I see these people four times a year. But the divorce rate among salesmen on the road is pretty high. It's almost like being a service wife."

Gregory is an old-fashioned guy doing an old-fashioned kind of job, the American archetypal traveling salesman, the man whose work supposedly embodies the freedom of the road. I have met his more modern counterparts every time I have boarded an airplane. They move between New York and Los Angeles or between Bahrain, London, New York or all the way around the globe. They know air schedules by heart and their most continuous relationships are with flight crews. The skies are now the open road, and if you live this sort of life, you need to check the phone directory to see what country you're in.

You don't have to work for yourself to be a Lone Ranger. When Dr. Robert MacLaughlin is summoned by a company that has an executive in crisis—alcoholism out of control, a breakdown well in progress—he finds that, consistently, the person in trouble "has no personalized connection with anybody other than themselves." Although the formal term for what Dr. MacLaughlin does is "executive crisis management," he thinks of it as "human salvage." What he most often needs to salvage is the executive's connection to other people: "They give up on the more human aspects of life. They're very separated from their families, don't know them at all. They have few if any close friends. They've been systematically denying their own needs, as though to have human needs is a threat to their ability to survive."

This seems more common in America than elsewhere. "American executives are the most encapsulated people," he says. "They lead narrow, channeled lives. All their satisfactions and efforts are located in one place. People who get to the top allow nothing to come between them and that goal, not family, not spirituality, not their own needs. They see themselves as personifications of the company, their jobs as extensions of themselves. It's an extension of the pioneer spirit—the strong, silent, entirely self-sufficient pioneer. American business has aligned itself with sports metaphors and military metaphors, us versus them, highly competitive and noncooperative metaphors."

Dr. MacLaughlin and I sat in a dark bar a few paces from Harvard Square. I had come to Cambridge in search of people who might be thinking about loneliness and work, particularly since Cambridge and Harvard in particular house a great percentage of the reputable people in this country who study organizations and the behavior of people in them. Few had addressed loneliness as an important issue. Dr. MacLaughlin —who struck me as a bit of a Lone Ranger himself, riding into a company, conducting his salvage operation and moving on to the next—was a provocative person to spend an afternoon with. His focus was entirely psychoanalytic. Circumstances— the structure of the organization, the nature of the work— interested him less than early experiences in the family. I had begun with the gender issue and with my observation that women spoke more often and with greater passion about loneliness at work, noticed the lack of satisfying relationships more than men did. Dr. MacLaughlin said that "women are less able to sublimate the need for relationships." I might have said that men are more able to deny that need and that corporate codes of behavior intensified that denial. He didn't want to talk that way.

"People who do well in organizations," he said, "are usually middle or younger children who had relatively trouble-free adolescences. They continue to visit Mom and Dad on Sundays. The parents praise them. These people tend to see the manager as the caretaking parent. Entrepreneurs tend to be older children, counterdependent males or women with strong repressed attachment to their fathers. Family systems theory is useful for looking at American business," he told me. "The way people function in organizations is dependent on historical themes—birth order, how they perceived their parents and their siblings." Still, his experience with crumbling executives had been experienced with men. And he has seen many men make the job, company or group the "significant other" in their lives. "How elaborate that relationship with the significant other becomes depends on how rich the fantasy is. For men, the company is perceived as female—Mom, a lover, the demanding, highly expectant lover who rarely comes across, always leaves a little something withheld."

Was someone lonely if he didn't think he was? I had interviewed many successful men—some I knew, some suggested by others—whose lives lacked human relationships, whose "significant other" was the work, but few said they felt lonely. This was especially true in Silicon Valley, where, instead of people in one's life, a person could have money, accomplishment, pride, patriotic fervor, whatever, and be, apparently, satisfied with it.

This kind of thing, Dr. MacLaughlin said, "works until it doesn't." He is called in when it doesn't. He finds a man in crisis, isolated. No one around him reaches out to help because "most people refuse to believe anything can be wrong. They view the senior executive as indestructible—they're modern gladiators; they don't get much sympathy; people say, 'Well, they're paid for it.' Part of their position is to be more than human."

If, in Dr. MacLaughlin's words, the crisis means the executive's "view of himself and his world is shattered," does it mean he becomes aware of his need for other people? "It becomes clear that's one of the major missing aspects. When they're climbing the walls and there's nobody to turn to and there's nobody to grab, it's hard to forget that." Happily, most of the executives recover and approximately one in three returns to his former job.

Less than a mile from Harvard Square, David Boyd was in his office at the *Harvard Business Review* scanning the data about more people who feel in their work that "there's nobody to turn to and there's nobody to grab." Boyd, along with David Gumpert of Northeastern University, had been studying loneliness among entrepreneurs. This research evolved from an earlier project in which the two investigated "stress" and discovered that some degree of reported stress among people who owned their own businesses was attributable to loneliness.

The data hardly seem conclusive, nor do they seem surprising. Inconclusive, I think, because there are questions not asked in this study. Feelings of "stress" and the high level of psychosomatic disorders these researchers found among owners of small businesses might, I would think, have something to do with "life style" in concrete ways. I wish they had asked everyone what their diets consisted of. Backaches, indigestion, insomnia and headaches—the symptoms their interviewees report—might be related to alcohol consumption, lack of exercise, anything. The interviewers seem surprised about what people said of their own business experience only because we have a taboo about admitting to loneliness. These are successful business people. Ninety percent of their businesses showed a profit. Still, as the authors say:

> Though entrepreneurs are usually surrounded by others— employees, customers, accountants and lawyers—they are isolated from persons in whom they can confide. "You can't go to anybody who could really help you because he's competing with you," explained one manufacturer. Long hours at work prevent entrepreneurs from seeking the comfort and counsel of friends and family members. The independence and freedom of entrepreneurs' positions may obscure their loneliness.

Boyd and Gumpert made no distinction in their study between the ways men and women coped with loneliness, but Boyd "had the impression" that the women handled it better. One woman, he said, was missing several people she had brought into the business who had then moved on elsewhere. As he described her, the story had a familiar ring to it. The Empty Nest syndrome. If companies are families, they only provide the solace and comfort the image invokes if they remain stagnant. Growth implies change. The woman mothered her employees; some grew up and left home. She felt lonely. Is the same true of men whose children grow up and move on? Surely it must be, although, until now, men have not been much encouraged to admit to these feelings. The Lone

Ranger is, after all, a man without a family.

The tide seems to be turning against the idea of the Lone Ranger, at least on the surface. Now corporations want "affiliative" managers, people capable of being part of a team, a family, a community. *In Search of Excellence* rides the tide of this turn; the Peters and Waterman book advocates more closeness on every level—close to the customer, close to the product, close to each other. Nowhere has the fact that "the Lone Ranger" is clouded in negative dust been more clear than in recent communiqués from the corporate front. When the Beatrice Companies announced reorganization within its ranks recently, Frederick B. Rentschler, president and chief executive officer of Swing/Hunt-Wesson Foods, first acquired by Esmark, Inc., then acquired by Beatrice, was out. The reason, a "source close to the company" told the press, "was that Mr. Rentschler's Lone Ranger management style did not fit into Beatrice's structured operation."

John Reed succeeded Walter B. Wriston as chairman and chief executive officer of Citicorp in the summer of 1984. As the press probed business associates to get a line on Reed, they came up with a conversion story. Until the mid-1970s, Reed was seen by his co-workers as "aloof," a "robot" and a "workaholic." Then, as the *New York Times* delicately put it, the change took place "as a result of the emotional stress his long hours and work-related travel had placed on his wife." A friend told the *Times* that "John rallied to her and to the family." His method of rallying may seem a bit exhausting: "To make sure he was home by six at night, he would be in the office at four-thirty in the morning." Wriston, who appointed his successor, was said by associates to have been impressed by Reed's "recognition of his family's needs" and Reed himself was said to have emerged from this crisis as "people-oriented" and "sensitive."

Back to Silicon Valley. Into Mountain View. Out of Mountain View. Up to Palo Alto. Down to Santa Clara. The issues come together and come apart. Local newspapers list compa-

nies that have folded, feature the ones that are starting, spot-
light the kingpins moving from one company to another like
ballplayers moving around the league. Company names become more familiar, take on character—Commodore, Versa-
tec, Tandem, Amidor—like baseball teams. "Us versus
Them" becomes part of daily conversation—the "Us" are us
in Silicon Valley, "Them" are the Japanese. I am doused with
the spirit of competition with the Japanese and the kind of
patriotism, pride in this country and what its technology and
its people can do, that I haven't heard on such a scale since
American cars dominated the world's market.

Jim Kouzes, director of the Executive Development Center
at the University of Santa Clara, equates the Lone Ranger with
the Green Beret. This, he says, is the myth, the kind of hero
emulated in Silicon Valley—"the personally self-sufficient
man who rides into town, does what he came for and goes
away, the man with no social needs." People like Kouzes absolutely believe you can't do things alone and are working on
programs to convince others. For the Lone Ranger, as an idol,
Kouzes would substitute Don Bennett, the amputee who
climbed Mt. Rainier. "You can't do it alone," he repeats. "The
individual wins trophies, but the team wins the champion-
ship." One of the programs he has initiated at the center is
called "My Personal Best," in which he gets Silicon Valley
executives to talk about what they have done well. It becomes
clear that success is a team effort. You can predict the success
or failure of an undertaking by listening to how often the
executive says "I" or "We." Venture capitalists always ask
who the rest of the team is—a star won't carry the day.

The "Personal Best" seminar has eighteen men in it, senior
executives in Silicon Valley. "Men," Kouzes says, "in their
forties, engineers, technicians. Their bottom salary is seventy
thousand dollars a year. Their eyes light up when they talk
about what they've done well," he says. "They cry. It's the first
time they've been asked to talk about success. We're trying to
get the men in top management teams closer to each other

and one way to do it is by getting them to talk about what they do well. Success is being defined as commitment. People report they're successful when they believe in something. It has a bottom-line payoff. Maybe the greatest reward is not making the most money. The more we emphasize individual success and individual careers, the more trouble we're in."

We come to talk about the idea of membership, of the feeling of belonging to something and of yearning for commitment to something. I have heard this everywhere in America. I have come to see it as part of our current mood related to where we have been, to our common history. The people who talk most avidly of their yearning for membership feel they had it once. They are usually people in their late thirties and early forties who participated, one way or another, in the social movements of the 1960s. They were campus radicals or antiwar activists or civil rights marchers, and if they weren't especially in the lead of those activities, they followed happily. Now they're grown up. They are wrapped up in individual success and individual careers, and it is easy enough from outside to say they have forgotten or moved on. I don't think many of them have forgotten, although they have surely moved on to different lives. The memory of membership, of doing things with other people that felt meaningful and, in fact, altered history, remains. This kind of longing lies behind the loneliness of people with what they consider adequate private lives—close friends, intimate connections, people to talk to, people to eat with or sleep with. Out of this loneliness, which seems massive, national and spiritual rather than political, comes a translation of focus—the company will provide that feeling of membership. Business will be what politics was.

In Los Angeles, before I came to Silicon Valley, I spent some time in the office of a broker at Merrill Lynch. He was one of those people, a civil rights activist turned stockbroker. Unlike the people in *The Big Chill,* a film that attempts to tell this very story of people who grew up in the Sixties accommodating to life in the Eighties, the broker doesn't see his engaged past as a nostalgic moment one does well to grow out of. He tries to keep some of it alive. And does so by comic distortion.

"Look out there," he says to me.

I look.

"What do you see?"

"People walking on the sidewalk."

"Right. And a lot of them are poor people. And what I'm doing here is making sure that fewer of them will be poor."

"Don't be fooled," Jim Kouzes had said, "by the fact that some of us are wearing suits." Hal Leavitt wears a suit. He is a professor of organizational behavior at the Stanford Business School. He worries about loneliness in the managerial class, pushing, in his theoretical and consulting work, for more "relational" management styles, for the necessity of creating a feeling of membership among people in any company, for choosing leaders capable of "affiliative" behavior. When we talked about loneliness in his office at Stanford, with people dropping by to say hello and leaving messages and bantering and belonging, we touched all the touchstones that define this problem: our national tradition of individualism, the lack of trust workers feel in their companies, the insistence by employees that "social relations" are part of having a good job. "If you assume that membership in a group is the other end of loneliness," he said, "most of the progressive companies in America are going that way." But then he stopped. The "progressive companies," the idea of "membership," the optimism Leavitt shared with Tom Peters, it came up short.

"I saw loneliness in spades the other day," he said. "I was down looking at a production line for fighter aircraft. A man there would come to work, punch in, go do his job. He'd see only his supervisor. He didn't know any of his co-workers. There are jobs in refineries where you watch dials all day."

527-9864.

If you're in Houston and you're in trouble, you can dial
527-9864, the Crisis Hotline. The phone rings in an office in
a three-story building that could, under other circumstances,
be full of people selling insurance, nestling the phone on a
shoulder, scribbling fast on a pad, but is, on a hot Sunday
morning, occupied by Naomi Hirsh and Steve Briggs listening
to pain.

"My brother has a drug problem."

"Tell me about it."

"Quaaludes. He's just taken six of them. My mother needs
to talk to someone. I'm at work and she just called me."

Naomi gives her a number to call.

"How many milligrams of Valium does it take to kill a person?"

Another woman. Naomi talks quietly. The woman calms
down. Steve is on the other line with a mother worried about
a son who married his high school girlfriend, left her, moved
home and started taking Mandrax. Naomi answers a call from
a Detroit woman whose boyfriend left her stranded on the
street penniless.

More than 60,000 calls a year ring at 527-9864. Most of
them come from people between eighteen and thirty-five
years old, almost twice as many from women. The busiest time
is between six and eight in the evening, after people have
come home from work. The hours between six and eight in the
evening are a kind of witching hour in the day, shaken loose
from the routines of work and the attendant safety of its structure on the one hand and, on the other, not yet immersed in
the activities, if they exist, of the night. Six to eight is the time
for "Happy Hour," the alcoholic, urban ritual of "hanging
out" or "letting loose" after a day's work and before an evening spent with the family or the television set. In another
class, this is "Miller Time," which, unlike Happy Hour, judging from television ads, only applies to men. If Happy Hour
implies mixed company, Miller Time is male camaraderie.

The fantasy aroused by the advertising is of conviviality among men, most of whom, judging from the commercials, have worked alone all day. Work in the world of Miller Time doesn't provide society and companionship, but beer does. With beer and other men, you can bitch about women and bitch about the boss or the foreman; you don't feel so alone. On weekends and holidays at the Houston Crisis Center, calls about wife-beating increase, testimony, perhaps, to the siphoning of energy that can occur at work.

Naomi Hirsch is a jovial woman with dark hair and an ebullient attitude. An old hand at answering crisis calls, she is a chemist and statistician with the Coca-Cola company during the week. Like many of the people she talks to on the telephone, Naomi was not born in Houston, but transferred several years ago from New Jersey. Like many of the callers, Naomi suffered what she calls "culture shock." She couldn't find a place to do her laundry and went around befuddled until someone explained to her that the elusive laundromat was, in this strange new place, called a "washeteria." She adapted to an unfamiliar place with few personal connections by volunteering to listen to other people's pain.

"The loneliness we're starting to see a lot of," she says, with considerable authority, "is in the people who come here with no resources. They come with very high expectations, bloated expectations. You come here and you find out"—she slips easily from "they" to "you"—"it's hot and humid, there are great big cockroaches, the traffic is the worst in the U.S., and the pay scale is lower, except for people transferred by their companies."

Steve Briggs is a more recent newcomer. Five months ago, he left his bank job in Utica, New York, for the pot of gold that is Houston. He was twenty-four years old with $1,500 in savings in his pocket. It took three weeks to find a job, but he did find a job. He was not without resources. The job was in industrial sales and the company he kept, the interactions Steve had with other people on the job, were not to his liking:

"I have difficulty relating to people who only want to go out and get smashed," he says. Steve is not nearly as priggish as he sounds, but he has landed himself in a cowboy culture and, within that, he's a bit of an Eastern dude. "I used to go to work and come home and stay in the apartment." He shudders. "You tend to go a little crazy. That's one reason I am working here."

The phone rings. Naomi answers. The volume has been turned up on the phone speaker. The man is crying. Steve and I listen as Naomi tries to get him to speak. He asks if she remembers him. He has called before. Yes, she does. But she asks him to repeat his story, remind her.

His wife left him a month ago. He'd only known her twenty-seven days when he married her; they had been married for three months and she was pregnant.

Where did she go?

"She moved back with her parents."

What made her leave?

"I blew up and hit her."

For me, it takes a second to absorb this, but Naomi goes on talking and Steve goes on listening. They have heard this story with variations many times before. The man on the telephone is about twenty-five years old and has come to Houston from North Carolina. Naomi urges him to find someone to talk to. He sounds calmer, but he says, "I never really had that many close friends. I go to school during the day and I work nights. I work in an area with only one other person."

I try to imagine him in his "area," which I take to be somewhere in the oil industry. Who is the other person? And I try to imagine this man at school, passing other students, teachers, saying nothing. He resists Naomi's suggestions, stymied and choked by the impulse to flee. "Indications all tell me," he says, "to get the hell out of Texas." And he hangs up.

There are jobs where you watch machinery all day. A man from Canton, Ohio, told the *New York Times* in the summer of 1984 that a former employee had been better off at one of those jobs. Don Williams, a funeral home owner, said his employee "was a good embalmer, but he just didn't relate to people. That's why he was better as a welder. He could just pull that mask down and be by himself." The man in question was James Oliver Huberty, who had walked into a Mc-Donald's restaurant in San Diego and massacred twenty-one people. Huberty had worked as a welder in Canton for thirteen years. Huberty had tried to call a mental health center the day before he carried his arsenal to McDonald's; they never called back.

Think of the people who don't call. In Houston, the sands shift as frequently as they do in Silicon Valley. The streets of Houston seem to be paved with gold, as the entire American continent once was for waves of immigrants. Work draws people here—the promise of blue-collar work when unemployment figures are high everywhere else; the necessity of transfer for managers in certain industries whose refusal to move to Houston would mean being stuck at a lower level somewhere else. All this movement dictated by work moved in two directions—both up and down. People do find work; people do move up. Others are disappointed, downwardly mobile. Take a ride sometime out to Pasadena, where Gilley's bar is, the scene of *Urban Cowboy,* and look at the pawnshops stuffed with symbols of dreams gone bad, the auto workers from the Midwest and the textile workers from the South who arrived in Houston to find no work, left their belongings in pawnshops before they turned around and went home.

"What you get in Houston," a management consultant says, "is the heavy hitter from some town who finds out he's no bigger than anyone else here." That's a corporate heavy hitter, someone with a good job. The consultant sees them come and go. This is the man who, with his wife, was entertaining some "heavy hitters" about to move to Houston. What about the ones who don't get entertained? Some do make a phone call. At the Houston Area Women's Center, Nikki Von Hightower gets a lot of calls from "women who are new to town.

The place seems so scattered. People don't know where to make contact."

Calls from single women newly arrived on their own are to be expected, but Hightower gets another kind of call just as often: "There are a lot of married women out in the suburbs who're lonely and terribly isolated. The neighborhood is made up of people who probably won't stay in Houston. Corporations bring them in and corporations send them out. They're here to make some money and take a step on the corporate ladder and then they're gone. The women are here because their husbands are here, but their husbands are plugged in, they have the corporation, business associates, an automatic setting. And she's sitting out there.

Everybody knows about this woman. She is one of the ghosts that haunt corporate life. In Fairfield, Connecticut, another center of corporate congestion, Dr. Vilma Allen, who runs a program of continuing education whose participants are mostly women returning to the work force after having raised their families, says you could ride up and down the tree-sheltered roads of Wilton or Weston, places that "have no center, where people don't know their neighbors," and behind the doors of those houses with "$200,000 mortgages" there would be executives' wives, "so used to being private, so unable to reach out." Allen has a vision of these women "just rotting." "Someday," she says, "someone will open the door and find a cadaver."

Everyone acknowledges this woman, theoretically, but points out, optimistically, how times are changing. More younger women pursue their own careers, disdaining the corporate "wifestyle"; more younger husbands prefer life this way, refusing transfers that would disrupt their wives' careers; more older women return to work. True. But the woman I am talking about won't go away simply because the world is changing around her.

If she's sitting out there in Houston and she's lonely enough, she might call the Women's Center to find activities to join and, depending on how troubled she is, she might call psychotherapist Ellie Chaikind. Chaikind's office is on the second floor of a modern office building off Westheimer. Its floors are covered with large pillows and those pillows covered with clients during therapy groups. One thing about her clientele is special—she sees a lot of transplanted wives and knows about the corporate "wifestyle" firsthand.

"In 1970," she tells me, "Shell came to Houston. They moved a thousand families en masse." Including the Chaikinds. "When we were first married, in the late Fifties, my husband would come home for dinner and then he'd go into his study and go to work. I felt impotent, hopeless, frustrated and very lonely. I considered it time off. He considered it time on." If being in the study after dinner seemed necessary then, it no longer does and Chaikind thinks there are men spending time off with their families now because the pressures of their careers have abated. Men are deciding they don't necessarily put the corporation first. "They're evaluating what their priorities are." Still, she knows what it is like on the other side of the closed study door or during an afternoon alone in a house while her husband is "plugged in" to a collegial atmosphere at work and the children are away at school. She knows what uprooting does to the women: "One friend of mine moved fifteen times in her career. No," she corrects herself, "in her husband's career. She said when she got here she was not going to move out of her house unless it was in a coffin. Moving is the most uprooting for the women in a traditional family—that's my experience. I'll talk from that."

She talks from that about waiting and silence. The corporate wife waits to be told what the next step is. This extends beyond the working day, the working years: "A friend's husband is about to retire. He has some future consulting plans and his wife still has certain responsibilities for running social activities for the other wives. She doesn't have any choice in that." Nor can she speak freely. If you're unhappy, you're taught "not to talk about it. You'd be disloyal to your spouse and to the company. These women identify themselves with the company. One friend talks about 'we,' never 'I.' The other half of 'we' is both her husband and the company." Most of the corporate wives who have come to her for help have not worked outside the home. "They have to learn," she says, "to make contact with people. They don't know how to go about making normal contact with the neighbor down the street."

Two things combine: the prohibition about sharing worries, about complaining or being disloyal, and the great accompanying fear of making a mistake, causing trouble for your husband, being responsible for his lack of advancement. Although many men I spoke to were fearful of revealing too much to their colleagues in the corporation, reluctant to give potential enemies information that could be "used," the men still had a sense that their own performance at work could outweigh any damage their loose tongues did. The women married to these men had no such confidence and were fearful. So the wary attitude with which many women in this position encounter other people, combined with situational factors like new neighborhoods and lack of daily contact with anyone, doom the company's efforts to provide a meeting ground for women in similar predicaments. At first, Ellie Chaikind doesn't see this. She is both inside and outside the problem. Although she is still married to a Shell executive, she took the "deviant" path of building a career of her own early on in their marriage. She often defends the company. Shell's social programs for wives—luncheons and fashion shows—are "a way for women to meet, a meeting ground," but, in fact, she says, later, that the relationships people can make under those circumstances are "very superficial." Eventually, a woman can crack.

Women seek Chaikind's help often because of alcoholism—"It's a direct reflection of loneliness. It's there when nothing else and nobody else is. Or they have an eating problem. Or they're depressed. They want to get fixed so they can then function in the same way they have before."

Sometimes, the "fix" for Ellie Chaikind's clients is a career and sometimes a woman's opting for a career leads to divorce and sometimes the women she knows take on careers and give them up because they "can't handle the stress." I ask what she means because I suspect she is not talking about the stress—whatever form it takes—of working. "The interpersonal conflict," she says. With colleagues? No, "the conflict between the spouses. The husband wants her available."

But we are talking here about dinosaurs, outmoded ideas about organizational structure and family expectations and antique notions of women as sweet young birds. Surely life is different among younger people. Surely there are bridges across some of those chasms.

I am in the workaholic center of the universe: New York City. Perhaps not, but it seems that way to me. I am in a place where people begin their business lives at seven in the morning over breakfast and where most can be reached in their offices late at night. The 100-hour work week here is not uncommon. This applies to women as well as to men. Young men working here, on the whole, have wives working as well. They have met their wives at business school or in some connection to their work. They see these things differently.

At the Yale Club, young men sit around talking, picking up drinks at the bar and finding seats in the large sitting room. One of them is a twenty-five-year-old securities trader, tall, lanky, with flopping red hair. He is wearing a dark suit and a red tie.

His work is lonely work. He looks down at his clothes: "I'm too well dressed," he says, "no one ever sees me. I could be sitting there naked." "There" is the place where he sits before a computer screen watching electronic credits. "I push paper and numbers around." He has a screen and a telephone. He describes his work, aside from its physical aspects, as "taking firm positions on stocks and bonds and options." He works for a foreign securities company and he's their only trader. "It's a very anonymous job," he says, "and one of the few jobs you can go into and come out poor. Traders' jobs are about risk and reward. They're judged on the bottom line." He chose this kind of work because "it's hard and fair. I don't like hierarchies. There aren't as many barriers to entry in this kind of job. And there's no yes-man about me."

I imagine him at his work, the screen and the telephone, no one else around. The telephone, I understand, is not a place for chitchat. So intense is the pressure of the working day, which ends when the markets close at 4:30, that no one says "Hiya, Joe, how's it going." When he calls brokers on the phone, he gets "fast information on a private line" and, he says, "I don't think they know it's me." The pressure is enormous. He explains short squeezes and corners to me. "Every time you don't do well," he says, "you have to work twice as hard. When you take a risk and you're wrong, you go to pieces. You can't do this forever."

For the moment, it's what he does. At Drexel Lambert, where he worked before, "the OTC traders came from Bay Ridge and they had all played in the same stickball game," so he didn't feel part of the culture there. In the company he works for now, he is the youngest person there—"I'd like to have some more young people"—and the rest are "a bunch of old men who haven't traded. They don't smile." When he says he's lonely at work, he means, in part, the lack of relationships in his office, but he means, also, that he has no one to talk to about what he does. None of his friends are involved in this kind of work. His father was a military man who doesn't understand it. His brother has dropped out of the business. On the floor of the Exchange, he says, "it's all father/son relationships. Here, no one can help me."

If anyone could, would he let them? I'm not sure. Several times, he has said to me, "You can't reveal your hand to anyone else." He means it to be a description of his attitude toward work and the people around him, but I'm not sure it stops there. He has been involved with a woman his age who is herself quite unsure how much time she wants to give to a relationship, how much she wants to concentrate on building her own career. He claims to have friends, men friends, but at the same time he tells me, "If you're a man in New York and you don't like sports, you're dead." And he doesn't much like sports, not the kind you talk about with other guys. In fact, we have met at the Yale Club because he comes here at the end of the day, every day, to work out. He swims, lifts weights and runs—all solitary activities. In the mornings, he rides to work on his bicycle, thereby avoiding the unpleasant but nonetheless interactive experience of looking at other people on the bus or subway. Then he sits down alone at the computer and the telephone.

"You can't reveal your hand to anyone else." It seems true, it seems an adaptive response to the world in which this man lives, to what his work requires, but it seems also to spill over into the rest of life's activities. This is a young man on the way up. Most people think he is doing well. He is, although "doing well" has an edge of fear to it, a precariousness that has something to do with his chosen profession. I have met another Lone Ranger. He's no monster, not even a neurotic. He is lonely and everything he does reinforces his loneliness. If he can't reveal his hand to anyone, how can he stretch it out to touch someone either?

CHAPTER 8

Out of Work

"Falling off the train"

Ten minutes out of Pittsburgh, you begin to see it. Whether you head west into Ohio and skirt the Ohio River or east down into what is called the Monongahela Valley, with the river of the same name running through it, the sight is the same. You think you know about the desolation of industrial America. You have read about it and seen it on television—the collapse of the domestic steel industry, for example—but no words approximate that first dismal sight.

The steel mills are massive structures, sidling up to the river, like oversize ferry boats tied to the shore. Except there are no passengers, no bands, no hoopla. The mills are huge, hulking and silent. At night, you can hardly see them. There are people in these places whose childhood memories have the smokestack going or the sputtering fire in nearly every frame. Their children will not have these memories. There are people in the Ohio and Mon valleys, and people like them elsewhere, whose lives revolved around these now-defunct steel mills. Towns were tied to them, like fetus to mother. There are the bars across from the parking lot entrance in almost every town, a dance hall still standing a few feet from the mill in quite a few places, a block where the whores worked ripped up only just before things collapsed. You can't walk through a steel town without looking down at the mill as you go along the steep streets, past the union hall, the houses, up the hills, past "For Sale" signs. It gets so that puffs of smoke, the sight of a working mill somewhere along the river, makes your heart leap up, forgetting the horrors of red lung and other attendant ecological disasters, your heart forgets because a working mill is a sign of life in what is otherwise a graveyard.

Life revolved around the mill. I am not speaking of the paycheck, although life surely revolved around that, but of the web of social connections, the fabric of family life, the friendships and continuity of relations emanating from the hub, the work, the mill. Or what happened in the union hall. Or at church. Or the bar. Or the bowling alley. Or the homes of fathers or grandfathers, uncles or cousins, where the conversation had, too, at its hub, this thing that is now shuttered and obliterated, the work at the mill and all that went with it. On this depended the folklore, the jokes, the outrages, the common references that made up a culture. What remains as that culture comes finally apart is not only forlorn desolation, but a pervasive sense of permanent extinction. As Tim Russell, who works at the Weirton mill in West Virginia, said: "I feel like I'm living in the belly of the dinosaur."

It was not so long ago. The dinosaur is not a remnant of nineteenth-century life, but of something that existed perhaps five years ago, less in some places, a short enough time for people to be shocked by its absence and unable to cope with the emptiness. The figures in my notebook are staggering. In 1981, the steel industry alone laid off 86,000 workers in the

Monongahela Valley. In the Pittsburgh Standard Metropolitan Statistical Area, there were 100,000 people working in the basic steel industry in 1980. Early in 1984, there were 40,000. In every town, someone will tell you the numbers. U.S. Steel's National Works in McKeesport, for example, had 3,500 people working there in 1982 and, at the time of my visit, there were 100. Homestead had 6,000 workers and now has a few cars in the parking lot. People will also tell you another number: the date on which they stopped working.

It is easier to begin to say what this situation has to do with loneliness by talking about what I did not see. I did not see Carl, for example. People in the bar across from the steel works in the Ohio Valley told me about Carl, but I didn't see him because he was dead. Before I even got into the bar, there was a steelworker leaving who stopped to talk. He, wary of strangers and wary of a woman, did not talk easily, but he told me how he was hanging on waiting for the mill to close officially so he could get his severance pay and move on somewhere. What had this done to him? He had developed some physical symptoms, he said and looked away. I knew I had to ask what kind. When he turned back, his lips were slightly parted and his chest was heaving: he had started to hyperventilate—that was the physical symptom and there it was again on some godforsaken street across from a hulking, dead mill. He told me to ask in the bar about Carl.

A few people had known Carl; others knew about him. Carl was twenty-eight years old and he was laid off down the river two years before. He had a wife and two small children. When the company offered a retraining program, Carl was one of the few who accepted. Most steel workers feel their lives are steel and the promise of being trained for hi-tech jobs, which is what will come to these valleys if anything comes, seems another world to them. Call them stubborn. Call them lost. Carl was more willing to go along with the reality he saw around him and he went for retraining.

His family life, like that of so many others in this place, grew rocky. They talk easily, these men, about the stress of economic hardship. Usually, they blame women. Women, they say, grow irritable with men who are not bringing in paychecks and sometimes the women run off. I heard innumerable stories of women running off to Florida with men who had jobs. Sometimes they took their children and sometimes they didn't. Sometimes they ran off to their parents' homes. Every once in a while, someone will say something about the men's part in the destruction of family life in these areas of high unemployment. There's hardly a country music station these days not playing a song about a guy sitting in a bar getting drunk—that's always been the stuff of country music—but this guy now has a family that's left him or one he can't bring himself to go home to and this guy now has lost his job and there's no other on the horizon. What comes through the songs and the meager talk of the men who can talk about it is a massive sense of depression, self-blame, worthlessness and loneliness.

Why loneliness? Many men felt the company and the job gave them a sense of belonging to something. That's gone. Many felt close to their families. That's often gone, both the closeness and, often, the families. But worse, far worse, if that is possible, than feeling disconnected from fellowship at work or intimacy at home was a feeling more cosmic and over-whelming—the feeling of being adrift in the universe, where no one cared. So halfway through the retraining program, while he was living at home with his family, Carl suddenly began to feel he had been duped. If he had some hi-tech skills, where might he use them? There were promises being made, industrial parks for the cities along the Mon Valley being drawn on drawing boards, hints that a major computer company was coming into Pittsburgh, but when Carl looked ahead, these things seemed very far off and the immediate future seemed absolutely bleak. And nobody cared. Or he felt nobody cared.

Is U.S. Steel supposed to care? The business of business is

business. Talk about caring seems not only out of place, but naïve. The hard-headed, the sensible, speak of profit and the bottom line. Those who speak of responsibility—perhaps a step toward caring—are the radicals or the softies. Yet there was much talk about not caring in the Mon and Ohio valleys, some of it radical, some soft, from men who hardly spoke this way about emotional life—a feeling of abandonment and betrayal, a sense of shock surrounding what had happened, inability to believe that the company really didn't care and perhaps, from indications that could be absorbed, the union didn't care either. All of these feelings are supported by reality —just drive along the banks of the rivers or stand in line where free food is being given away or walk into a house where a welder watches television all day with a beer can in his hand. And these feelings go above and under the concrete situation. Listen carefully: "They lied." "They promised." "They just walked out." "They don't give a shit."

Carl felt they didn't care. "They" was generalized—the company, the members of his family who urged him to stay with the retraining program when he knew in his bones it was futile, the union, the church, the world. In 1984, he put a bullet through his head.

"They don't care what happens to you. It's just tumbleweed." John Tirpak is talking. It is the winter of 1984 and we are driving along the Ohio River, starting in Yorkville and heading south toward Martins Ferry. Tirpak is my guide. Without him, I would have less access to stories like Carl's and to men like the one who hyperventilated in the street. Tirpak is also twenty-eight years old, a round, jolly man, hefty, funny, good-natured and out of work. Tirpak, too, has two young children. His life, too, has been steel. His father was killed in the Yorkville plant on his fifty-first birthday. He had worked there for twenty-five years. A tractor ran him over. "There wasn't a lawyer that would touch it." And, again, "they don't care what happens to you." Tirpak, not surprisingly, became safety chairman of the plant, and he can say with pride "there

were no fatalities when I was there," but it doesn't bring his
father back or the man he just heard about, electrocuted in the
plant two days before his wife had their first child. The company called it a heart attack. Tumbleweed. Tirpak says it to me
again: "They don't really care about anyone."

"They," of course, are the higher-ups, people who are not
really people, but functions, job titles. There are other people,
ones with names and faces, some he sees every day down at
the union hall or in church or at a market or a meeting and
those people—"they care about each other, but they're afraid
to say anything." I have to interrupt to tell you that John
Tirpak didn't lose his job in an ordinary layoff—the Yorkville
plant still employed 800 people—but because he had written
articles in the union newspaper that were considered inflam-
matory. When he talks about caring and fear, Tirpak means,
first of all, the support or lack of it he has felt close to home.
"You find out if you have any friends," he says, flipping the
stations on the car radio. "I've been through it and I can count
on two hands the people who helped me." In church, there
was whispering in the pews—"There's one of those radicals,"
they said—and Tirpak didn't know what to do about other
people's fear. He knows, though, where it comes from: "If
they can do that to him," he thinks other people think. . . . He
leaves the sentence unfinished as we drive up to the Pacoma
plant.

This was a USWA plant that shut down and moved to Tex-
arkana, where they were using nonunion labor. Like everyone
involved in the devastation of these valleys, Tirpak knew his
numbers cold: "They had a thousand people here." When we
get down to Martins Ferry, he says "there are only three hundred people here now; there were fifteen hundred before."
The body count goes on. Beans Foundry, which "forged every
manhole cover in the country, used to work twenty-four hours
a day. Two or three years ago, it shut down." We drive slowly
along the river and Tirpak talks about the life choked off—

"There used to be factories all along here." A closed auto painting shop. Galvanizing plant closed. There are six forlorn cars in the lot at Eastern Plating.

Bellaire, Ohio, was the national center of handblown glass. The Imperial Glass factory has a single car in the lot. The people who worked here were masters, Tirpak tells me, "They put everything they knew into pieces of glass." They had the kind of pride steelworkers talk about. We pull into the parking lot, climb out of the car and here, at last, we get an inside view. The steel mills are locked and guarded, but at Imperial Glass, we rap on the door and a mustached guard lets us in. I'm sure he can't imagine what we want to see, but we're welcome to see it.

A cap lies on the floor. A pipe sits on an ashtray. There are rows of workbenches on the second floor, empty, pieces of glasswork laid aside as though just for a moment. The furnace is shut. I walk carefully amid the ghosts. It seems everyone has vaporized, leaving the stuff of material life behind them. They were here just a moment ago. They must be out on a break, back soon. I think I hear a footstep, turn, find no one but Tirpak, who shares the eeriness, and the guard, who does not. It's just a shut-down plant. Tumbleweed.

The guard will be moving on soon. He has let us into this place because, unlike the men at the gates of the steel plants, he doesn't work for the company, has no attachment to it, but is employed by a guard service and moves from place to place, here a week and somewhere else the next, disengaged. He'll be moving on to Houston, where the police department has recruited him. He tells me he is happy to be single and able to move, glances at Tirpak as though, intuitively, he has understood that Tirpak is neither single nor able to move. Has he been to Houston, this man happy to have a future prospect? No. They came recruiting.

We descend the wooden stairs, walk the hallways, go out and down the steps, past the gift shop where Imperial Glass

sold right to the public who wanted to buy, and sit still in the
car for a while, the guard looking out at us and scratching his
head.

Tirpak's wife is watching television. It is a tiny apartment,
the bedroom just visible beyond the small living room in
which I sit on a couch looking at the enormous television set
and the three-year-old boy eyes me suspiciously from the corner. His wife hardly goes out. John takes the car and her family
lives a drive away. She is in her midtwenties, with long blond
hair and a sweet, bouncy kind of energy that I don't think has
been invented for a visitor. John Tirpak fills the apartment
entirely. She is reed-slim. She tells us who is having an affair
on the soap opera and we talk about those people on the
screen as though they are people we know, whose secrets we
have penetrated and whose sins we bring ourselves to feel
compassion for.

There were men I didn't see on this trip, men I was told
about, withdrawn into their homes and their beer cans and
their television sets, and there were men who had hanged
themselves or put guns to their heads, but equally striking was
the absence of women in public places, women to talk to.
There were no women in the bars we visited, none out for a
walk along the side of the road, none in the union halls. The
women were in their houses and they were in church, but most
of all they lived on the telephone. Or through the life on the
television sets.

I drove slowly. As I went north along the Ohio River I felt
that at my back was a place so annihilated I was at a loss to
imagine life taking over again. How romanticized the films
and stories about the Depression seemed; the sense of being
in the same boat together, of pulling together through the
hard times. Loneliness is a tumbleweed feeling, drifting along,
disconnected, surrounded by empty space. I could leave that
place; others couldn't. There were people who couldn't afford
to go to the bowling alley or didn't have the cash to buy gas
to visit their parents and uncles. There were people deserted

by a sense that anyone cared. Many were lost in denial—the mills would come back, the corpse would breathe, life would be as it was. Others gave up. Most pulled inward, in panic and terror. What was possible? The talk was of industrial parks and hi-tech jobs, another world, perhaps possible but not around the corner. In McKeesport, I had heard the mayor rejoice over the idea of building a dog track where the steel works now stand. A city official had shuddered at the thought, imagining a welder now selling tickets at a dog track. I drove past a Polish social hall, closed. An Elks club, shut.

Wheeling, West Virginia, is a place where one possible solution has been tried and, in limited ways with many caveats, seems to work. The workers bought the plant and have been operating it for two years. One of them, Tim Russell, was waiting for me on the porch of his brick house, his hands dirty from the mill.

Funny how fast hopelessness fades, how easy it is to forget. Tim's wife, Jody, is working in the kitchen, getting supper ready. Her sister is helping her. There is stuffing to cook for the steak and gravy, potatoes to set on the table, some apple cider and beer to drink. Four children run back and forth from the kitchen to the dining room table and out into the living room to stand shyly in corners and stare at a visitor. Not many strangers drop by. The world of these children and their parents is peopled by familiarity—brothers and sisters, cousins, people they all grew up with, people their parents grew up with. Steve, who is married to Jody's sister, is out of work, but otherwise things at the Russells roll merrily along, life seems very connected, isolation is unimaginable, the meal is good and lasts a long time and the people at the table are miraculously talkative to an outsider.

But this is an unusual household. Tim Russell, after his day's work at the mill, drove to Pittsburgh and got not only a college degree, but an MFA in the writing program. In 1982, Tim was laid off and he didn't go back to the Weirton mill until the end of 1983, when the workers bought it. His first child

was born five months after he was laid off. When he talks about
this time in his life, he is talking about a nightmare. He worked
in a tire shop, did odd jobs, and wrote a novel that still sits on
his desk. He, too, can recite the body count: "Four years ago,
there were twelve thousand people working here. Now there
are seventy-five hundred. Four thousand people have van-
ished." But he can write about these things, does. When he
says he feels like he's living in the last dinosaur, he brings out
a poem. This is the end of the poem, written to a younger
brother then in the army in Korea, a brother described in the
poem as someone with "so much/raw electricity in your body
/you glow at night in your bunk/but no one here thinks/
you're anything special." This is what he tells his brother:

> If you can help it
> don't come home.
> They'll get on your head
> with talk of medical benefits
> and the new regime at the mill.
> They'll batter you with pleas
> and warnings to forget paid holidays
> but to press for better pensions
> when the new contract comes up.
> They'll tell you how sorry they are
> for you because you're so young
> then ask you to have a look
> at their cars or their televisions.
> There's not a man left
> in the valley who can fix
> a leaky faucet or can lift
> more than twenty-five pounds
> without mechanical assistance.
> If you can help it
> don't come home because the moon
> here is a clipped-off toenail
> and you will always dream
> of the places you left.

He read me the poem. He said, "There are no bookstores here. There's one guy in the next town south that I can call and talk about writing. He looks up to me. There's nobody who works in the mill."

Steve, Tim's brother-in-law, shares something of this secret self, because Steve draws and illustrates, but he is also a twice-dislocated man. First, when he worked for Weirton Steel—which he reminds me, a sardonic smile cracking over an essentially boyish Midwestern face, used to be called "The Weirton Steel Family"—he was management. A white hat. In 1976, when he went to work, "management told me I shouldn't live in a blue-collar neighborhood—don't hang around with your old friends anymore." He didn't quite obey, but in all other respects, although he had an education and an option to leave the world of his grandfather, father and uncles, all of whom had worked for The Weirton Steel Family, he was happy to stay. "I was grateful for the job," he says, and proud. "I was still in my hometown. I know it's scuzzy, but I like it here. It's home. I was very loyal. I felt I was part of something. Jesus, I did artwork for the president on my vacation."

It went along like that until 1982. Two things seemed melded together in what has become Steve's nostalgia for the life no longer lived—the work was good and he felt part of things and there was a family, a large, extended family backing up this life, surrounding it, weaving in and out of it. I'm sure Steve would call the family the backbone. In 1980, he tells me, the whole family was here: "Hey, it's the Fourth of July, you could say. Let's play some poker and cook hamburgers."

The family isn't here any more. His father is still in Weirton, although he was "coerced to early retirement at fifty-three." One brother works for a gas company in another part of West Virginia. Another brother moved to Dallas to work as a computer programmer. His third brother still works in the mill, but his marriage has broken up. "So," Steve says, widening the lens a bit, "the kids are leaving and the people who live here have their grandchildren a thousand miles away."

The first management person at Weirton Steel was laid off in August 1981. Although he knew what was coming, Steve was "really shook up" when it did come and is shook up still. He thought he'd get his job back, but a staff artist doesn't seem a crucial part of the new Weirton Steel plan. He got depressed. He thought other people thought he was "a loser or a bum." He did some free-lance work. Friends started dropping away. Jobs were slipping away because people told him he was overqualified and because once you've worked for Weirton, other people think you'll be going back there.

The table has been cleared by the time we get to this part of the conversation. The women are again in the kitchen. The children are playing upstairs. We're talking about alcohol.

Steve is uncomfortable. He's still part of a world where you don't tell strangers your troubles and you don't admit you've got a problem. For reasons I can't really understand, except to say that Tim encouraged his brother-in-law to talk and that, like many of the people in the steel towns, these men feel their stories are important because they stand for other stories, that the dinosaur and the tumbleweed and the moon like a clipped-off toenail—whatever imagery they used to define the cataclysmic changes of the past four years—are things the world should know about.

"Yeah," he says, "I go out to bars and drink snowballs. I go with acquaintances." Pointedly, he doesn't say friends. "I come home at four A.M. drunk. I didn't do that before. I go to D.J.'s, which is full of Yuppies from Weirton—the girls are making twenty thousand a year more than I am."

They call him "Slouch" and now, embarrassed, he slouches in his chair and the women come silently back into the room to put coffee on the table.

"I'm not a stupid man. What kind of man am I? Melancholy."

Is there help to be had? Steve shrugs it off. Too much shame involved in asking for help. "Here, everybody knows. Everybody is related, one way or another. Word gets out. You're better off not asking for help." The pressure builds. A man feels put down and helpless and sorry for himself. Alcohol removes inhibitions. His frustration and rage find their target in his wife. No one will speak of it, except in generalities. I am compelled to ask.

The people at the table are silent. "Yes," Steve's wife says, "he once hit me."

I imagine she wants to take it back as soon as she has said it and I am prepared for cautionary looks from the others at the table, her sister, her brother-in-law, her husband. They aren't forthcoming.

Steve says yes, he hit her. In the talk that follows, it becomes clear that her measure of how hard she was hit is not the same as his, that Steve tends to think he hit her mildly and jokingly, that he excuses himself and that she has a different perception. She told his parents. They asked what she had done to provoke him.

"None of that ugly stuff happened before I was laid off," Steve says, looking at his coffee cup. "You just feel sorry for yourself." Then he looks at the napkin. "I'm just lucky she hasn't left me."

So the subject is open for discussion and the ghost comes out of the closet. One of Tim's neighbors "grew up with Weirton Steel," married a Thai woman, rode high, had a Trans Am, a Harley Davidson, a big stereo and got laid off. A few months after his unemployment ran dry, he was working part-time as a mechanic, smoking pot and drinking, and beating his wife. They had no medical care. A friend of Tim's wife, Jody, and "a sympathetic relative" intervened, got her a lawyer and helped her file for divorce. "I tried to talk to him," Tim says, "but I might as well have told this highchair to jump in the air." But the neighbor's wife didn't leave the house and got pregnant. It took her three years to leave, finally, for Galveston, and in those intervening years, she had a son, the husband of the sympathetic relative tried to molest her and Tim's neighbor got his job back. The child stays with his grandfather during the day.

It hangs there. It's a story. No one has much to say about it. It's how things are now. "The macho thing is in full operation in Weirton," Tim offers. "Tom Brokaw can't have the reasons to get drunk some of us do," Steve says. And it stays there.

One bright light. Without a job to go to every day, men in the steel towns spend more time with their families. Unlike executives I know of who put on coat and tie in the morning and pretend to go to work because they can't bring themselves to confess they have lost jobs, unlike managers who spend their days at the country club with other out-of-work managers, unemployment has pushed these steelworkers closer to their families, at least situationally. With less money in the bank, no golden handshakes to provide the cash to transport them away from wives and children, they are stuck at home. After a while, social life with people outside the family, which had never occupied a very prominent place, fell away. Less visiting back and forth. No nights at the bowling alley. No movies. Gas became a treasured commodity, travel a luxury. As those who could manage moved away—to Houston, to Florida, to California—the ones who stayed behind seemed thrown back on each other in a new way. For some families, this meant pressure, tension, resentment, disruption. For a few, however, it meant something good, although the value of a changed relationship with the family was not clear. John Tirpak had told me, as we drove along the Ohio River, that he had "two great kids I never knew I had." Tim Russell turned to his wife in the middle of dinner in Weirton and said, "I got the chance to meet her after ten years of interior exile." Jody smiled and pushed the potatoes around on her plate. "I wish," she said, "he was laid off again."

If the men were forced to be closer to home, some of the women were forced out of it. Steve's wife was working part-time as a maid at the nearby motel. A lovely woman in the Mon Valley had gotten a part-time job as a waitress. One might tentatively expect that the women would welcome opportunities to be out of the house—the dream of middle-class women in our time—to see some people, mingle in the world; but the work these women could get was so ill-paid and degrading, there seemed to be few "social" rewards. Most of them missed their families and couldn't wait to get back home.

And a dull light. Steve said if he ever got hired back at Weirton Steel, or even if he got a job somewhere else, he would have a different attitude toward his work, his employer and himself. "I wouldn't be the same kind of employee I was before," he said. He didn't look sorry, although for reasons that are understandable, he did sound defensive. "I'd look out for myself," he continued, "and take what I could get."

So things were starting to sound very up-to-date down in Weirton. Steve was starting to sound like the sons and daughters of organization men, people whose loyalty is only to themselves, people at whom an older generation shakes its head, wonders what happened to the world, why ideas like "The Weirton Steel Family" don't hold forever. He sounded like a person of his generation. The gray-haired elders shaking their heads would call him selfish, narcissistic. I call him a casualty.

It's a long way from Weirton, the Ohio Valley, the Mon Valley and Pittsburgh to a quiet street in a Houston suburb, a tidy house with a lawn and a sign supporting Kathy Whitmire, who would be elected mayor in Houston. Irwin Hightower had drawn the shades against the afternoon sun. In the rear of the house, at a slow pace, he had been building a greenhouse. But loyalty and continuity, the connection of employee to company and of employees to one another, were what he wanted to talk about or the lack of those things. His brother works for a large chemical company where employees feel connected to each other and to the corporation, so it's possible. What makes the difference? "Those that live by the quarter," he said. "They have disposable CEOs. If your boss's boss has no stability other than making a number at the end of the quarter, your relationship is the same way. It permeates the company. If you make the numbers, you've got another quarter to survive."

Why are we talking about this? "Well, it's a rude awakening if you've been with a company for twenty plus years and you realize that you're . . ." He stops for a long time. He looks out the window. He brings a cup of tea. "Realize you're . . ." The word he comes up with is "discardable."

This is what happened to Irwin Hightower. He went to work quite young in the rental car business and stayed with the company for more than twenty years. He also married young and stayed with his wife for more than twenty years. Rising in the company, he and his wife moved around from New Orleans to St. Louis to Tulsa to Fort Lauderdale to Tampa and West Palm Beach and Houston. By the time he was forty, he was an executive vice-president in the corporation with only two people between himself and the top. Then he was handed a plum that, in a way, became a grenade. The moving around stopped. "All you had to do was learn the street names," he says, "the places were the same because we were part of a company culture. Most people don't realize that when you're a corporate manager, you work twenty-four hours a day, seven days a week." His friends were people he worked with.

And this business of disposable people was seen, first, from his managerial point of view. The younger people he interviewed disturbed him because "they didn't want permanency. They were not there to build careers with the company particularly, even though they had been selected and groomed as potential managers. I grew up with a Depression mentality, long-range security, you got a job, you did it, if you worked hard you'd be recognized, you'd get promoted and rewarded. But the current generation doesn't start off with those ideas. They don't have that allegiance to begin with and so maybe they won't have the problem of waking up one day at the age of fifty, realizing you're disposable, having all your roots uprooted. Maybe they're right. Maybe the way to get ahead is to jump from one company to another. But," he says, suddenly avuncular, "you build no retirement, you have zero base," and he worries for a while about issues that are actuarial while the real point of our talk is about something highly emotional.

Hightower was a hotshot in the New York office by his fortieth birthday, and if you knew nothing else about the corporate structure, you would have known he was on the fast track because he was the person chosen to work with the computer people as the entire rental car operation was being computerized. The project started in 1969. It was not exactly conducted at a meditative pace. As he tells it, "the state of the art was going faster than we could have meetings. You couldn't even keep up with the changes from Sixty-nine to Seventy to Seventy-one if you were in the business. I had to learn everything. Four of us sat down in a hotel room in Long Island. Three people had expertise in computers and I had the expertise in the car rental industry. I learned to speak computerese and they learned to speak rental cars. That's the smartest way to automate a company—take somebody out of the rank-and-file who knows the business."

He learned; they learned; the project was carried out in a constant state of frenzy and tension. Then, one morning, he woke up in pain. It was a dull pain that traveled down the side of his neck and down his arm. He rested a little, but the pain got worse. Just a short while before, he'd read a magazine article about the symptoms of a heart attack. But no, not a man like Irwin Hightower, just past forty years old, who took vacations with his wife, Nikki, that were far from languid—scuba diving, skiing, not a hearty man like him who had worked those incredible hours under that incredible pressure to produce what is today called The Wizard of Avis, the computerized car rental system that speeds pressured travelers on their way. And the pain got even worse. He and Nikki called a doctor friend who lived nearby. It was early in the morning. It was spring. He was rushed to a hospital and told, among other things, that his arteries were barely open, not more than 10 percent open. He had a bypass.

This is the part of the story that makes Irwin Hightower teary. It's not the pain remembered or the sure knowledge that a certain kind of hotshot life was coming to an end that moves him. It is the compassion of the company president. In a world of disposable and discardable people, where you're only as good as that quarter's profits, where the idea of caring is as remote as the idea of Zanzibar, Hightower found he was working for a man with "compassion," although part of that compassion came from the president's self-interest—"It scared him 'cause he's not that old himself." Whatever his motivation, the president wrote Hightower a letter while he lay stricken in the hospital telling him to "take my time, come back when I wanted to, don't worry about it."

So he went back. He and Nikki had decided that the best thing to do was move themselves to a situation where there was less pressure. The president agreed to move them anywhere they wanted to go. He played "musical chairs" with various district managers and, eventually, the Hightowers moved to Houston. "My intention," Hightower says, "was to work in a more comfortable environment without the high level of stress I was under," but the intention never really reached fulfillment, although things started off well enough because the Houston operation was one he had managed years before and "I was back among friends. A lot of the people working here were people I had hired. It felt like a homecoming."

The homecoming was short-lived. The company was sold, a new set of managers arrived and, with them, what Hightower referred to all afternoon as "the disposable mentality. My new boss," he said, "was part of this disposable mentality. They had no . . ." He stops, stands up and stretches, looks around the room as though the word he is looking for lurks hidden in a corner. "No . . . sympathy? Respect?" Compassion, I think, is what he means—or whatever would be the opposite of "the bottom righthand side of the balance sheet is all anybody ever cares about anyway. They got into a mode of thinking if something isn't working, let's change the people instead of let's change what we are doing."

But Hightower wasn't fired. He was "producing." And he was going to his cardiologist for checkups and leaving the office with warnings. The pressure came from one person in particular, a regional vice-president who felt threatened, Hightower thinks, by having someone whose rung on the corporate ladder was lower but who obviously had more experience and more expertise. The idea of moving to an easier work situation wasn't working out. Tension between Hightower and the man he blames for the continuing pressure ended in a blowup in 1978. The cardiologist had done a sonogram and a stress test. "I think you ought to stop what you're doing," he was told. "It ain't gonna be long." He kept at what he was doing and then came the confrontation with the man he thought of as his enemy and he didn't quit, but said he'd declare himself on disability, which was, actually, leaving.

Like most people, Hightower remembers in vivid detail the day he "fell off the train," but the next day is a blur. He felt "totally lost." In the months that followed, he lived in "pure limbo." The story is familiar. "When I left the corporate nest so to speak, I discovered I had lost my whole family. For years, I hadn't had any friends outside the corporate structure other than my wife's friends. Your social life is built around that structure—it's always part of a manager's job—sales, creating a public image, belonging to trade associations, going to lunch. All of a sudden, when that's severed, you realize that your friendship with those people was purely tied to business. I don't care how close you were, it was business."

And, in fact, looking back, Hightower realizes that he has been talking about "ties" or "camaraderie," but not about what he would now call friendship. "People in business realize they need each other. You need allies. You can destroy somebody with allies. It's like weak animals—one gets sick and you pick on it. So, from a survival standpoint, you have close ties, but you may not want to have these people at your house."

Once you're gone, the ties, allies, affiliations disappear. Hightower never felt shunned, just faded out. "When you back away from business, you lose your ties. It's not that the drums roll and they tear your epaulettes off. It's just a gradual drifting apart. It just goes away. The parties are all about business and once you're out, you can't participate. You're no longer invited. You have nothing in common."

Six months after he went on disability, Hightower had a triple bypass. After that, it was clear he had gone from "a very rapid pace to a virtual standstill. You go from making fifteen or twenty decisions every couple of hours to a life where the biggest question is whether to buy skimmed milk or low-fat milk. You feel useless. You feel not needed and not wanted. You feel lonely, not only because you miss the people, even though your ties to those people turn sour in your memory the further you get from them and the clearer it becomes that without the business to talk about and the activity of ganging up on weaker animals as something you share, you're really out in the cold."

I was continually surprised at how wholeheartedly people working for large companies talked about company life, as though they were talking about family life, although no one rationally believed that company life was anything like family life. This was equally true among Pennsylvania steelworkers and corporate executives. The class difference seemed to be that blue-collar workers saw "the company" as a rejecting entity and managers focused on one particular person as the enemy. Steelworkers hardly ever blamed the man who delivered the pink slip; they knew he was a company slave. Executives always had someone concrete in mind when they talked about the pain and anger of losing their jobs.

Hightower was no exception. Feeling abandoned by the company meant feeling lonely, as though the world had walked away. It was the whole world that had walked away—at least for some part of this experience—but it was the hostile regional vice-president who was to blame. Although Boston psychologist Robert MacLaughlin says that most men, in their unconscious, see the company as female, the men I met focused all their feelings of rejection, abandonment and loneliness on other men. I didn't hear echoes, in this talk, of earlier experiences with mothers. I heard fathers.

A vice-president for finance at a Midwestern pharmaceutical company talked about not being paid enough attention by his boss. "I didn't get any feedback," he said. "I didn't have any comrades to talk to because I was the head of my department and the boss should have had some interest in what I did, but I never got any feedback from him." Once he asked his boss how he was doing and the man said, "I don't hear any complaints," which was hardly enough. So he felt left out and lonely at work—" 'Let's have lunch,' " he said, "meant someone was thinking of me"—and then he was let go. And nobody thought of him. Not a word from the boss and "of the eight people who reported to me, only one person called. They feel uncomfortable. They don't want to associate with you—it's like not wanting to visit people in the hospital. It's like a funeral. You offer condolences and what else can you say?"

Falling off the train, then, is a primal event that calls up images of loss—a funeral, a severe illness, a divorce. How people manage the severed connection, what they find to replace the tie to work, depends on what other resources they have in their lives, how entirely the attachment to work and the real or false relationships there have dominated their lives.

Here is Hightower walking to the rear of his house, where he is building a greenhouse. How can he, I wonder, with his health the way it is, but he can, because he works at his own pace, stops when he needs to, feels no pressure. We have moved from the living room, which has grown increasingly hot and stifling as the afternoon wears on, the windows closed, shades drawn, air conditioning turned off. The greenhouse is a huge space, the floors covered with shavings, a small breeze making its way through the room. He tells me, in a way, about a resurrection.

Some of this has to do with Nikki Von Hightower. At the moment, she runs the Houston Women's Center. Before that, she had been an ombudswoman on the city council and, before that, a talk-show host. She is a prominent and somewhat controversial figure in Houston and it was she who, hearing I was exploring the question of loneliness, thought I might want to meet with her husband. We had been talking about Houston's transience, the numbers of corporate transfers, the neighborhoods that were way stations in people's careers. Nikki added a category to our survey: "I've seen people get transferred here and lose their jobs. It's like you've been thrown off the train and you're out in the desert. Because social ties were almost exclusively through the job, the whole family gets cut off. It's a startling reality to discover how your life had been your job." Did she know someone in that situation? She said, "It happened to my husband."

In the greenhouse, Irwin Hightower said, "If Nikki had been the typical corporate quote wife unquote, if her occupation had been to keep the executive happy, if her friendships had been tied to the same well, we'd have been in trouble." Actually, they were in some trouble, but it might have been worse. In the months after his bypass operation, Nikki lost her job at the radio station. "We had never both been at home before," he said. They sort of asked each other "Who are you?" And "bad as it was, all the difficult emotions, everything from wanting to sleep all the time to being angry and frustrated—it was easier because she was there. We really had fun."

And life began to shift.

In her office, reaching behind her to turn the frigid air conditioning down to a bearable level, Nikki said, "Irwin was more saddened by what happened than I was. I worried about losing benefits and the car and the insurance, but I adjusted quickly. There was a lot of nostalgia; it was a separation from a youthful part of our lives. But by the time I got involved in the women's movement, I realized I had become caught up in his corporate life then lost it, and the women's movement gave me a feeling of belonging again."

And life shifted. Irwin got more involved in Nikki's life and her friends became his friends, and her concerns, including a campaign for a seat on the city council, which she did not win, became his concerns. "I guess," he said with a smile, "I'm a classic househusband now. I can say that now. I used to say 'I'm retired' or 'I'm semiretired.' 'Househusband' isn't okay. It's okay to say I'm managing the house and the investments."

It is no consolation, I know, to people whose unemployment leaves them in desperate situations, to observe that sometimes falling off the train gives you an opportunity to look again at the train and wonder where you were rushing to. For Irwin Hightower, though, leaving the corporation does have this tinge. The house is substantial; there are investments to manage and Nikki has a full-time job; economic comfort frees Irwin to stare at the train and say, "I don't know where I was all my life. I just missed it."

The "it" that was missed is vague and its articulation tends to sound propagandistic. "If you're deeply involved in a business, you don't have time to develop the right philosophical approaches sometimes. You lose it," he said. "It" has something to do with "emotions, experiences, feelings I didn't know existed." "It" has something to do with sex roles and with his lack of discomfort at being the support system for his wife's career. "You don't realize until you've taken on the task," he says, "how long it takes to run errands. The drycleaners, et cetera. It takes all day. Men involved in business don't know anything about all this and if they lose the spouses who are their full-time support people, they're really lost."

Yet something is lost, something is missed, as you might

expect. Just that day, Irwin had had lunch with the one friend he still has who is active in the car rental business. He brightened as he described what it meant to him: "He owns his own company and calls me from time to time. I think he respects my knowledge. He has no one to confer with because he is the boss. And that's a good feeling—the feeling of being needed."

But the "we" dies hard. "We" means me and my company, still, in some ways, for Irwin Hightower. He misses the job and dreams about it—dreams about making decisions like putting up a building. He misses being in the action. He knows he has a lot of company; that he is starting to see forced retirement sending people into the kind of tailspin he has already lived through. "Even though they're financially compensated, their ego is involved," he says. It's that feeling of not being needed or wanted, and it's happening to people in their fifties, sometimes in their forties now. "We" is still me and my company. You still hear them say we did this well—we made the best steel, we really cared about our customers, we trained our people better than anyone else did.

It is a contradictory kind of attachment in a culture from which the Lone Ranger idea has not really disappeared. But Irwin Hightower and a lot of other people recently fallen off the train are, as Irwin said earlier, products of relatively old-fashioned ideas about work and the self, companies and people. He and others always believed that once you hooked up with a company, you were hooked for life, the attachment was unbreakable, your progress was meant to be upward in the company, not lateral. Falling off the train is made worse by believing that the train is the only train and that it hurtles through an empty, barren world in which there is no sustenance, no progress, no sense of self and no pleasure. In other words, the experience of people who have given their lives to the company and who have never seen any other alternatives for themselves when they fall off the train is the experience of being left in a black field. Alone. And the caboose light in the distance, fading.

Falling off the train is an interesting metaphor, implying that one has somehow slipped, that it is a person's own fault, or one of life's odder accidents. It doesn't imply being pushed. Being "on the street," another image for unemployment, carries no blame, but, still, implies that the rest of the world is inside, where it's warm, inside, where there is home, inside, where there are other people, inside, where you can stay put. I've also heard the phrase "losing your place in line," equally forlorn, lonely, cast out.

There are enough studies, governmental and private, of the impact of unemployment on mental health for it to be understood that losing a job can lead to depression and, sometimes, suicide. The Mon Valley is not the only place where people know about, are frightened by and speak in whispers about those who killed themselves alone in that dark field, those who felt stranded and furious as the train sped on. As the economy shifts and changes, the cracks open and close. Companies whose stability, ten years ago, seemed assured, are now merged or acquired at a frantic pace and the human cost of such shifting grouping and regrouping is usually overlooked. In 1984, *Fortune* magazine estimated that the ten largest mergers of the previous year had changed the lives of up to 220,000 employees. One for whom "change" meant "destruction" was Chris Donahue, a thirty-eight-year-old economist who worked at Heublein, Inc., which was taken over by R. J. Reynolds Industries. Donahue thought his boss, chief executive Hicks Waldron, would become Reynolds' chief executive and that he would follow along to corporate headquarters. This was a "friendly takeover," but things didn't work out so well, and Donahue was let go with eleven weeks' severance pay. He hanged himself in the basement of his suburban Massachusetts home. "Tell someone at RJR that I loved their generosity and compassion," his bitter suicide note read. "They owed me more."

At approximately the same time, in New York City, Elizabeth Peer, *Newsweek* magazine's first woman foreign correspondent and the first woman foreign bureau chief, dressed herself in a blue nightgown, put a record on the stereo, drank some wine and poured pills down her throat. She was forty-eight years old and had been fired without warning. Peer had told a friend that she was "no longer Elizabeth Peer of *Newsweek,* but 'Lizzie who?' " and there were some among her colleagues who said that Peer, who had been with the magazine for twenty-six years, "desperately needed that old sense of office family in her life" and found "the increasingly impersonal tone and corporate character of life at the office" hard to take. The day after she was fired, she had written in her journal, "I shunned those others who'd been sacked, beaming cordially and running for cover whenever these pathetic ghosts of colleagues roamed the corridors. Why should it be any different for me?"

The "pathetic ghosts of those who have been sacked" haunt corporate life. The pathos comes, interestingly enough, for a psychological reason much more than an economic one. In blue-collar communities like the steel towns, the stories of those who have been sacked are stories about economic destruction—how the house had to be sold, how people moved in with their parents, how the children wore torn underwear to school. In white-collar communities, however, corporate folklore grows up quickly around those who have been sacked and has little to do with bread-and-butter issues, either because they don't exist or because there is a tendency to minimize them.

What is haunting is that people fallen off the train threaten those who remain on board. That they might thrive outside the walls or initiate satisfying lives for themselves by themselves is an intimidating idea. Ghostly former members of the corporate family must be forgotten because the colleagues left behind function best believing that the corporation cares, enjoying the security of their jobs, riding the train and fantasizing endlessly about what they would do with the freedom they don't have and don't really want, how they would love to go into business by themselves, be off the train.

"Once you've worked for a major corporation, you're too deep into the system to quit and go do it yourself. You lose too much," Irwin Hightower had said, adding, "I wouldn't work for a large corporation again unless they paid me a million dollars for six months. I think I could walk backwards for that length of time." So if a heart attack puts you off the train or a merger does or if you're sacked or if you just decide to walk away—you become a ghost. There is no train but that train. The rest of the world is a dark lonely field.

One example of a man struggling with issues of being off or on the train, hooked up with a corporate family or wandering alone, is a morbid, indulgent and embarrassing account written by John Koffend, a former editor of *Time* magazine. His book, *A Letter to My Wife,* is a long, rambling exploration of his feelings about his marriage ending—falling off the family train —and of his eventual decision to leave *Time* in what then managing editor Henry Grunwald called "the most spectacular departure since Gauguin left for Tahiti."

The book begins with a psychiatrist's evaluation. "Social skills are superior to very superior. . . . At present, Mr. Koffend feels friendless and without any warm human relationships." The contradiction notwithstanding, when Koffend writes in his own voice, he says that "outside the office, Franzl's [a bar] is my only important human connection." He is alone for the first time in his life. "Man isn't designed to live alone," he says. He drinks too much, takes a lot of Valium, watches television on weekends and goes to work. He dreams of leaving and then, more than a hundred pages into the book, decides to do it. He's going to Pago Pago. No one thinks he will do it, but he does. As he is about to announce his decision to Grunwald, he writes in his journal:

> I wish there were someone at *Time* to whom I could confide before going to HAG [Henry A. Grunwald], but there isn't.

. . . Boy, does the hole close in fast after you're gone. Who misses Mike Demarest? He wasn't even replaced. George Love —the indispensable George Love? Not a tear or a trace.

The list of the departed goes on and then he thinks of how his brothers and sisters don't write to him—"Why did ticking off all those departed *Time* staffers remind me of my brothers and sisters? . . . Queer, the associations of the mind."

His relations with other people on the magazine are attached and disconnected at the same time, are and are not important human connections. There is, masking the loneliness, a misleading conviviality:

Just after seven, ran into Fred Golden, who suggested one drink. We turned into Ho Ho's, just next door, for our one drink and found a full table of convivial *Time* people. So the one drink multiplied into three. Then they all left, and as Fred and I drained the last of our glasses another *Time* contingent came in and the evening began all over.

One reason I hate to do covers is that I begin writing them on Mondays. Things aren't as they should be. They're out of pattern. And then I must eat dinner alone. Everyone else has gone home, which makes me uneasy too.

[Grunwald's] reaction to my news was impassive. He said the predictable things, but tonelessly. . . . I left with my stomach somewhere down around my knees and went out to a semibibulous lunch with Marcia Gauger, a researcher. . . . I wanted support and didn't get it. Announcing to HAG cut the last connecting thread. . . .

I simply can't imagine missing *Time*. Some of the people, yes; I learned to know them better in the year I lived alone, and to appreciate more than ever those I learned to know. I needed them, and need forms friendships.

Koffend left. The announcement that he had arrived in Pago Pago said he would be covering the South Pacific for the magazine, so some connection was kept. In the last letter to his wife, he said, "To borrow inspiration from one of those old barroom songs: I had nineteen beers with the wrong woman. Now I'm going to have nineteen beers by myself." Then he killed himself. The hole closed in fast. There were no "important human connections." The train moved on.

Unemployment seems to be a slightly different experience for women, at least for some women. This makes sense. Until recently, it wasn't even possible for women in significant numbers to invest all their needs for attachment in their work lives. Although the female workaholic is becoming a more familiar figure in our landscape, most women value family life and friendship as highly as they do work. They don't expect work to provide "real human connections." Among women I talked with who worked in towns where textile factories are closing down, loneliness was rarely mentioned as part of the experience of being unemployed. Most had close ties to their families—spouses, children, parents, cousins—and continued to see the women they had worked with even when the plant closed. Whether they met at church groups or at the market, staying in touch seemed a natural part of their lives. One woman did say, however, that the experience of looking for work had its lonely side—she had, that day, driven to a nearby town to see if there was any hiring, and in the factory office there were no people, just a table with application forms and a box to put them in.

It is unimaginable to think of men's magazines devoting the space women's magazines do to the issue of "love versus work." We expect women to work and still continue to care for home and family. Some of the tension around this issue comes from women themselves, attempting to "have it all," which means a satisfying work life and a satisfying personal life, which women rarely define as synonymous. Women have larger networks of friends than men do and the maintenance of friendships, which don't usually originate in the workplace, is more important to women. So it follows that the loss of social connections at work—and the loss of self-esteem that follows falling off the train—is a somewhat different experience for women.

"No," Roberta said, "losing a job isn't like a divorce. Not at all. Jobs aren't like people. There will be other ones."

We are in a comfortable Soho loft in Manhattan, the afternoon's traffic chugging away below and the streets there clogged with natives and gapers. The loft is huge, hung with photographs and peaceful. She has collected baskets from all over the world and several pieces of sculpture that appear to be Eskimo. The comfort here is tenuous. If she doesn't find a job by the end of the month, she will have to move.

Roberta started out in the theater, where she produced two Broadway shows that became long-running hits. She moved to Hollywood, where she did several movies of the week and then a series. When a new cable company started, she headed the West Coast office. Can such a person fall off the train? Of course. The train rattles as it rushes along and, contrary to popular belief, changes course unexpectedly.

The cable operation "went under" unexpectedly and dramatically. Roberta and her staff were given notice ninety days before she drew her last paycheck. In the space of six months, she discovered that her mother was dying and Roberta's health problems resulted in a hysterectomy. She drank Scotch and milk in the morning, sometimes a glass or two of wine during the day, and although no one else would have said so, "caught herself" on the road to alcoholism and joined AA. She moved out to the beach at Santa Monica, where the air was better. Looking for another job, she realized something about the way she had conducted her career.

She didn't have a "network" or a "support system" within the industry. She explains this in various ways in the course of our afternoon together. The easiest explanation is that men have the Old Boy Network and Roberta, being female, wasn't part of it. But some of the responsibility for this absence was her own. "I heard about support systems, but I didn't think it applied to me. I thought I had positioned myself well. I thought my life was moving in the direction it was supposed to.

"I managed," she says, "not to be part of anything." She tells me how she didn't fit in Hollywood, was able to sell her product with difficulty, always felt she was speaking a different language. She spent a good part of 1983 looking for work in Hollywood, running into her lack of cemented relationships within the industry and into the backlash against women that followed a period of hectic and easy hiring. She decided to come to New York and no one doubted she would find a good job.

A publishing company was setting up its own video department and hired Roberta to assist the man running it. Roberta became the executive producer of that unit. From the start, there were two problems. The man she worked for was "in a terrible emotional crunch, going through a terrible divorce and didn't show up most of the time. What I was expected to do was make him look good while he wasn't there and coddle him when he was." But Roberta is not a naïve woman and, looking back, she thinks that had she not been so shaky because of the operation, her mother's death and the shake-up of her life, she would have "stood up for myself better." The second problem was that the unit was badly set up and, if you were looking, it would have been clear that it was not going to last. Roberta wasn't looking. She did what many women do on the job—set her nose to the task at hand and paid little attention to the gestalt around it. She produced her programs. The unit started to fall apart. She knew it, but "I didn't risk picking up the phone and parlaying the job into another one. I was afraid they'd hear I was telling people they were in trouble, call me disloyal and I'd be fired. I was scared I'd get killed, but I got hurt."

She "lost my place in line" in the fall of 1984, when her boss said, "You're gonna have to go" and asked her to be out by the end of the day. She took the weekend to finish up what she felt responsible to the clients for. Secretaries left notes on her desk. The young woman who had been part of her group and had given her the most trouble also gave her "more support than anyone" when she fell off the train. When Roberta and I met, she had been "out there looking" for several months. Nothing had "clicked." She was living through what she called "a piece of my ultimate nightmare." Your sense of yourself gets shaken. You're alone with yourself, you stand by yourself, you're not Roberta So-and-So of this big company, you just are what she calls "your personhood." She speaks of unemployment as a "confrontation" with loneliness and "á total confrontation with yourself, with having to accept your life and your dependence on other people."

Roberta's relationships with people are so different from her relationship to work that it appears, for a moment, that another person has moved into the armchair and sat herself down in Roberta's jeans and white sweater, smoothed her blond hair and gone on talking. "I have always been steady, clear, clean," she says, "in the formation of friendships. At all my high-powered jobs, a friend could call in the middle of a great crisis and I could pick up the phone and communicate something. I've always been able to do that. All during the day in all my jobs, I had a need to be interrupted by friends or by the possibility of love coming." Roberta isn't pleased with this aspect of herself. She thinks that the need to assuage a lifelong loneliness distracted her, kept her from concentrating on her career—not on the work, which she always excuted well, but on parlaying one job into another, building a network of allies, hedging against falling off the train. I'm not as sure that the attention to relationships, the investment of energy in private life, has served her so badly. Having fallen off the train, in fact she is finding that the attention paid to people now rebounds. I think it is saving her sanity.

There is, in this urgent period of need, a "new piece of information," as she puts it. Her friends have come through. Although she may not have a "support system" on the train, she has one in the dark fields outside. Her bank account is drained. For the first time in her life, she has had to borrow money. People have come through. Friends call other friends. People set up contacts. Friends help her endure the piece of the ultimate nightmare. If she has the impulse to withdraw, to give up, she has resisted well. Withdrawal is "a blasphemy against life." All day long, she goes out to see people, developing ideas, looking for a job or a project. Many people think her overqualified and can't imagine why she would be after the jobs they have to offer. Roberta keeps on. The friends are a wedge, standing between herself and absolute loneliness. The worst thing would be "to be lonely going into that world out there where people are all strangers."

CHAPTER 9

Communities

"There is, everywhere in America, a terrible need to belong to something"

Strike up the band. Actually, it's an orchestra, close to forty people, more women than men, eyes on the conductor. Everyone wears black pants and white shirts and the expressions on their faces have the seriousness and concentration one might expect at a moment like this one—waiting for the conductor, the buzz in the audience quieting down—but they have, too, a look of pleasure bordering on merriment. They are gleeful. In comes the conductor, striding. His arms lift. Bow arms lift in the orchestra. A pair of hands poises over the piano. The music begins.

"Bridge on the River Kwai." Hoop de doo. "Dance of the Chameleons." A waltz. "La Cumparcita." The music has been chosen and arranged for this particular group of players—mostly string players, mandolins and violins. A portion of a Tchaikovsky piano concerto precedes the finale, one of

Brahms's Hungarian dances, performed with a great flourish. The program, which lasted a little over an hour, might seem odd, and so too might this assemblage of players. This is the Senior Citizens' Orchestra of Miami Beach. All of its members are over sixty, a great many over seventy, quite a few over eighty. Far from being odd, the orchestra is a rather average example of how the need to belong to something can and is being met all over the country, in surprising places and heartening ways.

The orchestra members are packing up their instruments. The room is a large "social hall" just off the lobby of a highrise called the Tower Building, decorated in tones of orange on the walls and the floors and watched over by a large sentry of a chandelier made of huge glass globes. Beneath the globes, there has been a meager audience. The people who live in this building, Henry Osman, the orchestra's conductor, scoffs, "would rather play cards." But it doesn't seem to matter to the players.

"On account of this I survive." Miriam Tracht snaps her mandolin case closed. She is a hefty woman who bustles around greeting other players, folding music stands. Mrs. Tracht played in the orchestra at Auschwitz. When her sister was killed she "turned to music" and, forty years later, still does. Rose Shapiro is the pianist—"I'm all the instruments we don't have." Without this orchestra, she says, looking around the room, "these people would get sick and some would die. This is their life. They would die before their time."

There is, as you might expect, much talk among the orchestra members about sickness and death. Henry Osman says that when the orchestra got organized—in 1971—its members started going less and less often to doctors. This has something to do with physical health, but much more to do with attitude, with mental health. People felt happier, more engaged, less lonely. "Nobody died for four years," he says, proud. By common consent, the orchestra is good medicine and the longevity of some of its members is considered proof.

Harry Rose, the cellist father of the renowned cellist Leonard Rose, had just died at ninety-three, and Osman insisted it was the hospital that killed him. A ninety-five-year-old woman named Rosemary Garelick, who had also recently died, had only begun to learn to play the mandolin when she turned seventy. When the orchestra travels to nearby condominiums, the audience often consists of people young enough to be the players' children. And there they are, the ones in their seventies and eighties, on stage, hands whipping over the mandolin strings, bows flying over the violins, heads bobbing. It makes you want to polka.

Pauline Avrutis invites me home to her apartment on West Avenue, a ten-minute drive from the Tower Building. Transporting players to and from performances has fallen to Henry Osman, who has been driving a van and picking up those who cannot arrive under their own steam. Pauline is one of them. She is now eighty-nine years old, which does not win her the mantle of "oldest member," since mandolin player Joseph Garelick is ninety-six. Pauline may, however, be its sprightliest and most outspoken member.

The apartment is small and decorated with African violets, painted china and photographs of Pauline in orchestras, string ensembles or alone with her violin. She has been playing since she was twelve years old and the music is, to her, a legacy from her father, a "wonderful baritone," who "used to go down to the cellar to sing" in his family's home, but "they didn't pay attention. They were too poor, too ignorant." She loves to sing. She loves to play—both mandolin and violin, although the mandolin sound is a bit "tinny" for her. Sometimes, though, she'll pick up the mandolin and go visit one of the other women who live on her floor: "I'll go into the apartment and just start playing Russian Jewish songs." The decline of Jewishness in Pauline's family worries her. Her divorced son worries her. Her grandson, whom she "helps financially," worries her a bit too. She has two brothers, one ninety, the other eighty, who call her every Saturday morning. But the

people she speaks of with love are not family but friends,
musical friends.

"Oh, she was a beautiful pianist, this Christian lady." Pauline puts the photograph down. It looks like it was taken thirty
years ago. "Once a year, we play for Irving Gavorin's group.
. . . Mr. Cohen taught me to play the recorder. . . . Rose
Shapiro knew Mrs. Kotovsky, a very great mandolin player.
. . . Eddie Meyers always loved my singing. . . . I bought this
violin from Mr. Osman. Henry Lowry repaired it. It's a little
heavy, but I need a new chin rest."

She may need a new chin rest, but she doesn't need to feel
she belongs to something because Pauline does. The "something" she belongs to seems so simple, yet it eludes so many
of us. Pauline's community—which is what the orchestra provides—encompasses not only living people with names like
Mr. Cohen and Eddie Meyers and Rose Shapiro, but an activity that has meaning to the members of the community. They
are not saintly people—there is a fair share of pettiness and
bickering and a surprisingly minimal dose of competitiveness
among them—but they do seem to feel the need, as Pauline
said, "to do what we can for each other," a sense of being
needed by one another.

Pauline brings tea and we sip it slowly. That morning, she
tells me, as though it were a lifetime ago, she felt sick. She was
dizzy. She took the pill for her blood pressure, but it didn't
help. She felt like saying, all day long, "Please take me to the
clinic. I feel that my head is breaking." But she had to go and
play. Now she feels fine. "I forget everything," she says, "and
I just feel so good. You know, without the orchestra, some of
us would just pine away."

On Monday and Thursday mornings, the orchestra re-
hearsed at the South Shore Community Center in Miami
Beach. Some people arrived an hour or two early for rehearsals. Some people went out for lunch together when rehearsals were over. For the ones who could not climb on buses to
make their way home, there was always a ride. Pauline Avrutis

had learned to drive at age sixty, but she no longer did so. A few got married; a few died; a few bickered. Some simply came to rehearsals and concerts and then went their own ways, but most people stayed in touch, played in other groups together, simply got together to make music.

Henry Osman was not only the orchestra's conductor, but its social center. He picked people up and brought them home. He arbitrated disputes. He kept telling people who felt ill to stay away from doctors and hospitals, although he once admitted that he was worried about his own health and had been taking an ulcer drug for three years when he had been told to take it for only three weeks. If someone said, as someone usually did, "I can't play today. I feel too confused," he nursed them through the confusion and they went home feeling better. Anyone who wanted to be in the orchestra could do so. There were no auditions. Osman simply said to the newcomer, "Sit down and play." One man had made a whistle out of two coffee can lids.

Mostly, the players played mandolins and violins and Osman arranged the music to suit the kind of orchestra it was. Although he moaned and complained about his players, who sounded sometimes like his children and his charges, Osman was rewarded for his labors. He had seen the orchestra grow from the eighteen people who showed up for the first rehearsal—fifteen mandolins, two concertinas and a piano—to the fifty members it has today. He had seen it become substantial, an institution. "Long before I started to conduct the orchestra," he said, "the senior citizens of Miami used to gather on the beach to play, and those that couldn't play would listen. This was a wonderful way to overcome their loneliness. What I did was to create dignity to their performances by giving them formal concerts and getting the bank to provide funds to hire bus transportation for them so they could perform as far away as Palm Beach." The bank, the Washington Savings Bank, paid for transportation, gave Osman a salary of $12,000 a year and a car, paid the pianist

$50 a month and the orchestra's secretary $25 a month.

So the orchestra was a life-support system, its members extremely aware of the desert in which many of their neighbors lived, people who lacked the companionship music provides by itself but, even more, the community of people making music together. But the life-support system was more intricate and more worldly, involving, as it did, buses and cars, music stands and sheet music, a large amount of Henry Osman's time and the funds provided by the bank. "Community relations" motivated the Washington Savings Bank. Every time the orchestra played, they displayed a banner with the bank's name on it. Most members of the orchestra kept their money in that bank.

The plug was pulled on this life-support system at the end of 1983. Osman arrived at rehearsal and told the orchestra he was through. There appears to have been some trouble with the bank about the fact that he had taken the car they paid for to Canada and had an accident there. But that was only part of it. The bank had been taken over by a California bank—it was now called First Nationwide Savings & Loan—and there was a consensus that the time had come to support other community groups.

The next time I saw the orchestra, they were rehearsing again. It was springtime, 1984; the sun beat at the windows; the large room at the South Shore Community Center was cool; and about forty members of the orchestra were making their way with zip through the opening bars of "Oklahoma." There was a new conductor, a wiry, dark man named Alfredo Baldassarri.

I sat down on one of the folding chairs that lined two walls of the room. There were several senior citizens scattered about, many with their eyes closed, tapping their feet. They weren't orchestra members, just people who came to listen. And they looked proud of the players. Next to me was a very sun-tanned woman in a loose white dress who used to play with the orchestra but recently moved to Puerto Rico. She had come to visit and to show how well, after a recent serious illness, she was. She patted her side. There had been an operation for colon cancer and she wore a surgical bag. Another woman sat on the other side of me and, next to her, her brother, holding his violin case. Her brother was near ninety and she wanted him to play in the orchestra, but he was shy. He clutched his case. This time, she said, he would just listen, but she would bring him again to the next rehearsal.

I watched Pauline Avrutis play her violin with gusto. When the rehearsal was over, she put into my hands some documents she had brought for me. I began to understand how the orchestra had been saved. Pauline's letter was written on white paper in a careful hand. She had dated it December 24th and then written in the margin that it had been mailed on the 27th. This was all less than a week after Henry Osman announced his departure and the withdrawal of funds. The letter, addressed to the bank, said:

> I am pained and disappointed because of your decision to withdraw your sponsorship of our orchestra and Henry Osman, our conductor. It has been [10 or 12] years the orchestra has been playing a minimum of 4 concerts a month to condominiums and club organizations. It is now a Fla. institution.
>
> Please reconsider your decision and reinstate the orchestra, which is one of the greatest community relations projects in all [Southern Florida]. In the final analysis, you will benefit [from] extraordinary good will among the senior citizens of this great area. With increasing numbers of retirees flowing in . . . from the north, 1st Nationwide will be in 1st place to receive this new influx of saving dollars. I have this day removed my funds from the Nationwide regretfully.

Everyone in the orchestra had written to the bank and withdrawn their money. One member, Ann Zimmerman, had asked her violin teacher to take over the conducting duties and he had agreed to do so without pay until things could be sorted out. Mrs. Zimmerman had become the orchestra's president. The bank was reconsidering, although the promise held out was for partial funding; there would have to be other sources.

There were, as there were bound to be, sour notes. A chorus of complaint had risen against Henry Osman. It was mostly composed of women in the orchestra. The men were silent on the subject, as though they had no grasp of what had gone on. The women spoke of having felt sad and crying at the thought that the orchestra might be disbanded. Some were angry. They felt abandoned by Henry Osman. He ought to have gone on without pay. He ought to have fought.

When Osman appeared at the morning rehearsal that spring day, backs stiffened throughout the room. The new conductor was on the stand. The group started and restarted "Oklahoma." Rose Shapiro could hardly see the sheet music on the piano. Osman, whose purpose in being there was to see me, could not keep himself in the background. He got up to look through a pile of sheet music. He talked constantly about the need for new musical arrangements. At one point, he stood before the orchestra and tried to correct some phrasing. Baldassarri, the new conductor, did not consult with him; Osman simply stepped out of the way.

At the rehearsal's end, Osman gathered a group around himself, the pro-Osman faction; Ann Zimmerman, on the other side of the room, gathered a contra group. Pauline was in the middle. Each group planned to go out to lunch. For a moment, it looked as though the wound would be healed, both groups would go together. Pauline and I left the room and sat on a bench outside, waiting for the arrangements to be made. Cars pulled up. Instruments were piled into trunks. People left.

She trembled. The dissension upset her terribly. She managed to see both sides of the problem at once—that Osman deserved tribute for what he had done and that the orchestra now needed to proceed without him. Pauline was not naïve, but she was an ensemble player. For my part, as it became clear that the factions were about to go their separate ways for lunch, and in general, I felt forced to choose sides. In the interests of getting the side of the story I had not yet heard, I went with Ann Zimmerman and her friends. I drove Pauline home and sat in the car for a moment watching her sorrowful, retreating back.

We ate at Wolfie's on Collins Avenue, one of the late Meyer Lansky's favorite hangouts. The waitress threw a basket of rye bread at us and argued with us about our orders. Miriam Tracht sat next to Rose Zatz and Ann Zimmerman sat beside me, unable to touch her food. Although she and the other women at the table probably deserve the credit for saving the orchestra, they were remarkably lacking in pride about what they had done. They were all upset by the dissension. They tried hard to contain their anger with Osman.

Ann Zimmerman, who had little experience organizing anything, had simply taken over at the end of the year when it seemed things were absolutely falling apart. She had gone to the bank and told the man in charge of disbursements that withdrawal of funds for the orchestra would "kill" its members. She went back again and again. Eventually, she extracted a promise of reconsideration. She had been responsible, too, for reorganizing the orchestra. It now had a board of trustees and a decision-making apparatus. "We never had a meeting before," she said, "it was a one-man show."

The transition from one-man show to essentially more democratic structure is one that many institutions and communities have undergone in recent memory. Although many formal and informal communities in America had their beginnings as one-man shows—Brigham Young leading his followers into Utah, or any religious sect, for that matter—the idea of "community" has taken hold so completely that membership in a community has come to mean active participation in making decisions about how it is run. The senior citizens of Miami Beach have not escaped the surge of activism that leaves people feeling they must "have a say" about their lives. The relentlessness with which Ann Zimmerman searched for ways to keep the "life-support system" going is not unusual, nor is the fact that the "one-man show" was transformed into not quite a one-woman show, but a show heavily influenced by the leadership of several women.

A woman appeared at our table. She had, she said, seen the instruments the others were carrying and wanted to know if they belonged to an orchestra. They said they did. The visitor took out an engagement book. She was program chairman for a social group. Could she book the orchestra to play for them? Ann Zimmerman looked at her calendar.

At home, I thought, Pauline Avrutis might be feeling dizzy and lying down or she might have gone to visit the other women on her floor to play some old songs for them on her violin. Maybe her new chin rest had arrived. At any rate, upset as she was by the trouble in recent memory, there were many things she could not possibly have been feeling that afternoon —that she was alone in the world, that nobody cared what happened to her, that there was no one to talk to, nothing to be part of, that she was doomed to solo playing for the rest of her days.

About a half hour's drive south of the essential gaiety and bustle of Wolfie's and the sweet sounds of people making music together was a place where "membership" was perhaps even more crucial to survival. Settlement House is a halfway house for mental patients. It is, its director Marshall Rubin said, "a stepping stone to the community." Rubin's work is almost entirely devoted to helping people overcome loneliness. He looks not to the center of our culture, but to the fringe. The people who face a loneliness other people don't, he says, are those in prison, on heroin, suffering from cancer, living on unemployment and welfare. And the "members" who live at Settlement House, who are, as many of them told me, "lonely for the community" and who live together in what

Rubin calls "a community made up of individual little loneli-nesses."

All of the people I spoke with saw loneliness as longing not for a friend or a lover but for something they seemed to consider tangible and concrete—the community. As I listened to each of them, I kept seeing a medieval town, walled and foreboding, and a small stranger outside the gates, looking in, wan, timid and somewhat afraid.

"I feel labeled. I feel I can't go out in the community and totally express myself."

"People are afraid of your disease. I want to tell them it's not contagious. They shout at you from cars when they ride by this place and they write graffiti about us on the walls."

"Before I came here, I was a prisoner in my own apartment."

"I sleep to combat loneliness."

"Medication is a form of loneliness. It puts you out of touch with everyone around you. You live in your own world."

"I face it every day. I keep thinking if I can make it past breakfast without lying down and crying because I feel so lonely . . . if I can make it past lunch . . . if I can make it past coffee break."

Bob had white hair and wore glasses. Francine was a black woman in her early twenties. Evelyn interviewed me while someone else ran the videotape machine—a souvenir for the Settlement House library. Each of these people was a "member" of Settlement House. Some lived there; others lived in supervised apartments; some lived on their own. Rubin sees his job as relieving the social isolation many of the mentally ill feel. He talks about "family," and about a "group culture." In every social service organization I encountered, these were the keys. To help people who needed help, it was clear, the first step was to address their loneliness, to connect people in trouble with others in the same boat so no one need feel alone in the universe, struggling with a problem that felt unique to them. "A burden shared is a burden halved," perhaps, but there was a second step—to provide care, to color the cold world of people in trouble with warm colors, assure them that someone cared.

A woman was being shown around Settlement House the afternoon I was there. She had come because she cared and wanted to help and had money to give. She was an elegant blond woman, a former fashion consultant, fashionably dressed. The members of Settlement House seemed intimidated by her and I thought I sensed them draw closer to each other as she spoke with them. She told me she thought loneliness came from "the lack of a big family" and "you're not going to solve it in the nuclear family." As she spoke, it became clear to me that her visit to Settlement House was motivated, at least in part, by her own loneliness, by her desire to be part of something, that her generosity was prompted, at least in part, by her personal need for connection. "It's a shame," she said, "the very rich and the very poor have it better." Better than whom? The middle class, living in nuclear families. Eventually, she spoke about herself. She was divorced. She lived alone. "My mother," she said, "lives just two minutes away from me and some days I'm alone all day and she's alone all day and we're both really miserable, but we don't call each other. I don't know why."

The image came back to me: the walled town and the stranger full of longing to be let in. This time, however, the walled town was Settlement House itself, a community of sorts, a place where there was always someone to talk to and someone who cared, where if you didn't show up for meals someone came looking for you to find out if you were all right, where people cooked together and ate together and wished each other well as they struggled to get from breakfast to lunch to coffee break, to find jobs, to connect to the world. Outside the gate this time was the blond woman in beautiful clothes with money to give.

One of the cataclysmic changes in our social arrangements is the relatively recent banding together of people previously outside the gates. The anomaly, the "weirdo," has, in the past twenty years, managed to find other anomalies and weirdos and to huddle with or, put more positively, to attempt to build a community based on likeness, usually, of situation. Just as immigrants with strong ethnic and national ties can arrive on America's shores and hunt up specific communities—places where people share language, custom, habit, perhaps dress, food, ritual, whatever seems shared, common and familiar— new groups have formed from fragments, the people previously scattered are building communities in what previously felt like wilderness.

Communities? Associations? Groups? It is impossible to tell, looking in, whether the single people living in a "complex" on the outskirts of Houston live in a community or the lesbians in New York or the gay men in San Francisco or the widowed Jewish women in a communal house in Los Angeles do. It is an American tendency to form associations, as de Tocqueville observed almost two centuries ago—a tendency in ironic counterpoint to the one that praises independence and the act of living alone, fighting alone, managing alone. The tendency to associate—usually with a purpose—is not new, but the specific associations newly sprouted around the country are: parents of suicide children, victims of child abuse, parents of children with drug problems, lesbian mothers, single fathers, women writers, women in computing, the West 105th Street block association. I am picking randomly through the associations that have been visible to me, without any effort on my part, in the past few days. These associations may or may not be communities, may answer the terrible need to belong to something, or they may not.

For lesbians and gay men, the possibility of a community exists where it never did before. A homosexual in the Fifties, as any number of memoirs, confessions and painful personal recollections show, was likely to be among the loneliest people in America. The issues that plague all of us at every stage of life and that express themselves as loneliness—where do I fit in? who cares about me? who is there to touch and talk to? —were more intense where the direction of desire was considered "perverse," shameful, sick and was, as a result, generally hidden.

This is Toby Marotta's story. Like most of the gay people with whom I spoke, Toby thinks of loneliness first in terms of that period in his life when he was trying to be "straight." He had come to Harvard and although he had already experienced several homosexual relationships, decided it was time to "become an adult and stop all that." He stopped and, as he looks back at that time, Marotta sees himself "cut off entirely from intimacy, empathy, acknowledgment, rapport." Being lonely, for him, meant "not being known, not being understood, not being with kindred spirits." In spite of himself, he says, he "gravitated" to a "very intense male relationship," one that was not sexual for quite some time, and that relationship became "my basic connection to the human species."

Marotta is talking nearly twenty years after that time at Harvard. We are sitting on a window seat in a large house in the Berkeley Hills that belongs to friends of mine. Around us are the sounds of a family in motion. A three-year-old girl and her five-year-old sister dash in and out, intrigued by the visitors. The wife in this family is upstairs writing a paper on female psychological development; her husband is fighting the traffic on the Bay Bridge on the way home from his work as a psychiatrist at Mt. Zion hospital. This house and the family that fills it is one of the least lonely I know—the bustle of family life and professional life often colliding, the friends on the phone, the sister coming by, the atmosphere of warmth and affection, the nearly visible thread that binds the people who live in this house to one another, to the people around them, to the larger world, brings me happily here again and again. At times like this, as Marotta recounts his lonely days at Harvard and a chill settles over both of us, the problem of loneliness seems so wasteful, so odd, and its opposite, connectedness, seems so simple, although it only takes a moment to remember that it isn't.

Marotta's story has a happy ending and a dimension larger than the personal. The man with whom he had formed a relationship became his lover and life partner. "I certainly don't think that sexual contact eliminates loneliness," Marotta says, "because in the gay male subculture there is an enormous amount of sexuality. The loneliness that comes from never being physically intimate with another person is something gay men rarely have. But I think eliminating loneliness is a quality of a sustained relationship." He and the man in his life became what Marotta, who is now a social scientist, calls a "bonded pair." And then they wanted something else. "We yearned," he says, "for community. For like-minded, like-living souls. Particularly because it was so difficult to find in Cambridge or Boston, we moved out here. We came to San Francisco to find gay community."

Marotta is a trim, earnest, light-haired man who speaks as though he were lecturing at Harvard, from which he received a doctoral degree in government and education. He has made the study of male homosexual life his professional career, writing several books on the subject, carrying out studies of the gay life style for various foundations, including an ongoing study of homosexual prostitutes. His observations about the initial failure to find community and the reversal of that failure over the past decade blend a personal pilgrimage with the more impersonal interests of a social scientist, although, he sighs, "the whole state of the art, of understanding the gay male subculture is so primitive."

Ten years ago, a gay man arriving in San Francisco would gravitate to the area around the Tenderloin. "He'd feel dirty," Marotta says, "it would be like arriving in Times Square. He'd feel despicable, he'd be surrounded by ugliness." He would not find a community. Instead, he would find the traditional institutions of gay male life, those facilitating sexual encounters—bars and bathhouses. The changes, accomplished in less than a decade, can be seen most strikingly in the bars that run along Castro Street—"the Castro" is often synonymous with "the gay community." As Marotta tells it: "The bars used to be places where you went to score, like singles bars, but now they're more like families. They have the same crowd, the same bartenders. They offer low-priced meals." The bars are bright and airy, with plate-glass windows so you don't have to look out at the world through a glass darkly. And the bars are full all day long, every night.

I bristle at Marotta's descriptions of bar life. Life laced with alcohol hardly seems to me unlonely. In fact, the chief of mental health services for the city of San Francisco, Alan Leavitt, had only that morning called his city "the last refuge of the lonely" and pointed out that San Francisco has the highest mortality rate from cirrhosis of the liver in the country. He considered that a good index of loneliness. Marotta counters by saying that most of what is consumed in bars around the Castro is beer, unlike "straight" bars. He insists that the bars are what social scientists call "mediating structures" and that one of the casualties of gay life in the Castro is the gay teenager who, because he is under age, can't get into the bars and "can't make those connections."

If you're looking for loneliness in the Castro, Marotta says, you'll find it among the kids—"They've run away from home because they've fought with their families about homosexuality. They turn to hustling. It's hard for a gay teenager to avoid it. Most gay adults are reluctant to have anything to do with younger people."

"Most gay adults"—male adults—form the basis of the community Marotta is describing. In the decade we are talking about, they have become a powerful entity, a force to be reckoned with in the city of San Francisco and, to a lesser degree, throughout the country. Have they become, also, this elusive thing called "community"? Marotta thinks so. He points to the institutions that now exist for gay men in San Francisco: a service to help people find roommates, a gay Olympics, writers groups, musical choruses, an array of self-help groups. "Connections," he says, "are no longer solely sexual."

But although "community" may be a feeling, it is often more tangible—a place, an institution, a series of rituals, a means of support. This, too, has marked the gay community in San Francisco. In economic hard times, the community was thriving. Businesses made money; houses were renovated. There was no First Nationwide Savings Bank in the story to withdraw its money and throw the community into a state of peril. This sense of a boom town that you get talking to gay men in San Francisco stands in stark contrast to what gay women say about faltering attempts to build communities, to found institutions, to translate a feeling of "membership" into tangible things. "Gay men," Marotta says, "are men and they have more money than women do. They're single; they pool their resources; they're mobile and privileged as men; they don't have dependents."

Does this mean, then, that Marotta and his lover moved to San Francisco, helped build the community thriving there, and lived happily ever after? Hardly. In fact, Marotta and his lover broke up or, as he puts it, "dissolved our couple relationship." Here, rather than dwell on his personal story, Marotta turns to recent psychological theories to help explain the demise not only of his relationship, but the kinds of emotional difficulties that prevent gay men from forming the kind of close personal and lasting bond that, after all, he considers the only antidote to loneliness. A couple without a community may feel lonely but so too, although perhaps less so, will a community member—or at least Toby Marotta—without someone to love. "There's a dimension of loneliness that comes from not being known, from being unable to form a sustained emotional relationship, that plagues gay men partly because they've been socialized as men and partly because the gay subculture facilitates sexual connections, but not the rest. We have a much more difficult time finding, building, remaining in and being nourished by sustained relationships. The psychological problem in same-sex relationships is often about suffocation rather than connection. Heterosexual couples complain about not being able to connect; gay men complain about suffocation and the adaptation usually is a more open relationship."

Although the study of problems in same-sex relations is very much in its infancy—both the interest of professionals and the willingness of homosexuals to discuss their emotional lives openly is quite recent—Marotta has evolved a way of living that combines his need for membership and for intimacy: "I'm living with a man who's been married for seventeen years. He has his wife and children about twenty minutes away and he spends weekends with them. During the week, he and I live together. I'm very much included by his wife. I think I have a nice relationship with her, the kids and her family."

He rises to go. The lights have come on across the Bay, and the kitchen of the house I am sitting in is alive with the sounds and smells of dinner cooking. The husband of this family stands at the stove, stirring a pot of pasta. It has not been lost on me that this happy family, so glaring an example of non-loneliness, has its problems and its crises and there have been times any of the four people who live in this house must have felt lonely, but, even more importantly, their choices are conventional ones. They live, essentially, in a world of professional white people, couples with children, close to the norm, sanctioned absolutely, unlike Marotta, in the bonds they have chosen.

Before he leaves, Toby Marotta points me northward. Guerneville, he says, a town on the Russian River, is a perfect example of what he has been saying about communities. Guerneville is "an extraordinary social phenomenon. It's been settled by gay people, mainly gay men. It's charming. It's beautiful. The gays have bought these old decrepit resorts and houses and transformed the town into a healthy, happy, visible gay community."

If you take the road along the ocean, the drive from San Francisco takes several hours, winding north of Muir Woods and Stinson Beach and Bodega Bay through towns, after a while, that look as though people make year-round lives there, where feed stores and hardware stores replace snazzy restaurants and shops selling suntan oil. You turn inland at Jenner and after a while the trees come up and across the road, forming arcades and tunnels. The redwoods grow thicker and thicker, interspersed with madrones and fir trees. The ridges rise, sometimes to 800 feet and, between them, you drive along the valleys. Guerneville sits in a valley. Main Street runs five blocks long. At one end is the Stumptown Inn Pizza Parlor, which was the scene of my first Guerneville encounter and, across from it, the Rexall drug store, where you can book appointments for a complete physical examination for thirty dollars. A cardiogram is extra. In the drugstore, on one of the days I was there, a woman asked a clerk if there were greeting cards to congratulate someone on getting a new job. The answer was yes.

Along Main Street are the bank and the Safeway supermarket, which is about to be closed and replaced by a new Safeway being built right behind it. There is the Rainbow Cattle Company, a gay male bar, standing next to the Guerneville 5¢-and-10¢ store, then a tackle store, then Neeley's, which is owned by one of the town's oldest families, and Pat's, a luncheonette with a counter and booths, Danish brought in from a nearby bakery in the morning, jello and rice pudding in glass display cases and a big sign over the counter showing the location of the best fishing places in the Russian River area.

The river itself is puny at this point—and dangerous. You can walk two blocks from Main Street and look at the muddy water from a small pebbled beach. At rest, it is hard to imagine the raging floods that periodically swamp the valley. If you continued east from Main Street, you would drive through the heart of the Sonoma landscape on your way to Santa Rosa, the county seat. Along these roads, east and south of Guerneville, lie the dairy farms, the huge green expanses and low rolling hills that drew Christo to this place and led him to create one of his famous "outdoor art" pieces, a thin fence running from hill to hill. Christo thought this one of the most beautiful places in America.

Toward the end of the nineteenth century, Guerneville was at the heart of the lumber industry. Originally called "Stump-Town," the name was changed to honor a founder of the first mill, George Guerne. Rail transportation followed the lumber boom, and when the redwoods had been "logged off," the trains began carrying tourists coming from San Francisco for day trips, who built summer cabins and eventually provided patronage for the resorts and hotels that replaced the big red trees. The car replaced the train and the town continued to grow as a "watering hole" long after the last run of the Guerneville branch of the San Francisco and North Pacific Railroad in 1935.

Bob Jones told me the rest of the story. Jones is the minister of the Guerneville Community Church, and in the time he has lived there he has seen the foundation of what he calls three separate communities. The first are now referred to as the "old families," essentially "stable, retired folks from the Bay Area who moved into their summer homes." There are about 10,000 retired people in Reverend Jones's parish. There is, in this community, both tradition and memory. Jones speaks of funerals and weddings as indications: "Recently two hundred to three hundred people showed up for the funeral of a ninety-four-year-old woman. When somebody dies, the whole town turns out. And they do for weddings. They are honoring those connections." For twenty-five years, he tells me, the "old community" had an annual ritual called the Pageant of Fire Mountain, where they enacted the Romeo and Juliet story on the mountain and lit torches up and down its face. "I still remember Jim Neeley running around with his fire department putting out the fires. Now we have a jazz festival every year."

He does not seem discontent with his own life in Guerneville—far from it—or with the eventual shape the community would take, but Reverend Jones sounds nostalgic for its past, particularly in terms of the connections that seemed to come more easily in what was a rural, almost frontier town. Neeley ran up and down with his fire department. People always went into each other's houses—nobody locked doors—and left notes for one another when no one was home. The river, of course, holds people together and some of Reverend Jones's memories of community are of pulling together in the disasters caused by floods. "The Lynch family," he says, "would call everybody in the canyon after a flood to see if they were all right. When there's a spate of high water, even today, normal operations shut down. We ferry people about the flooded river and complain about it together."

Although I live on an island and am constantly reminded of the rivers that run along each side of it, I have never been endangered by those rivers, nor have the people who live near me mobilized to face that kind of threat. I cannot help thinking, though, watching the smile on Reverend Jones's face as he recounts "pulling together" in disaster, a smile that will cross the faces of the other people I will come to know in Guerneville, an equally warm memory regardless of how many floods each person has lived through, of other disasters in other places. On my urban island bounded by rivers, the feeling of vulnerability has still come from nature. In the two power blackouts that I lived through in New York City, when the lights failed, the sky seemed to close in. We did not spend much time in easy relation to the sky, we New Yorkers, and we banded together, helping each other, propelled by a sense of communal vulnerability.

So the river was a great leveler, particularly when it posed a danger to the community in Guerneville. People pulled together, Reverend Jones had said, lines were crossed. These lines were drawn clearly by the second and third waves of émigrés to Guerneville, the establishment of communities within communities. The second wave came in the Sixties and was made up of hippies. I could see remnants of this wave on Main Street from time to time—women in long skirts wearing silver jewelry, men with long hair and beards. They looked like displaced persons. In fact, although many people came to Guerneville and remained there, the "hippie" migration did not take root in the community. The "elders," Jones says, did not like these hippies—"They're more upset about people who have long hair than about homosexuals." They owned few businesses. They occupied few positions in the organizations that run the town.

The gay migration to Guerneville, which began half a dozen years ago, had an entirely different impact on the community. Gay people bought property and opened resorts and restaurants and attracted other gay people, and the town's economy improved. It is a precarious economy, the one brought by the gay tourist trade, and a seasonal one. The old town ritual on Fire Mountain, transformed into a jazz festival, has been set for a week after Labor Day in order to extend the usual tourist season. The resorts and many restaurants close in the dead of winter.

Still, a core of gay men were property owners and business owners, sat on the Chamber of Commerce, founded the Russian River Gay Business Association and became, in effect, stable members of the community.

Between the time Toby Marotta first told me of the glories of Guerneville and my own visit there, more than a year had passed. In that time, a new threat had come into public view and grown to frightening proportions. As I talked with Reverend Jones, watching the sun dart in and out of the clouds illuminating his serious and rather boyish face, listening to him talk about the apple trees that surround his porch and his own increasing movement toward more solitude in his personal life, his "meditative" responses to the blooming apple trees, people were dying of the disease that had come to be called AIDS. Since it mostly strikes gay men, AIDS posed a distinct threat to Guerneville's new community.

Sam was in a panic. He also had a flair for melodrama. He was waiting at the Stumptown Inn on Main Street, drinking coffee and smoking Camel cigarettes. We sat near a window, where we could watch Main Street and Main Street could watch us. Hardly an appropriate spot for an encounter that resembled Bernstein and Woodward's with "Deep Throat." Sam said he knew secrets. He said no one would tell the truth about Guerneville, but he would.

Some of Sam's truth had little to do with AIDS, but a great deal of it had to do with loneliness. He had been in Guerneville for several months, having come from Houston. He arrived with two goals in mind: "To make money and human contact." The money part came easy at first. Sam started renting canoes to tourists and summer people. "A month after I arrived," he says, "I was referred to as an overnight success. I swept the River away with blind ambition." Then the tourist season passed. As for finding other things to do, Sam says, "There's no such thing as meaningful work on the River." So he was broke and disenchanted and talking about moving away, but it was the thwarting of the second need, the need for human contact, that seemed to most distress him.

"I've been groped by every businessman in town, but I've never had anybody ask to buy me a cup of coffee or how I'm doing."

He looked out the window. He ordered another cup of coffee.

"There's nothing to congregate around here except happy hour. The Rainbow Cattle Company," just down the street, "opens at six A.M. There's a lot of heavy drinking."

Fear of AIDS exacerbated the distance. In the case of Guerneville, according to Sam, this was one danger that sent people scurrying into the woodwork rather than calling up and down the canyon to see if everyone was safe or hauling

together to face the threat. Sam was obsessed with the hypoc-
risy about AIDS that he said existed in Guerneville. He had a
list of horror stories. One man had been bitten by a spider and
the hospital refused to treat him. There is, in fact, no local
hospital; the nearest are in Santa Rosa or Sebastopol, each
sixteen to twenty miles away. This was Santa Rosa, Sam said,
and they refused to treat the spider bite because they thought
the patient had AIDS. Which hospital and why they thought
this and the man's name were all unknown to Sam. He had
other stories. An epileptic had died of a seizure while he was
sitting in his pickup truck. The hospital refused him. The
funeral home wouldn't accept his body. They thought he had
AIDS. And he had stories—a list, actually—of people in town
he claimed actually had AIDS. "But the Chamber of Commerce claims there's no AIDS in Guerneville," he said, "and
I think we probably have more AIDS per capita than anywhere
else."

It was easy to dismiss Sam. He was tense, belligerent, defensive. His voice bordered on a whine. If he had no lover, no
friend and no feeling of membership in a community, I was
tempted to say, it was his own bloody fault. But fault was not
the question. Experience was. And Sam's experience in
Guerneville turned out to be illuminating. It actually did cast
light on what had brought me there—the question of what
holds us together and what pushes us apart.

The effect of AIDS on gay communities across the country,
but particularly in Guerneville, where I could see it firsthand,
was devastating. Literally, what community existed was torn
asunder by death—friends and lovers dying—and the grief
and mourning that accompanied it. It brought with it an atmosphere of suspicion that was difficult to overcome. In part, the
suspicion came from "outside"—the AIDS epidemic was used
by opponents of gay rights and generally homophobic people
everywhere to justify the idea that homosexuals were sick,
diseased and dirty. In San Francisco, the police were issued
masks and gloves to wear in case they had to handle suspects

who might be homosexual. Inside the community, the force of suspicion was equally strong. Other people became suspect, potential carriers of death. The impulse to connect, particularly the impulse to connect sexually, was short-circuited. Some hailed this as progress, an end to the rampant promiscuity of gay male life and a move toward more "regular" living. Many gay men I know gave up sex altogether. But in Guerneville I could see it leading to something else.

Sam and his list reminded me of Senator Joseph McCárthy and his. The potential for a new kind of witch hunt was enormous. There was no evidence, no opportunity to defend oneself, little interest in truth but a large tide of hysteria and panic. The community was awash with rumor. This man had it. That man had it. One Guerneville resident told me that a group had met and decided that anyone who had AIDS and was still sexually active was guilty of manslaughter. They had someone in mind. In the time I was there, no one in Guerneville had acted on this decision, but it was suddenly not hard to imagine a vigilante action, a gang in white sheets, a lynching or a castration.

"We never had a better chance than here," Sam said. He did feel part of a "we."

One of the problems was that there were many "we's" among the gay men in Guerneville and their interests, particularly when it came to AIDS, were in conflict. Some were more worried about tourism than they were about danger. To face down the rumors, acknowledge the threat of AIDS, would be to frighten away the visitors who filled the resorts and brought dollars to the Russian River. Everyone I spoke with said tourism had already fallen about 50 percent because of fear of AIDS. The collective impulse of one part of the community was to sweep the whole question under the rug.

Leonard Malevich is a decorated Vietnam War hero, active in conservative politics and owner of the Stumptown Inn, which features a picture of Barry Goldwater on the wall. If anyone has membership in the community of Guerneville, he does—he sits on the board of directors of the Chamber of Commerce and other civic organizations, including the Republican Club. Like many people in the town, he says that when he arrived, three years ago, he felt like he had found a home at last. Malevich described himself as a former army brat who, at last, found a place to "put roots in," an "old-fashioned guy who believes in a front yard and a back yard."

It was lonely at first. "I'm not a party person," he said, acknowledging how much of the gay life of the town is a bar life. He coped with this loneliness in conventional ways—he bought a pet (a cat) and he threw himself into work. Although even three years ago, he said, there was hostility to gay people settling in and opening businesses, Malevich can mark the abatement of that hostility quite clearly: "fag bashing" used to be rampant and unreported; now "you're likely to get an accurate account of what happened." The trees outside the pizza parlor tell him the same story: this Christmas, the lights with which he decorated the trees remained in place; a year ago, they would have been gone. And Malevich glows with the happiness and relief I have seen in so many people who feel themselves to have been wanderers who found "home" at last. He tells me with pride how an eighty-year-old town resident says hello, how the town kids say "Hi, Leonard." He has become a "River Rat," someone who has been there long enough to pass through the initiation rites and acquire his own kerosene lamps and rubber boots.

"People help people in trouble," Malevich says. The litany of Guerneville.

And AIDS?

Malevich turns the question aside.

Steve Piezo, an editor at the *Russian River News,* wandered into the pizza parlor. I asked again about AIDS. Both men dismissed the talk of it as "hysteria." As a newspaper person, I said, wasn't Piezo interested in tracking down some of the rumors, particularly the ones about people being turned away from hospitals? There was nothing to them, he said. That, I thought, made a good story. He disagreed. It was not news. I felt like the stranger who had ridden into town to stir up trouble. Why wouldn't I leave the Russian River pieties alone?

One characteristic of communities is the necessity of closing ranks against the outside world. This is especially true of places where people have carried out that great American enterprise, the errand into the wilderness, the establishment of refuge in a hostile environment. Guerneville was no different in this way from other communities in history. Whenever I thought of Sam, he took on a kind of cockeyed messianic quality—the loner inside the community saying things are not what they seem here, that no one is telling the truth, and being shunted aside for saying so. My association was not American. I thought of Spinoza in seventeenth-century Amsterdam whose inquiries and dissension so threatened the solidarity of the endangered Jewish community there that he was urged over and over again to submit to communal will, to make himself part of a "united front" against the rest of the world, and when he refused he was punished, according to the traditions of the community, by being forced to lie on the steps of the synagogue and have the community walk over him. Sam hadn't Spinoza's stature, but he did have Spinoza's problem.

By the time I returned to Guerneville, I knew a lot more about the problem. In Berkeley, Susan Griffin, writer, activist, someone "outsiders" consider a member of the lesbian community, told me, "Aside from my childhood, my initial period as a lesbian was the most painful of my life. Lesbianism in the Seventies was supposed to solve all your problems. But I realized," she said, "that now I had only begun to learn what love was all about. It was not as easy to make a lasting relationship as I thought." Susan Griffin faced the same difficulty finding an intimate relationship that she had faced as a "straight" person, except the terrain was different and the kind of connection she sought was truer to her actual need. "I couldn't share this loneliness with anybody," she said.

"One felt terribly ashamed as a lesbian to be lonely and, especially, you didn't want straight people to know."

Writer Kim Chernin spoke of the "feeling of the mythological community. It's not like the Jewish community," she said, "where, if you want it, it's meeting in the synagogue and you go there and get it, you can find it."

Susan Griffin clung to the mythological community at first in a way she no longer does. It represented "the family connection," she said, "and my way to hold on to it was to do less of my art and more politics."

I drove back to Guerneville a second time, taking the inland route on a bright spring day, the hills startlingly green and the cattle grazing in amazing repose and then, off the highway, the road darkened by redwoods, the dip into the valley, passing through shade and light, going along Main Street again, driving up to Armstrong Woods Road, where two people who saw themselves as pilgrims of a sort had come to live in Guerneville. By then, I knew a great deal more about what threatened the community and what held it together, where some of the cracks were and who was falling through them.

Some of the cracks had little to do with gay life. As Sam had pointed out, in spite of the resorts and cabaret acts, Guerneville was a poor place. Last year, the town was the recipient of surplus cheese provided by the United States Department of Agriculture to needy communities. By the time the cheese arrived in Guerneville—1,800 pounds of it—the cheese was moldy; still, town residents decided to keep it, see what they could salvage. The poorest people in Guerneville, the poorest people in America, are women living alone supporting their children. Reverend Bob Jones had seen a group of those women move for a moment out of their isolation and then back into it. "There's no meeting down at the well," he said, so he had used his church to bring people together, to provide the well.

"There are more and more of these younger women living alone with children here," he said, "and they're coping against all kinds of odds." Recently, the Salvation Army and Pacific Gas & Electric offered to help pay the utility bills of some of those women. They came to the church to work out the arrangements. They started talking to each other. "One had a three-hundred-dollar bill; another had a sixty-dollar bill. They were talking about that, and suddenly there was a spontaneous community. It's like the Spanish women living here who can't speak English. Their husbands learn at work; their children learn at school. The one thing that's important is to get these people together." But the loneliest people he knew in Guerneville, Jones said, were not women, who always seemed to have some kind of network, but older men who had "lost their wives." Jones seemed stymied about what to do for those men. He echoed what others had said: "We men still seem to channel our relationships through a woman." And he stopped, as though both his imagination and his compassion failed him. No remedy came to mind. No well would bring them in touch with each other.

Joyce and Bob Goldberg hardly saw the older men who lived alone, but on the porch of their house on Armstrong Woods Road, Joyce's teenage son was standing around the barbecue with three friends. They grunted at me as I came up on the porch, then went back to figuring out what to do with the rest of the afternoon.

Joyce is a slim woman in her early forties, with curly hair, a raspy voice and a knowing way about her. Bob is several years younger, dark, serious and worried. Like everyone else, they have heard the stories Sam told, and the stories have changed some in transmission—the man with the spider bite had become a man with a concussion, or perhaps it is yet another man refused admission at the hospital. Bob sits on the floor with his back to the wood stove and draws on a cigarette. "What if I'm unconscious," he says, "and I get brought in to the hospital by gay men? Or men someone thinks are gay?"

"There's an investment in saying that's not going on here," Joyce says.

Still, Bob and Joyce insist that they live in a "tight" community, that the general spirit of Guerneville is "cooperative rather than divisive" and that the river's threat keeps that spirit honed. "When the water comes," Bob says, "it doesn't matter whether you wear a tutu or not." That winter, the water had come. Their road was flooded. They couldn't leave.

Like many others, Bob and Joyce came to Guerneville from somewhere else. The community, Bob says, is "people who gathered in a place and felt safe. They had a fear of being somewhere else." Among the émigrés, who outnumber the original residents, a heterosexual couple like Bob and Joyce is rare. They call themselves "the token traditionals." What drew them from Los Angeles and to the river is, in part, the kind of tolerance they found in Guerneville, what Bob refers to as "a willingness to accept diversity" and Joyce calls "a degree of no judgment about life style." There is another reason and Joyce hesitates before she says it. She knows how it will sound. She tucks her feet under her on the couch and lights another cigarette.

"I feel called to the river."

Yes. Well. I clear my throat. I am accustomed by now to California talk, to that blend of the cosmic, the mystic, the apocalyptic, a language of blurred edges and gurgling sentence structures. I am accustomed, too, to the mix of this leftover Sixties language with a hard take on reality, particularly material reality. Joyce is, after all, talking mystically about being on the edge of an economic boom. This is hard to tell at first. What do you say when a perfectly rational woman sitting on a couch with boys barbecueing outside and a dog snoring on the floor tells you that "we have the potential and have been chosen to be a dot on the map, the leading edge to turn the world around"?

You say, first, that this is the American spirit, that it has a familiar ring—Brigham Young coming over the mountain ridge and looking down at what is now Salt Lake City, no less than the founders of all the original American colonies and the settlers pushing west. This is the place. The New Jerusalem.

The Guerneville sense of being on a new frontier is an amalgam of passionate convictions about tolerance, devotion to building a settlement where people of different "life styles," they would say, live comfortably together, and of having been smart enough to pick a place just on the edge of an economic boom. Surely not everyone in Guerneville shares this vision—some simply live there—but enough residents do to make it a vision that holds the community together nearly as strongly as the treacherous river does.

Signs of the coming revival are visible everywhere to the believers, like Joyce and Bob. Santa Rosa, just sixteen miles away, is one of the fastest growing cities in the nation, its growth based on the expansion of hi-tech industries. "A boom is coming," Bob says, "based on Santa Rosa's growth. This will be a suburb with a river, like Venice, California. This will be Mill Valley to the max. We felt the energy."

This is how the energy has manifested itself so far: Safeway is building a new supermarket; Union Bank is opening a branch in Santa Rosa catering only to large corporations; condominiums are going up in Guerneville; investment capital, while not exactly pouring in, is surely trickling.

Reverend Bob Jones had been less than enthusiastic about this energy. "Santa Rosa coming west," he said, "is going to make this more like other communities. Until recently, we had no condos or apartment buildings. The houses were all different; they all had different signs on them and different size mailboxes. It's been a community of middle-of-the-road free spirits. I think we're going to start getting a normal kind of middle-class loneliness. Our middle-class culture gives people the means to build fences in their yards."

While Joyce and Bob Goldberg wait for the boom and remain in a house that has no fence, they are negotiating

Guerneville as it is. They have come to a new place. Each applied the expertise in advertising they had accumulated in Los Angeles to starting their own agency. Although one of their reasons for moving to the river was to get away from the "workaholic mentality" of LA, they find themselves working long hours in order to get established. Joyce looks out the window as she tells me this. It is a sparkling, clear day and the sun is beginning to set. "I wonder," she says, "why I'm not out hiking more."

The process of making friends has been different for each of them and, for both, different from what it was in Los Angeles. Joyce finds the people around her "more gracious" and "less likely to judge you based on your financial status. There is not so much stigma about being poor. For my fortieth birthday, a woman I know brought me an etching and made me a frittata. I know she's on welfare, but people here are not stopped by poverty. They have style." She does miss her circle of women friends and the way they used to "skip-talk" together. There are not many professional women in Guerneville. She misses the "camaraderie of bitching to another wife" about how Bob doesn't "hold down his responsibility in the home, like taking out the trash." Lacking a group of friends with similar experience, she and Bob have been thrown closer to each other than either is comfortable with.

"Well," she says, "we decided to jump in the same canoe together. But as a couple, we need to do more things separately. I say 'Guess who I saw today?' and he says, 'Yeah, I know, I was there.' "

Bob is having an easier time making friends, although "things move slower here." He likes the fact that he is "liable to do business on Monday with someone I saw on Sunday" and doesn't at all miss the "anonymity" or "crowds to hide in" of Los Angeles. For the first time in his life, he is making friends with women. "I have platonic women friends—gay women—and I get to share things with men that didn't seem available in LA. I have buddies because men hang around in groups."

There was a group of us at dinner the next night, five to be precise, in the dining room at Fife's, which is the first resort you come to as you leave the center of town, just across the creek. Peter Pender was there. He owns the place and is credited by some people with being the spearhead in the revitalization of Guerneville. Or the gentrification. Or the gayification. Or the brave new world. How you see it depends on who you are. Pender sees it as the brave new world. So do Joyce and Bob Goldberg, who had dressed themselves up for dinner— he was wearing a tie; she was wearing a soft black costume. The fifth person was Dave, who helped run the place. Dave looked to be in his late twenties, with well-muscled arms, curly dark hair and clear blue eyes. It was a large, beautiful room, newly remodeled, with a fire crackling in a fireplace near our table and a high cathedral ceiling supported by triangular wood struts.

Peter Pender is from Main Line Philadelphia and is a world-class bridge player. He is tall and thin and serious-looking, and he reminded me a lot of Tony Perkins. Some say he bought Fife's because he was rich and bored; others that he has a mission. That morning, Peter had been on a golf course, which is not usual, but it was spring coming and he was thinking about exercising. Golf is part of his past, the Main Line and a world of men from which he generally felt excluded and in which he usually felt stigmatized. He had been alone, putting and driving, when a group of men asked him to join them. Reluctantly, he did. And it had turned out fine. In fact, he'd had a good time. In fact, his reluctance seemed to him, sitting there at the dinner table in his own place surrounded by friends, with the fire going and the new menu sitting in his hands, another one of those instances where there had been a choice between isolating himself or risking rejection and joining in.

The waitress is nervous, serving the boss. Peter and I share a pasta dish, a new item on the menu. We all eat well and drink good California wine. No one mentions AIDS or the expansion of Santa Rosa. When I bring either subject up, it disappears into the food and wine and general conversation. I haven't the heart to go after it.

At one table, three men in their fifties or sixties, all wearing red suspenders, are laughing. At another, an elderly man and woman, who look like country people to me, are having a quiet meal. Near us, two women are deep in discussion of their relationship. On the other side, a young black man wearing a jersey cut off at the shoulders and a baseball cap is sitting across from a blond man in a white shirt open nearly to the waist. They can't keep their hands on their utensils; they keep stroking each other's arms and looking longingly into each other's eyes. One man is eating alone. Peter says he works in the kitchen. An old man wanders in, the gardener, whom Peter "inherited" from Fife's previous owners, a grizzled fellow who goes straight to the bar.

It happens sometimes, these moments when the walls seem not so much to fall as to never have existed. I am struck by the ceremony of eating together and the odd combination that we five are and how unorthodox the mix in the entire dining room is. I understand that the "dream" of Guerneville is nothing more than the dream of making a big buck for some people and nothing less than the dream of an unharassed sensual heaven for others. I understand that those who are serious about "community" here are largely white men and that the power they have so far absorbed does not embrace women or nonwhite people as much as it ought to, to be a community admirable beyond qualification. I know that not far away that night there is someone like Sam, who feels like an outsider. I know that the Indians abandoned this part of the land because they believed the redwoods to be poisonous. Still, we finish the meal and fool around with some video games in the bar. Peter always wins. Joyce beats me. A group of people are watching a Diana Ross special on television in another room. Someone throws wood on the fire. I can't remember, at this moment, what loneliness is.

Index